This book is a work of nonfiction created for educational purposes.
All examples, scenarios, and illustrations are original and intended to help readers understand software development concepts.
This edition is distributed through multiple platforms by Draft2Digital.
For inquiries, feedback, or permissions, please contact:
business.logicladder@gmail.com
First Edition

Preface

I'll be honest with you - design patterns used to scare me. For years, I'd hear terms like "Factory Method" and "Decorator Pattern" in meetings and nod along, secretly wondering if I was the only one who didn't get it. The explanations I found were either too abstract ("patterns are reusable solutions to common problems") or so technical they felt like reading a dictionary.

Then I had my "aha!" moment. I realized design patterns aren't some mystical programming magic - they're just **common sense solutions to problems we face every day as developers**, packaged with fancy names.

This book is the guide I wish I had when I started. It's written for developers who, like me, learn best by doing, by seeing real code, and by understanding the "why" behind "what."

Who is this book for?

This book is for every developer who has ever:

- Stared at a giant if/else statement and thought "there has to be a better way"
- Created multiple similar objects and wondered about the copy-paste smell
- Struggled with code that breaks every time you add a new feature
- Wanted to write code that your teammates will actually enjoy working with

If you know C# and understand basic object-oriented programming but find design patterns confusing or overwhelming, you're in the right place.

What makes this book different?

We learn through building, not just reading. Instead of abstract theory, we build a complete pizza ordering system from scratch. You'll witness the transformation from messy, hard-to-maintain code to a clean, professional architecture - one pattern at a time.

Each pattern comes with:

- 🍕 Real pizza shop analogies that make complex concepts stick
- Working code you can run and experiment with
- "Oops Moments" that show exactly what problems each pattern solves
- Mini-challenges to test your understanding
- 🏆 Interview-ready questions and exercises

What will you learn?

By the end of this journey, you'll not just understand design patterns - you'll think in patterns. You'll look at code problems and immediately see which pattern fits. More importantly, you'll know when NOT to use patterns (because sometimes simplicity wins!). You'll master all 23 Gang of Four patterns by building something real, not by memorizing definitions.

How to use this book? 🎉

01 **Read the Pattern Story**

Each chapter starts with a real problem from our pizza shop. Read about the "pain" - it will make the solution much more satisfying!

02 **Get the Analogy**

Imagine each pattern as a character in our pizza shop drama. The Singleton is the "One and Only Manager," the Factory is the "Pizza Chef Specialist," the Observer is the "Kitchen Announcement System."

03 **Code Adventure Time!**

This is where the magic happens! When you reach the refactoring code section:

- Clone the GitHub project and run it yourself
- OR Create your own project step-by-step following the patterns
- Break things! Modify the code and see what happens
- Add your own features using the patterns you just learned

04 **Conquer the Mini-Challenge**

Each chapter ends with a fun coding challenge. Don't skip this! It's where the pattern truly becomes part of your toolkit.

05 **Become Interview-Ready**

Test your knowledge with our pattern puzzles and interview questions. You'll be surprised how quickly you can spot patterns in real-world problems.

A Quick Word of Encouragement

If you've ever felt intimidated by design patterns, I've been there too. This book breaks down that intimidation barrier by showing you that patterns are just named common sense. They're the vocabulary that lets us communicate complex ideas simply.

So grab your favorite drink, fire up your code editor, and let's build something amazing together. By the end, you won't just understand design patterns - you'll wonder how you ever coded without them!

Happy coding! 🍕💻

P.S. The code examples work, the analogies are delicious, and the learning is genuine. Let's make design patterns your superpower!

TABLE OF CONTENTS

PART 03

STRUCTURAL PATTERNS — ORGANIZING THE SYSTEM

PART 04

BEHAVIORAL PATTERNS — DEFINING BEHAVIOR

PART 05

WRAP-UP

✨ PART 1: WELCOME TO THE PIZZA UNIVERSE

Where Code Meets Crust! 🍕
Welcome to the delicious world where programming patterns become as familiar as your favorite pizza toppings! In this opening act, we're not just learning theory - we're opening our very own virtual pizzeria. Get ready to meet the quirky Design Pattern Family who'll be working in our kitchen, discover why your code might be giving you more headaches than a busy Friday night rush, and witness the birth of our pizza app in all its glorious (and slightly messy) beginnings. This is where we roll out the dough and prepare for an amazing coding adventure!

What's Cooking in This Part:

- Meet your new coding BFFs: The Builders, Architects, and Strategists
- Witness the "before" picture of our pizza app (spoiler: it's chaotic!)
- Discover why design patterns are like having secret recipes for coding success
- Get ready to transform messy code into a well-oiled pizza-making machine

Perfect for you if:

- You've ever felt like you're reinventing the wheel with every new project
- You want to understand the "why" behind design patterns, not just the "what"
- You learn best by seeing real problems and real solutions
- You believe learning should be as enjoyable as eating pizza!
-

Grab your apron and let's start cooking up some beautiful code! 👨‍🍳👩‍🍳

Chapter 1

What are Design Patterns – And Why Should You Care?

Have you ever found yourself stuck copying and pasting the same bits of code, again and again? Or maybe you wrote a feature that worked fine—until adding a tiny change caused your whole program to break? If this sounds familiar, don't worry — you're in good company.

Design patterns are here to save the day. Think of them as secret recipes, handed down from generations of experienced developers that show you the best way to solve common coding problems. Instead of struggling to invent your own solutions every time, you follow these time-tested blueprints — and your code becomes cleaner, smarter, and easier to work with.

What Exactly Are Design Patterns

In the simplest terms, a **design pattern** is a reusable solution to a recurring problem in software design. But it's more than just a piece of code or a trick. It's a guiding idea that helps you organize your code so it's easier to read, maintain, and extend.

Imagine you're running a pizza shop. Each pizza you make has the same basic steps: prepare the dough, add toppings, bake it, and deliver it. Over time, you develop a recipe that works perfectly — you don't have to guess what to do next every time. That recipe is like a design pattern for your code: a reliable, tested plan for getting the job done well.

Why Should You Care About Design Patterns?

Without design patterns, your code can quickly turn into a tangled mess:

- You might copy-paste the same code everywhere, leading to bugs that hide in dozens of places.
- Adding new features becomes a headache because everything is tightly connected and confusing.
- New teammates may stare blankly at your code wondering, "What on earth is going on here?"

Design patterns help avoid all this chaos. They provide a shared language and set of best practices that make your code:

- **Clean:** Easy to read and understand
- **Flexible:** Simple to extend without breaking existing stuff
- **Reliable:** Fewer bugs and unexpected crashes

Meet the Design Patterns Family

Design patterns come in three big families — each with its own personality and role in your code:

The Builders

Family Name: Creational

What They Do: They create objects — the building blocks of your program. Like chefs crafting pizzas from scratch.

The Architects

Family Name: Structural

What They Do: They organize and arrange objects, making sure all parts fit together perfectly — like an architect designing the pizza shop layout.

The Strategists

Family Name: Behavioral

What They Do: They manage how objects communicate and behave — like the kitchen staff coordinating orders and deliveries.

Think of them as a quirky but talented family working behind the scenes to make your pizza app a success!

Introduction to the Family Members

Welcome to the Design Pattern Family — a quirky team of coding superheroes. Each member has a special power, and they show up only **when the time is right** to fix your app's problems. You'll meet these family members throughout our pizza delivery story. Let's take a quick family photo:

The Builders — *Creational Patterns*

These are the creators. They help you build flexible and efficient ways to create objects — especially when things start getting repetitive or complicated. This family includes:

Singleton

"The One and Only"

Ensures only one instance exists

Factory Method

"The Pizza Selector"

Chooses the right object to create

Abstract Factory

"The Kitchen Setup"

Creates families of related objects

Builder

"The Customizer"

Builds complex objects step by step

Prototype

"The Cloner"

Copies existing objects like magic

> **Memory Trick**
>
> **S**mart **F**rameworks **A**re **B**uilt **P**recisely
>
> (S = Singleton, F = Factory, A = Abstract Factory, B = Builder, P = Prototype)

The Architects — *Structural Patterns*

These folks know **how to arrange things.** They make sure parts of your app fit together in the cleanest, most maintainable way. The members of this family are:

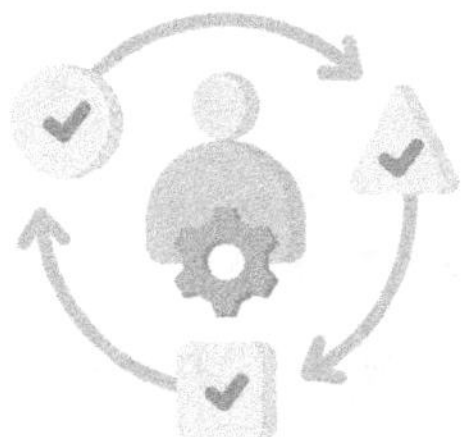

Adapter

"The Translator"

Makes incompatible things work together

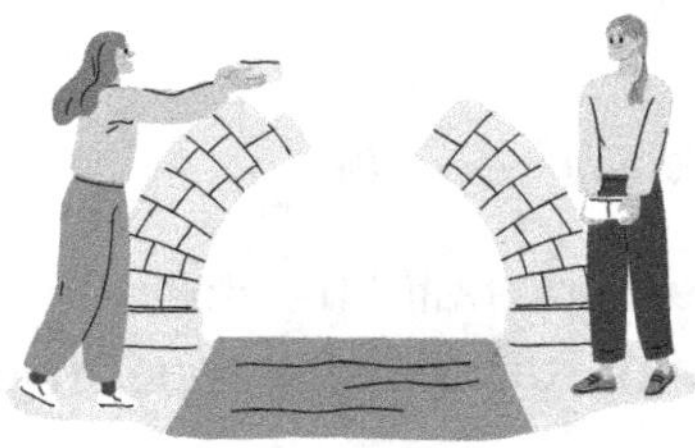

Bridge

"The Divider"

Separates abstraction from implementation

Composite

"The Group Leader"

Treats individual and groups as one

Decorator

"The Enhancer"

Adds features without changing original code

Facade

"The Front Desk"

Simplifies complex subsystems

Flyweight

"The Memory Saver"

Shares data to reduce memory use

Proxy

"The Gate Keeper"

Controls access to another object

> **Memory Trick**
>
> **A**rchitects **B**uild **C**omponents, **D**ecorating **F**acades **F**or **P**erformance.
>
> (A = Adapter, B = Bridge, C = Composite, D = Decorator, F = Facade, F = Flyweight, P = Proxy)

The Strategists — *Behavioral Patterns*

These are the thinkers and coordinators. They manage **how objects talk, react, and behave.** This family member includes:

Observer
"The Notifier"
Keeps others updated automatically

Strategy
"The Game Planner"
Switches algorithms on the fly

Command
"The Remote"
Turns actions into objects

State
"The Mood Switch"
Shifts behavior with state

Chain of Responsibility
"The Pass-it-On"
Passes requests along a chain

Iterator
"The Tour Guide"
Provides a way to access elements in a sequence

Mediator
"The Messenger"
Manages communication between objects

Memento
"The Time Traveler"
Saves and restores object state

Template Method
"The Skeleton"
Defines a skeleton and lets steps vary

Visitor
"The Inspector"
Adds actions without changing structure

Interpreter
"The Language Guru"
Interprets and processes grammar

Memory Trick

Only Smart Coders Solve Critical Issues, Making Meaningful Tools Very Interactive.

(O = Observer, S = Strategy, C = Command, S = State, C = Chain of Responsibility, I = Iterator. M = Mediator, M = Memento, T = Template Method, V = Visitor, I = Interpreter)

A Family That Grows With You

📖 You won't meet all these members at once. Some will arrive early when your code is still small. Others will step in as your app grows and gets more complex.
But don't worry — every time there's a problem, **the right family member will show up to help you fix it.**

> 🍕 *"Every great pizza needs the right ingredients. Every great app needs the right patterns."*

👀 As your pizza story unfolds, watch how the kitchen evolves — with new tools, helpers, and solutions coming to the rescue.

🧭 Get ready... our journey begins now. And our first helper is already warming up in the kitchen...

Chapter 2

The Story Begins — A Pizza App Is Born

Setting The Stage

Before we invite our Design Pattern Family to the kitchen, we need to see **how the app looks without them.**

> *In this chapter, you'll:*
> 1. **Meet the Requirements:** What does our pizza shop want the app to do?
> 2. **Sketch a Simple Architecture:** A hand-drawn-style diagram of components, without fancy UML.
> 3. **Show the Initial, Messy Code:** A single, straightforward C# implementation that tries to handle everything at once.
> 4. **Spot the "Oops" Moments:** We'll annotate the code with pop-ups — little callouts — to explain what each block is doing and where it breaks down.

By the end of this chapter, you'll understand exactly why we need design patterns. Ready? Let's fire up the oven.

2.1 Core Requirements of the Pizza Business

Our imaginary pizza shop — ***"Delizioso Pizzeria"*** — has a very simple vision:

- Customers can **order pizzas** (e.g., Margherita, Pepperoni, Veggie).
- Some orders are **combos** (pizza + drink + dessert).
- Prices can vary (add-ons, weekday deals, coupons later).
- The kitchen must **bake → pack → deliver**, then send notifications.
- We **reserve ingredients** (inventory) and take payments via a third party.
- We keep **orders in memory** for now and print basic reports.

For now, no fancy web front end or actual database. We'll simulate **"Data Storage"** with **"In-memory Lists".** As you'll see, even this "simple" functionality quickly becomes a tangled ball of code if we're not careful.

2.2 A Simple Architecture Sketch

Below is a **hand-drawn–style sketch** of how we imagine the app, before any patterns.

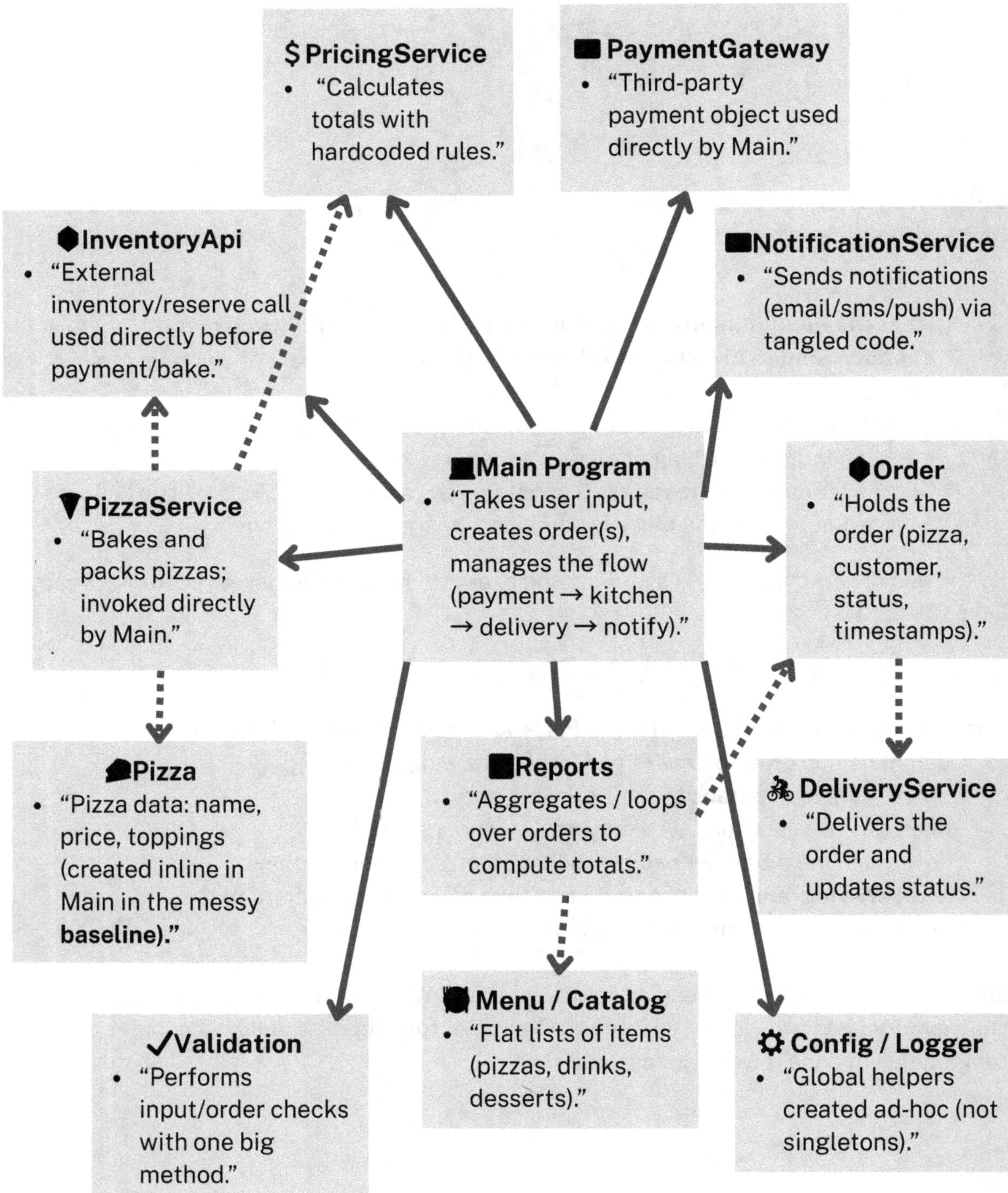

2.3 The Initial Code — Everything in Action (with No Patterns)

Below is a **complete, runnable C# console application** that meets the requirements **without using any design patterns.** (We've added pop-up callouts to highlight what each section does — and where it starts to get messy.)

⬣ Remember: This code is intentionally "ugly." Our goal is to show the pain points. In later chapters, design patterns will swoop in to rescue us.

Scan Pizza App

Pizza.cs

```
// File: Pizza.cs
using System.Collections.Generic;

public class Topping
{
   public string Name { get; }
   public Topping(string name) { Name = name; }
}

public class Pizza
{
   public Pizza(string name, decimal price, IEnumerable<string>
toppings,
            bool extraCheese, bool stuffedCrust, bool glutenFree = false,
bool doublePepperoni = false)
   {
      Name = name;
      Price = price;
      Toppings = new List<Topping>();
      foreach (var t in toppings)
      {
        Toppings.Add(new Topping(t));
      }
      ExtraCheese = extraCheese;
      StuffedCrust = stuffedCrust;
      GlutenFree = glutenFree;
      DoublePepperoni = doublePepperoni;
   }
   public string Name { get; set; }
   public decimal Price { get; set; }
   public List<Topping> Toppings { get; set; }
   public bool ExtraCheese { get; set; }
   public bool StuffedCrust { get; set; }
   public bool GlutenFree { get; set; }
   public bool DoublePepperoni { get; set; }
}
```

1 This constructor has too many parameters and flags. Adding more options will make it unreadable and confusing.

2 Add-ons like "extra cheese" or "gluten-free" are stored as booleans here. If we add more toppings, this class will explode with flags.

3 Duplicate topping objects — wastes memory unnecessarily.

4 No cloning method — copying pizzas requires repetitive manual code.

```
public class Drink
{
    public string Name { get; set; }
    public decimal Price { get; set; }

    public Drink(string name, decimal price)
    {
        Name = name;
        Price = price;
    }
}

public class Dessert
{
    public string Name { get; set; }
    public decimal Price { get; set; }

    public Dessert(string name, decimal price)
    {
        Name = name;
        Price = price;
    }
}
```

Config.cs

5 **Config object made in many places — settings can get messy**

6 **Too many copies of config — no single place for rules**

7 **Static config here — not safe if many things run at once**

```
// ========================
// File: Config.cs
// ========================
public class Config
{
    public string Currency = "USD";
    public string Region = "US";
}

public class Logger
{
    public void Log(string msg) => System.Console.WriteLine("[LOG] " + msg);
}

public static class IdGenerator
{
    private static int _next = 1;
    public static int Next() => _next++;
}
```

Menu.cs

```
// =========================
// File: Menu.cs
// =========================
using System.Collections.Generic;

public class Menu
{
    public List<string> Categories = new() { "Pizzas", "Drinks", "Desserts" };
    public List<string> Items = new() { "Margherita", "Pepperoni", "Veggie",
"Coke", "Brownie" };
}
```

8 Just a plain list — no easy way to handle single items and groups the same way

THE PIZZA APP

InventoryAPI.cs

```
// =========================
// File: InventoryApi.cs
// =========================
using System;

public class InventoryApi
{
    public bool ReserveIngredients(Pizza pizza)
    {
        Console.WriteLine($"[Inventory] Reserving ingredients for
{pizza.Name}...");
        return true;
    }
}
```

9 Direct remote call — no caching, retry, rate-limiting, or authentication in place

Validation.cs

```
public static class Validation
{
    public static bool Validate(Order order, out string error)
    {
        if (order == null) { error = "Null order"; return false; }
        if (string.IsNullOrWhiteSpace(order.CustomerName)) { error = "Name
required"; return false; }
        if (order.Pizza == null) { error = "No pizza chosen"; return false; }
        if (order.Pizza.Price <= 0) { error = "Invalid price"; return false; }
        // ... dozens more checks
        error = null;       return true;
    }
}
```

10 Single giant validator — all checks jammed together

Order.cs

11 Using raw strings for order status

12 No snapshot/restore of order state before payment/cancel

13 No notifications when order status changes

```
// =========================
// File: Order.cs
// =========================
using System;

public class Order
{
   public int OrderId { get; set; }
   public string CustomerName { get; set; }
   public string Address { get; set; }
   public Pizza Pizza { get; set; }
   public string Status { get; set; }
   public DateTime TimeOrdered { get; set; }
   public DateTime TimeDelivered { get; set; }
}
```

Reports.cs

14 Callers loop raw lists everywhere

15 Status is just a string

16 Ignores add-ons/discounts; no extensibility

17 Brittle type checks for each new report type/op

```
// =========================
// File: Reports.cs
// =========================
using System;
using System.Collections.Generic;

public class Reports
{
   public static int CountDelivered(List<Order> orders)
   {
      int c = 0;
      foreach (var o in orders)
         if (o.Status == "Delivered") c++;
      return c;
   }

   public static decimal SumRevenue(object[] items)
   {
      decimal total = 0;
      foreach (var x in items)
      {
         if (x is Order o) total += o.Pizza.Price;
         else if (x is Pizza p) total += p.Price;
      }
      return total;
   }
}
```

PaymentGateway3rdParty.cs

```
// ========================
// File: PaymentGateway_3rdParty.cs
// ========================
using System;

public class PaymentGateway3rdParty
{
    public bool Pay(decimal amount, string currencyCode, string
rawCardToken)
    {
        Console.WriteLine($"[3rdPartyPay] Charging {amount}
{currencyCode} using {rawCardToken}...");
        return true;
    }
}
```

18 Awkward 3rd-party method signature we don't control

THE PIZZA APP

PricingService.cs

```
// ========================
// File: PricingService.cs
// ========================

using System;

public static class PricingService
{
    public static decimal CalculateTotal(Order order)
    {
        decimal total = order.Pizza.Price;

        if (order.Pizza.ExtraCheese) total += 1.00m;
        if (order.Pizza.StuffedCrust) total += 1.50m;

        var day = DateTime.Now.DayOfWeek.ToString();
        if (day == "Tuesday") total *= 0.9m;

        return total;
    }
}
```

19 Discount logic is hardcoded with if/else

DeliveryService.cs

```
// ========================
// File: DeliveryService.cs
// ========================
using System;
using System.Threading;

public class DeliveryService
{
   public void Deliver(Order order)
   {
      Console.WriteLine($"Delivering #{order.OrderId} to
{order.Address}...");
      Thread.Sleep(300);
      order.Status = "Delivered";
      order.TimeDelivered = DateTime.Now;
   }
}
```

NotificationService.cs

20 Notification logic tightly coupled
Channel × Provider (email/sms/push × smtp/twilio/...) all mixed together

```
using System;
public class NotificationService
{
   public void Send(string channel, string provider, string message)
   {
      if (channel == "email")
      {
         if (provider == "smtp")
            Console.WriteLine($"SMTP email: {message}");
         else if (provider == "ses")
             Console.WriteLine($"SES email: {message}");
      }
      else if (channel == "sms")
      {
         if (provider == "twilio")
            Console.WriteLine($"Twilio SMS: {message}");
         else if (provider == "nexmo")
            Console.WriteLine($"Nexmo SMS: {message}");
      }
      else if (channel == "push")
      {
         if (provider == "fcm")
            Console.WriteLine($"FCM Push: {message}");
      }
   }
}
```

PizzaService.cs

```
// ==========================
// File: PizzaService.cs
// ==========================
using System;
using System.Threading;

public class PizzaService
{
  public bool BakePizza(Order order)
  {
    Console.WriteLine($"Baking {order.Pizza.Name}...");
    Thread.Sleep(500);
    order.Status = "Baked";
    return true;
  }

  public void PackPizza(Order order)
  {
    Console.WriteLine($"Packing {order.Pizza.Name}...");
    order.Status = "Packed";
  }
}
```

21 Baking is synchronous, blocking thread → No queue/async.

22 The sequence of steps is hardcoded, fixed pipeline

23 Pizza status transitions scattered in random places.

Program.cs

```
// ==========================
// File: Program.cs
// ==========================
using System;
using System.Reflection.Emit;
using System.Text.RegularExpressions;

class Program
{
  static void Main()
  {
    var pizzaService = new PizzaService();
    var deliveryService = new DeliveryService();
    var payment = new PaymentGateway3rdParty();
    var notifier = new NotificationService();
    var inventory = new InventoryApi();

    Console.WriteLine("Welcome to Delizioso Pizzeria!");
```

24 Adapter pain (odd API)

25 Bridge pain (channel x provider)

26 Proxy pain (direct remote)

```
    Console.WriteLine("Available pizzas: Margherita, Pepperoni, Veggie");
    Console.Write("What would you like? (e.g., 'Pepperoni' or '2x
Margherita + Coke'): ");
    string input = Console.ReadLine();
```

27 INTERPRETER pain — ad-hoc parsing will grow messy

```
    var match = Regex.Match(input, @"^(?<qty>\d+)x\s*(?<item>.+)$",
RegexOptions.IgnoreCase);
    int qty = match.Success ? int.Parse(match.Groups["qty"].Value) : 1;
    string choice = match.Success ? match.Groups["item"].Value : input;

    Pizza chosenPizza = null;
```

28 FACTORY METHOD pain — long if/else to create objects

```
    if (choice.Equals("Margherita", StringComparison.OrdinalIgnoreCase))
    {
      chosenPizza = new Pizza("Margherita", 5.00m,
        new[] { "Cheese", "Tomato Sauce" },
        extraCheese: false, stuffedCrust: false);
    }
    else if (choice.Equals("Pepperoni",
StringComparison.OrdinalIgnoreCase))
    {
      chosenPizza = new Pizza("Pepperoni", 6.50m,
        new[] { "Cheese", "Tomato Sauce", "Pepperoni" },
        extraCheese: false, stuffedCrust: true);
    }
    else if (choice.Equals("Veggie", StringComparison.OrdinalIgnoreCase))
    {
      chosenPizza = new Pizza("Veggie", 6.00m,
        new[] { "Cheese", "Tomato Sauce", "Bell Peppers", "Olives" },
        extraCheese: true, stuffedCrust: false);
    }
    else
    {
```

29 ABSTRACT FACTORY pain — ad-hoc "family" creation (pizza+drink+dessert)

```
      if (choice.Equals("Combo1", StringComparison.OrdinalIgnoreCase))
      {
        chosenPizza = new Pizza("Margherita", 5.00m,
          new[] { "Cheese", "Tomato Sauce" }, false, false);
        var drink = new Drink("Coke", 2.00m);
        var dessert = new Dessert("Brownie", 3.00m);
      }
      else
      {
        Console.WriteLine("Sorry, we don't have that.");
        return;
      }
    }
```

```
      for (int i = 0; i < qty; i++)
      {
        int id = IdGenerator.Next();

        var order = new Order
        {
           OrderId = id,
           CustomerName = "Walk-in",
           Address = "Counter",
           Pizza = chosenPizza,
           Status = "Received",
           TimeOrdered = DateTime.Now
        };


       if (!inventory.ReserveIngredients(order.Pizza))
       {
          Console.WriteLine("Out of stock"); continue;
       }

        var total = PricingService.CalculateTotal(order);
        if (!payment.Pay(total, "USD", "card-..."))
        {
           Console.WriteLine("Payment failed");
           continue;
        }


        pizzaService.BakePizza(order);
        pizzaService.PackPizza(order);
        deliveryService.Deliver(order);


        notifier.Send("email", "smtp", $"Order #{order.OrderId} delivered");

        Console.WriteLine($"Done #{order.OrderId}");
      }
    }
}
```

30 Not a proper Singleton/Thread-safe ID generation

31 Prototype pain — reusing same instance

32 State as raw string

33 FACADE pain — Program orchestrates everything directly

34 Strategy pain (if/switch rules)

35 Fixed step sequence written manually (will repeat in many places)

36 Command pain — no queue/retry/undo)

37 MEDIATOR pain — services talk directly (Pizza → Delivery → Notifier) As system grows, each new service needs to know about all others.

2.4 Where the Mess Begins — Spotting the "Oops" Moments

As you look at this code, you'll notice several pain points. Below are the **major "Oops" Moments,** each of which a design pattern can help fix later:

Oops Moment 1 — Too Many Parameters in Constructor
🔴 The constructor takes several parameters plus flags. This makes it hard to read, hard to maintain, and error-prone when creating pizzas.
💡 Who will help? — Builder Pattern will let us create pizzas step-by-step without dumping all parameters into one big constructor.

Oops Moment 2 — Add-ons Stored as Booleans
🔴 Storing extra toppings, drinks, or sides as bool fields means we'll need to keep adding more booleans for every new add-on. The class will grow messy and rigid.
💡 Who will help? — Decorator Pattern will let us attach features to a pizza dynamically without modifying the base class.

Oops Moment 3 — Duplicate Topping Objects
🔴 Every pizza creates its own topping objects, even if they're identical. This wastes memory and slows things down for big menus.
💡 Who will help? — Flyweight Pattern will share topping objects between pizzas to save resources.

Oops Moment 4 — No Cloning Method
🔴 If we need to duplicate a pizza (e.g., "same as my friend's order"), we must manually copy every field — slow and error-prone.
💡 Who will help? — Prototype Pattern will let us clone pizzas instantly with all their properties intact.

Oops Moment 5 — No Single Source of Truth for Configurations
🔴 The configuration object is created anywhere in the app with different settings. There's no guarantee that all parts of the system are using the same values.
💡 Who will help? — Singleton Pattern will ensure there's only one configuration instance that everyone shares.

Oops Moment 6 — Multiple Instances, No Global Policy
🔴 Having multiple config objects floating around makes it easy for parts of the app to go out of sync.
💡 Who will help? — Singleton Pattern will centralize configuration and enforce one global state.

Oops Moment 7 — Naive Static Approach

● A static config may seem simpler, but it's not thread-safe, not flexible for unit tests, and can't be easily reloaded from a file or database.

Who will help? — Singleton Pattern with proper initialization will give thread safety and flexibility.

Oops Moment 8 — Flat Menu Structure

● The menu is just a list of individual items. If you want a "Family Combo" that contains pizzas, drinks, and desserts, you can't treat it the same way as a single pizza. You'll end up writing special code for every group type.

Who will help? — Composite Pattern will let us treat individual items and groups uniformly.

Oops Moment 9 — Raw Remote Call to Inventory API

● The code calls the inventory service directly every time, without caching results, retrying failed calls, controlling request rates, or securing access. This can make the app slow, fragile, and potentially unsafe.

Who will help? — Proxy Pattern will wrap this remote call to add caching, retries, rate limits, and authentication without changing the calling code.

Oops Moment 10 — Monolithic Validation Logic

● All validation rules are crammed into one big method/class. If you want to add, remove, or reorder checks, you have to edit this whole block. It's hard to extend and even harder to reuse parts of it in different scenarios.

Who will help? — Chain of Responsibility Pattern will let you break validation into smaller steps, each handled by its own class, and chain them together in flexible orders.

Oops Moment 11 — Fragile Order Status

● Order status is just a string like "Pending", "Paid", "Cancelled". Typos or invalid values can slip in, and logic for transitions is scattered everywhere.

Who will help? — State Pattern will model each status as its own class, ensuring only valid transitions happen.

Oops Moment 12 — No Undo for Orders

● Once you update or cancel an order, there's no way to "roll back" to a previous snapshot. If payment fails halfway, the system can't restore the old state.

Who will help? — Memento Pattern will let us capture and restore order snapshots, making rollback safe.

Oops Moment 13 — Silent Status Changes

● When an order status changes (e.g., from "Pending" to "Paid"), nothing else in the system is informed. The UI, reports, or notification service have no way of knowing.

💡 Who will help? — Observer Pattern will allow automatic notifications to other parts of the system whenever status changes.

Oops Moment 14 — Raw List Iteration Everywhere

● Reports manually loop through every list of pizzas, drinks, and desserts. Any new collection (like combos or coupons) means rewriting loops again and again.

💡 Who will help? — Iterator Pattern will let us traverse collections uniformly, without exposing raw list internals.

Oops Moment 15 — String Status in Reports

● Report logic depends on raw strings like "Completed" or "Failed". If these values change in the Order class, reports break silently.

💡 Who will help? — State Pattern ensures consistent handling of statuses, shared between Orders and Reports.

Oops Moment 16 — Discounts Ignored

● Reports only calculate totals for base menu items. Discounts, coupons, or special add-ons are ignored, requiring hacks in multiple places.

💡 Who will help? — Decorator Pattern (or a Strategy for discount policies) will let us add pricing rules cleanly.

Oops Moment 17 — Brittle Type Checks

● Reports use long if/switch blocks to handle different item types. Every time you add a new type (say, GiftCard), you must edit all the type-checking code.

💡 Who will help? — Visitor Pattern lets you add new operations without modifying existing report item classes.

Oops Moment 18 — Awkward Payment Gateway Signature

● The payment gateway is a 3rd-party library with its own method names and parameters. Our code must bend around its signature, spreading adapter hacks everywhere.

💡 Who will help? — Adapter Pattern will wrap the external API in our own clean interface, so the rest of the app stays simple and consistent.

Oops Moment 19 — Rigid Pricing Rules

🔴 Right now, discounts and promotions are baked into the service with simple if/else checks. As new rules appear (e.g., "Tuesday discount", "Buy 1 get 1 free", "Holiday offers"), the code will quickly become a giant branching mess.

💡 Who will help? — Strategy Pattern will let us define each discount rule separately and swap them in/out without changing the main pricing engine.

Oops Moment 20 — Tangled Notification Logic

🔴 Right now, the service directly ties together channels (Email, SMS, Push) with providers (SMTP, Twilio, Firebase, etc.). Every new combination means more code duplication and mess.

💡 Who will help? — Bridge Pattern will separate what we send (channel) from how it's sent (provider). This way, you can add a new channel or provider without touching everything else.

Oops Moment 21 — No Async/Queue for Pizza Operations

🔴 Baking uses Thread.Sleep, blocking the main thread. If many pizzas come at once, the system will freeze or slow down.

💡 Who will help? — Command Pattern can queue and execute tasks asynchronously.

Oops Moment 22 — Rigid, Hardcoded Pipeline

🔴 The sequence "Bake → Pack → Deliver" is fixed in code. If tomorrow we add "Cool Down Pizza" or "Quality Check," we must rewrite methods.

💡 Who will help? — Template Method Pattern makes the pipeline flexible by defining steps in a reusable structure.

Oops Moment 23 — Scattered Status Transitions

🔴 Pizza status changes (Baked, Packed, etc.) are raw strings sprinkled everywhere. Easy to mistype, hard to manage when states grow.

💡 Who will help? — State Pattern keeps all status logic organized and prevents chaos.

Oops Moment 24 — Adapter Pain (Awkward Payment API)

🔴 The payment gateway's API doesn't fit our needs (strange parameters, odd return types). We call it directly, so any change will break us.

💡 Who will help? — Adapter Pattern wraps the awkward API in a clean interface.

Oops Moment 25 — Bridge Pain (Notifier Coupling)

🔴 We hardcode "email" + "smtp" in the notifier call. If we add SMS, push, or another provider, this call explodes with if/else.

💡 Who will help? — Bridge Pattern separates notification channel from provider.

Oops Moment 26 — Proxy Pain (Direct Remote API)
● We hit InventoryApi directly. No caching, retries, or rate-limiting. One network hiccup = broken order flow.
💡 Who will help? — Proxy Pattern gives a safe wrapper for remote calls.

Oops Moment 27 — Interpreter Pain (Messy Input Parsing)
● Regex parsing "2x Margherita + Coke" is brittle. Adding more grammar (combos, extras) will make this unreadable spaghetti.
💡 Who will help? — Interpreter Pattern builds a small grammar for menu input.

Oops Moment 28 — Factory Method Pain (Long If/Else for Pizza Creation)
● Each new pizza requires adding another else if. Very repetitive, not scalable.
💡 Who will help? — Factory Method Pattern centralizes object creation.

Oops Moment 29 — Abstract Factory Pain (Combos Built by Hand)
● Combo1 creates pizza + drink + dessert manually in Program.cs. Every combo would repeat this.
💡 Who will help? — Abstract Factory Pattern creates whole "families" of products consistently.

Oops Moment 30 — Singleton Pain (Thread-Unsafe ID Generator)
● IdGenerator.Next() is static but not safe in multithreaded scenarios. Could give duplicate IDs.
💡 Who will help? — Singleton Pattern with thread-safe initialization.

Oops Moment 31 — Prototype Pain (Reusing Same Pizza Instance)
● We reuse the same chosenPizza for all orders. If one modifies it, all orders change.
💡 Who will help? — Prototype Pattern lets us clone pizzas safely.

Oops Moment 32 — State Pain (Raw String Statuses)
● Status like "Received" is just a string. Easy to mistype and scatter across code.
💡 Who will help? — State Pattern models order lifecycle properly.

Oops Moment 33 — Facade Pain (God Program)
● The Program.Main coordinates inventory, payment, baking, packing, delivery, notification — everything! It's bloated and knows too much.
💡 Who will help? — Facade Pattern gives a clean "OrderProcessor" entry point..

Oops Moment 34 — Strategy Pain (Pricing Rules Explosion)
🔴 PricingService.CalculateTotal() is if/switch based. Adding new rules like "Tuesday discount" will clutter fast.
💡 Who will help? — Strategy Pattern keeps each pricing rule separate.

Oops Moment 35 — Template Method Pain (Rigid Workflow)
🔴 The sequence Bake → Pack → Deliver is hardcoded here (and repeated elsewhere). No flexibility if steps change.
💡 Who will help? — Template Method Pattern defines workflows in a reusable skeleton.

Oops Moment 36 — Command Pain (No Queue/Retry/Undo)
🔴 Bake, Pack, Deliver are direct calls. If one fails, there's no retry, no undo, no logging.
💡 Who will help? — Command Pattern wraps each step into queueable, retryable commands.

🔴 **Oops Moment 37 — Services Talking Too Much**
Right now, the PizzaService, DeliveryService, and NotificationService know about each other directly. The moment we add more services (cashier, kitchen screen, loyalty points, etc.), the number of connections will explode. Every service has to call every other service it depends on — creating a spaghetti of dependencies.
💡 Who will help? — The Mediator Pattern will act like a central "kitchen manager." Instead of every service talking to every other one, they all talk to the mediator. The mediator decides who needs to be informed, keeping communication clean and decoupled.

2.5 Wrapping Up Chapter 2

You've now seen our **initial, pattern-free implementation** of the pizza app. It "works," but:

- It's tightly coupled.
- It's hard to change and extend.
- It mixes responsibilities.
- It's brittle (lots of risk for typos, duplicate code, and freeze-ups).

In the next chapter, we'll call in our first helper from the Design Pattern Family: the **Factory Method**. We'll refactor this code so that **adding a new pizza** type doesn't require hunting down every if-else or hardcoded list. Step by step, each pattern will arrive right when we need it, turning this messy code into a well-structured masterpiece.

> **Next Up: Chapter 3 — Factory Method: Making Pizzas Without the Copy-Paste Mayhem**
> Ready to see how one small change can make your life infinitely easier? See you there!

🍕 PART 2: THE APP BEGINS–CREATIONAL PATTERNS

Where Objects Get Their Start! 🎉

Meet "The Builders" - the master creators who bring our pizza objects to life! This is where we master the art of object creation without the mess.

What's Cooking:

- **Factory Method:** Specialized chefs crafting perfect pies
- **Abstract Factory:** Combo meal masters
- **Builder:** Custom pizza artists
- **Prototype:** Lightning-fast pizza cloner
- **Singleton:** The one-and-only manager

You'll Master:

- Creating objects without if/else spaghetti
- Building complex objects step-by-step
- The secret to single-instance control
- When to clone vs. create fresh

Perfect if you've ever:

- Written new Something() and wondered "there's got to be a better way"
- Had constructors with too many parameters
- Copied object creation code everywhere

Get ready to become an object-creating maestro! 👨‍🍳✨

Chapter 3

Factory Method — Making Pizzas Without the Copy-Paste Mayhem

Setting The Stage

Our pizza app has been running on sheer determination and caffeine, but the cracks are showing. Every new pizza type feels like defusing a bomb — one wrong edit and something else breaks. Before we roll in the Factory Method to save the day, let's take a good look at the mess we're in.

> *In this chapter, you'll:*
>
> 1. **Spot the Pain Points:** See how adding a single pizza requires touching code in multiple places.
> 2. **Understand Why It's Risky:** Learn why scattered creation code can slow us down and cause bugs.
> 3. **Peek at the Existing Code:** We'll walk through the current approach line by line, highlighting exactly where it hurts.
> 4. **Prepare for the Fix:** We'll set the stage so that the Factory Method feels like the natural, obvious next step.

3.1 Hook: What's the Pain?

"Every time we add a new pizza, we have to open multiple files, update long if-else chains, and pray we didn't miss something. It's like juggling pizzas in one hand and code bugs in the other. Not fun."

3.2 The Problem in Our Pizza App

Let's revisit the messy code from Chapter 2. Our Main() method in Pizza.cs is choked by a long if/else chain that creates pizza objects *(Oops Moment: 28)*.

```
if (choice.Equals("Margherita", StringComparison.OrdinalIgnoreCase))
        {
            chosenPizza = new Pizza("Margherita", 5.00m,
                new[] { "Cheese", "Tomato Sauce" },
                extraCheese: false, stuffedCrust: false);
        }
        else if (choice.Equals("Pepperoni", StringComparison.OrdinalIgnoreCase))
        {
            chosenPizza = new Pizza("Pepperoni", 6.50m,
                new[] { "Cheese", "Tomato Sauce", "Pepperoni" },
                extraCheese: false, stuffedCrust: true);
        }
        else if (choice.Equals("Veggie", StringComparison.OrdinalIgnoreCase))
        {
            chosenPizza = new Pizza("Veggie", 6.00m,
                new[] { "Cheese", "Tomato Sauce", "Bell Peppers", "Olives" },
                extraCheese: true, stuffedCrust: false);
        }
```

Why This Hurts:

- **Duplication:** This creation logic is duplicated anywhere we need a pizza.
- **Tight Coupling:** Main() is tightly coupled to every concrete Pizza constructor.
- **Rigid Extension:** Adding a new pizza type means hunting down and modifying every one of these if-else chains.

3.3 The Quick Fix: Simple Factory

The simplest way to fix this is to centralize the creation logic. We're not using a "design pattern" yet, but a common-sense technique often called a **Simple Factory.**

3.3.1 Pattern Definition (Simple Factory)

A **Simple Factory** is a class with a method that handles all the object creation in one place, based on a parameter. It's not a formal GoF pattern, but a fundamental step towards them.

3.3.2 Refactored Code: The PizzaFactory Class

We create a static class whose only job is to create pizzas.

PizzaMaker.cs

```
using System;
using System.Collections.Generic;
public static class PizzaFactory
{
    // Centralized registry: Pizza name -> Creation function
    private static readonly Dictionary<string, Func<Pizza>> _pizzaRegistry =
        new Dictionary<string, Func<Pizza>>(StringComparer.OrdinalIgnoreCase)
        {
            { "Margherita", () => new Pizza("Margherita", 5.00m, new[] { "Cheese", "Tomato Sauce" }, false,
false) },
            { "Pepperoni", () => new Pizza("Pepperoni", 6.50m, new[] { "Cheese", "Tomato Sauce",
"Pepperoni" }, false, true) },
            { "Veggie", () => new Pizza("Veggie", 6.00m, new[] { "Cheese", "Tomato Sauce", "Bell Peppers",
"Olives" }, true, false) }
        };

    // ✅ The public method everyone will use
    public static Pizza CreatePizza(string name)
    {
        if (_pizzaRegistry.TryGetValue(name, out var createPizza))
        {
            return createPizza();
        }
        return null; // Or throw a helpful exception
    }
}
```

Now, our Main() method becomes beautifully simple:

Program.cs

```
// ✅ After: Clean, declarative, and decoupled
Pizza chosenPizza = PizzaFactory.CreatePizza(choice);

if (chosenPizza == null)
{
    Console.WriteLine("Sorry, we don't have that.");
    return;
}
// ... rest of the order process
```

FACTORY METHOD

Why This Matters (Simple Factory):

- **No More Spaghetti:** The if/else chain is gone from Main().
- **Single Source of Truth:** All pizza creation logic lives in one file.
- **Easier Extensions:** To add a Hawaiian pizza, we only need to update the _pizzaRegistry.

3.3.3 Mini-Exercise: Add a Hawaiian Pizza

Add Hawaiian to PizzaFactory:

```
{ "Hawaiian", () => new Pizza("Hawaiian", 7.00m, new[] { "Cheese", "Tomato Sauce", "Ham", "Pineapple"
}, false, false) }
```

Then order "Hawaiian" from the console. Did it work without changing Program.cs?

3.4 The Formal Pattern: Factory Method

The **Simple Factory** is a great solution for our current problem. But what if our needs become more complex? What if different franchises of our pizza chain need to create slightly different versions of the same pizza?

This is where the formal **Factory Method** pattern shines.

Pattern Definition

> *"**Factory Method** is a creational design pattern that provides an interface for creating objects in a superclass, but allows subclasses to alter the type of objects that will be created."*

3.5 Understanding the Pattern

The Real-World Analogy: A Franchise Model

The full **Factory Method** pattern is like a pizza franchise. The head office (the abstract *PizzaFactory* class) defines the entire blueprint for how to create a pizza order: *prepareDough(), addToppings(), bake(), box()*. However, the head office knows that a pepperoni pizza is made differently in New York than it is in Chicago. So, it declares that the step for *CreatePizza()* (the **Factory Method**) must be handled by a local, specialized kitchen.

When a customer orders a pizza at a *NewYorkPizzaFactory,* the head office's proven process is followed, but it's the New York kitchen that creates the authentic, thin-crust pizza. That same process runs at a *ChicagoPizzaFactory*, but the Chicago kitchen creates a deep-dish pizza. The process is consistent, but the end product depends on which specialized factory is implementing the "create" step.

In Code Terms: The *PizzaFactory* base class defines a method for creating objects *(CreatePizza())* but lets its subclasses override that method to decide the exact type of object to instantiate. The base class can then use the created object (via its interface) without knowing its concrete class.

3.6 The Implementation Blueprint: Factory Method Steps

Before we refactor, let's break down the implementation into a simple, repeatable recipe. Whenever you need to implement a Factory Method, follow these steps:

1. Isolate the Product: Identify the objects that need to be created. Define what they have in common by creating a common interface for them (e.g., *IPizza*). Your code will depend on this interface, not the concrete classes.
2. Create Concrete Products: Implement the product interface in multiple concrete classes (e.g., *MargheritaPizza*, *PepperoniPizza*). Each class provides its own specific implementation.
3. Define the Creator Class: Create an abstract creator class (e.g., *PizzaFactory*). This class will declare the factory method (e.g., *CreatePizza()*), which returns an object of the product interface. Crucially, the creator's core business logic (e.g., *OrderPizza()*) will call this factory method.
4. Implement Concrete Creators: For each variant of the product, create a concrete creator subclass (e.g., *StandardPizzaFactory*) that overrides the factory method to instantiate and return the correct concrete product.

Let's see this blueprint come to life in our code.

3.7 Implementing the Full Factory Method

Step 1: Isolate the Product (Define IPizza)

First,we need a common interface for all our products. This is the foundation that allows our code to be flexible.

FACTORY METHOD

IPizza.cs

```
// File: IPizza.cs
public interface IPizza
{
    string Name { get; }
    decimal Price { get; }
    void Prepare();
    void Bake();
    void Box();
}
```

Step 2: Create Concrete Products (MargheritaPizza, etc.)

Now,we create the specific pizza classes that implement this contract.

MargheritaPizza.cs

```
// File: MargheritaPizza.cs
public class MargheritaPizza : IPizza
{
    public string Name => "Margherita";
    public decimal Price => 5.00m;

    public void Prepare() => Console.WriteLine($"Preparing {Name} with fresh basil and
mozzarella...");
    public void Bake() => Console.WriteLine($"Baking {Name} to perfection...");
    public void Box() => Console.WriteLine($"Placing {Name} in a classic box.");
}
```

(Similar classes would be created for *PepperoniPizza, VeggiePizza*, etc.)

Step 3: Define the Creator Abstract Class (PizzaFactory)

This class defines the Factory Method (*CreatePizza()*). It can also contain other core business logic that uses the products the factory creates.

PizzaFactory.cs

```
// File: PizzaFactory.cs
public abstract class PizzaFactory
{
  // This is the Factory Method. Subclasses MUST implement this.
  protected abstract IPizza CreatePizza(string type);

  // This is a core business method that uses the factory method.
  // It doesn't know the concrete class of the pizza, just its interface.
  public IPizza OrderPizza(string type)
  {
    // ☑ The power: This code works with ANY IPizza, thanks to the factory method.
    IPizza pizza = CreatePizza(type);

    if (pizza == null)
    {
      Console.WriteLine("Sorry, we don't have that pizza.");
      return null;
    }

    pizza.Prepare();
    pizza.Bake();
    pizza.Box();
    Console.WriteLine($"Your {pizza.Name} is ready! Price: ${pizza.Price}");

    return pizza;
  }
}
```

Step 4: Implement a Concrete Creator (StandardPizzaFactory)

Finally,we create a subclass that makes the decision about which object to create.

StandardPizzaFactory.cs

```
// File: StandardPizzaFactory.cs
public class StandardPizzaFactory : PizzaFactory
{
  // The Factory Method implementation
  protected override IPizza CreatePizza(string type) {
    switch (type.ToLower()){ // This is where the creation decision happens.
        case "margherita": return new MargheritaPizza();
        case "pepperoni": return new PepperoniPizza();
        case "veggie": return new VeggiePizza();
        default: return null; }
  }
}
```

How We Use It Now:

Program.cs

```
// ===============
// File: Program.cs
// ===============
// ... other using statements ...
using FactoryPattern; // Assuming your factories are here

class Program
{
    private static PizzaFactory _pizzaFactory; // Declared outside Main

    static void Main()
    {
        _pizzaFactory = new StandardPizzaFactory();

        // ... other initializations ...

        // ✅ Factory Method in action: Delegate creation to the factory.
        IPizza chosenPizza = _pizzaFactory.OrderPizza(choice);

        if (chosenPizza == null)
        {
            // Handle combo or invalid order
            if (choice.Equals("Combo1", StringComparison.OrdinalIgnoreCase))
            {
                // ... combo logic ...
            }
            else
            {
                Console.WriteLine("Sorry, we don't have that.");
                return;
            }
        }

        // ... rest of the code ...
        // Note: The following code will need refactoring to use IPizza (a TODO for later chapters)
        var order = new Order
        {
            // Pizza = chosenPizza // ❌ This will be the next refactoring step!
        };
        // ...
    }
}
```

3.8 Why the Factory Method Matters

- **Architectural Flexibility:** The *OrderPizza()* method is completely independent from the concrete pizza classes. We can create new PizzaFactory subclasses (NYStylePizzaFactory, ChicagoStylePizzaFactory) that produce different styles of the same pizza type without touching the *OrderPizza* logic.
- **Deeper Decoupling:** The application is now coded to interfaces (*IPizza, PizzaFactory*), not concrete implementations. This is the foundation of maintainable, large-scale software.
- **The Open/Closed Principle:** We can introduce new types of pizzas and new stores by extending the code (adding new classes), not by modifying existing code.

3.9 Mini Exercise: Expand the Franchise

Your pizza app is a huge success! Now you need to open new franchise locations that create regional styles of pizzas.

Your Task:

1. Create two new concrete factories: *NewYorkPizzaFactory* and *ChicagoPizzaFactory*.
2. Implement their *CreatePizza* method to return different styles of the same pizza type.
3. Update the *Main* method to use the new factories.

3.10 When to Call the Factory

- **Use a Simple Factory** when you need to centralize the creation of a family of objects and your creation logic is relatively simple and static. It's a pragmatic, quick win.
- **Use the Factory Method Pattern** when you foresee a need for flexibility and extension. When the core process should be defined in a base class, but the exact product to be created must be decided by subclasses.

3.11 Transition to Chapter 4

We've now mastered creating individual pizzas, first with a simple helper and then with a powerful, extensible pattern. But our customers are hungry for more! They want combos: a pizza, a drink, and a dessert. Wiring these together by hand in our code would bring back the old mess. We need a way to create families of related products. This is a job for the **Abstract Factory pattern.**

> **Next Up: Chapter 4 — Abstract Factory: Crafting Complete Meal Families**
> Ready to build entire pizza combos without the wiring chaos? Let's assemble the whole package.

Want to see this pattern in action? Scan me!

Chapter 4

Abstract Factory: Crafting Complete Meal Families

Setting The Stage

Our pizza creation is now clean, but customers are hungry for more! They don't just want a pizza; they want a combo: a pizza, a drink, and a dessert.

> *In this chapter, you'll:*
> 1. **Spot the Pain Points:** Identify the problem of creating families of related objects.
> 2. **Understand the Pattern:** Learn the Abstract Factory pattern to solve it.
> 3. **Refactor Combo Creation:** Refactor our combo creation to be as elegant as our pizza creation.
> 4. **See the Magic of Patterns:** See how patterns work together to build a robust architecture.

4.1 Hook: What's the Pain?

"Every combo meal forces us to manually wire together a pizza, a drink, and a dessert across different classes. Adding a 'Family Feast' combo means hunting down and updating code in a dozen places. We're back to copy-paste mayhem, but now with entire meals!"

4.2 The Problem in Our Pizza App

Our code is still plagued by the hand-rolled combo we saw in Chapter 2 and Chapter 3: *(Oops Moment: 29).*

```
if (choice.Equals("Combo1", StringComparison.OrdinalIgnoreCase))
{
    chosenPizza = new Pizza("Margherita", 5.00m,
new[] { "Cheese", "Tomato Sauce" }, false, false);
    var drink = new Drink("Coke", 2.00m);
    var dessert = new Dessert("Brownie", 3.00m);
    // no family factory; everything wired by hand here
}
```

Why This Hurts:

- **Inconsistency:** Nothing guarantees that a "Combo1" always has a "Margherita" pizza and a "Coke". A typo could break the combo.
- **Rigidity:** Adding a new combo (e.g., "*VeggieCombo*") means duplicating this code and manually changing the products.
- **Coupling:** The client code (*Program.Main*) is tightly coupled to the concrete constructors of Pizza, Drink, and Dessert.

4.3 The Formal Pattern: Abstract Factory

Pattern Definition

> *"**Abstract Factory** is a creational design pattern that lets you produce families of related objects without specifying their concrete classes."*

In Simpler Terms: It's a factory for factories. You first create a factory object (e.g., a *ComboFactory*). This factory object then has the methods to create an entire set of related products (a pizza, a drink, a dessert). The client code uses this factory without knowing the specific classes of the products it gets — it just gets a perfectly matched set.

4.4 Understanding the Pattern

The Real-World Analogy: The Combo Meal Kit

Think of the Abstract Factory as the **central combo menu** in our app. Right now, we manually assemble a "Combo1" by calling *new Pizza(), new Drink(), new Dessert()* separately. This is like a cashier running to three different kitchens to get each item. Instead, we will create a *IComboFactory* interface that represents the idea of a combo. Its methods (*CreatePizza(), CreateDrink(), CreateDessert()*) promise to return a perfectly matched set.

A *Combo1Factory* class will implement this interface. When our app needs a "Combo1", it will just ask the *Combo1Factory* for the entire meal. The factory handles the concrete instantiation, ensuring the Margherita pizza, Coke, and Brownie are always created together correctly. The main code no longer worries about the "how" – it just gets a ready-to-serve combo.

4.5 The Implementation Blueprint: Abstract Factory Method Steps

Before we refactor our combo, let's break down the implementation into a simple, repeatable recipe. Whenever you need to create families of related objects, follow these steps:

1. **Define Abstract Product Families:** Identify the different types of related objects you need to create. For each type, define a common interface (e.g., *IPizza, IDrink, IDessert*). Your code will depend on these interfaces, not the concrete classes.
2. **Implement Concrete Product Families:** Create concrete classes for each product variant that implement these interfaces (e.g., *MargheritaPizza : IPizza, Coke : IDrink, Brownie : IDessert* form one family. *VeggiePizza : IPizza, Juice : IDrink, FruitCup : IDessert* form another).
3. **Declare the Abstract Factory:** Create an interface for the abstract factory (e.g., *IComboFactory*). This interface declares a set of creation methods, one for each abstract product type (e.g., *CreatePizza(), CreateDrink(), CreateDessert()*), each returning its respective abstract product type.

4. **Implement Concrete Factories:** For each variant of the product family, create a concrete factory class that implements the abstract factory interface (e.g., *StandardComboFactory*, *VeggieComboFactory*). Each factory is responsible for instantiating and returning a full, compatible set of concrete products.
5. **Write Client Code Against the Abstract Factory:** The client code is written to work with the abstract factory and product interfaces. It is configured at runtime (e.g., via dependency injection) to use a specific concrete factory. It then uses that factory's methods to create entire families of products, without ever referencing their concrete classes.

4.6 Implementing the Abstract Factory Method

Step 1: Define Abstract Product Families

First, we need interfaces for our products. We have already created *IPizza* in the previous chapter. Lets create same for *IDrink* and *IDessert*.

IDrink.cs

```
public interface IDrink
{
   string Name { get; }
   decimal Price { get; }
}
```

IDessert.cs

```
public interface IDessert
{
   string Name { get; }
   decimal Price { get; }
}
```

Step 2: Implement Concrete Products

We already created MargheritaPizza.cs, lets create same classes for Coke and Brownie.

Coke.cs

```
public class Coke : IDrink
{
   public string Name => "Coke";
   public decimal Price => 2.00m;
}
```

Brownie.cs

```
public class Brownie : IDessert
{
   public string Name => "Brownie";
   public decimal Price => 3.00m;
}
```

Step 3: Declare the Abstract Factory

IComboFactory.cs

```
public interface IComboFactory
{
   IPizza CreatePizza();
   IDrink CreateDrink();
   IDessert CreateDessert();
}
```

Step 4: Implement a Concrete Factory

First, we need interfaces for our products. We have already created *IPizza* in the previous chapter. Lets create same for *IDrink* and *IDessert*.

StandardComboFactory.cs

```
public class StandardComboFactory : IComboFactory
{
   public IPizza CreatePizza() => new MargheritaPizza();
   public IDrink CreateDrink() => new Coke();
   public IDessert CreateDessert() => new Brownie();
}
```

What Those Methods Are Doing?

Those methods are the ***CreatePizza***, ***CreateDrink***, and ***CreateDessert*** methods promised by the ***IComboFactory*** interface.
Think of the ***StandardComboFactory*** as a vending machine for Combo #1. When you call:
comboFactory.CreatePizza() ■ it gives you a MargheritaPizza.
comboFactory.CreateDrink() ■ it gives you a Coke.
comboFactory.CreateDessert() ■ it gives you a Brownie.
Its only job is to create and return those specific objects. It doesn't need to contain any other logic. The power is that the rest of your code only knows it's getting an ***IPizza***, an ***IDrink***, and an ***IDessert***. It doesn't know or care that they are specifically a Margherita, a Coke, and a Brownie. This is the decoupling the pattern provides.

Step 5: Client Code (Usage in Program.cs)

This is the crucial refactor. We replace the manual combo creation with abstract factory. In your Program.cs (where you handle the order):

Program.cs

```
//💬 Check for a combo FIRST, before trying the pizza factory
if (choice.Equals("Combo1", StringComparison.OrdinalIgnoreCase))
{
   //💬ABSTRACT FACTORY IN ACTION: Get a family of products with one factory.
   IComboFactory comboFactory = new StandardComboFactory();
   chosenPizza = comboFactory.CreatePizza();
   chosenDrink = comboFactory.CreateDrink();
   chosenDessert = comboFactory.CreateDessert();
```

```
    Console.WriteLine($"Combo1 selected! You get:");
    Console.WriteLine($"  - {chosenPizza.Name} (${chosenPizza.Price})");
    Console.WriteLine($"  - {chosenDrink.Name} (${chosenDrink.Price})");
    Console.WriteLine($"  - {chosenDessert.Name} (${chosenDessert.Price})");

    decimal comboTotal = chosenPizza.Price + chosenDrink.Price + chosenDessert.Price;
    Console.WriteLine($"Total for combo: ${comboTotal}");
}
else
{
    //■ Not a combo? Let the Pizza Factory (from Chapter 3) handle it.
    chosenPizza = _pizzaFactory.OrderPizza(choice);
    if (chosenPizza != null)
    {
        Console.WriteLine($"You ordered: {chosenPizza.Name} (${chosenPizza.Price})");
    }
}
```

The Key Separation of Responsibilities:

- **The Factory's Job (StandardComboFactory):** To **CREATE** the objects. ("Here are your products.")
- **The Client's Job (Program.Main):** To **USE** the objects. ("Let me tell you what you got and calculate the price.")

This separation is what makes the pattern so powerful. You can change what gets created (by using a different factory) without changing how it's used (the code that prints the receipt).

Key Points to Test:

1. Ordering "Combo1" should create a *MargheritaPizza*, a *Coke*, and a Brownie automatically.
2. Ordering "Pepperoni" should still work using the original _pizzaFactory from Chapter 3, proving the patterns work together.
3. Adding a new combo (e.g., "VeggieCombo") would now only require creating a new *VeggieComboFactory* : *IComboFactory* and adding a single if condition in the client code. The core logic for creating the products is encapsulated in the new factory.

This code cleanly separates the concerns and sets the stage for easily adding new product families. Test this structure in your project, and it will demonstrate the power of the pattern perfectly.

4.7 Why the Abstract Factory Matters

- **Family Consistency:** Ensures that all products created by a factory are compatible (e.g., you don't get a meat pizza in a veggie combo).
- **Decoupling:** The client code is completely independent from the concrete classes of the products it gets.
- **Swappable Factories:** You can easily swap the entire family of products by passing a different factory (e.g., switch from *StandardComboFactory* to *PremiumComboFactory*).

4.8 Mini Exercise: Create a Premium Combo

Your Task: Create a *PremiumComboFactory* that produces a *GourmetPizza*, *CraftSoda*, and *Cheesecake*.

4.9 When to Call the Abstract Factory

"Whenever you find yourself manually assembling groups of related objects (like UI elements, meal combos, or platform-specific components), it's time for an Abstract Factory."

4.10 Transition to Chapter 5

"Now that we can seamlessly create whole families of objects, our customers are getting more demanding. They don't just want a pre-defined combo; they want to customize everything! Extra cheese, no olives, double pepperoni, gluten-free crust... Supporting every possible combination through subclasses would lead to an explosion of classes. Next, we'll learn how to construct these complex pizzas step-by-step using the Builder pattern."

> **Next Up: Chapter 5 — Builder: Crafting the Perfect Custom Pizza**
> Ready to give your customers infinite customization without the constructor chaos? Let's build their dream pizza, one step at a time.

Scan to View Abstract Factory Pattern Code

Builder — Customizing the Pizza

Setting The Stage

Our pizzas are now created efficiently, but customers demand customization — extra cheese, stuffed crust, no onions, double pepperoni. Using constructors with countless parameters is messy and error-prone.

> *In this chapter, you'll:*
> 1. **Identify the pitfalls:** Identify the pitfalls of complex object construction.
> 2. **Learn the Builder pattern:** Learn the Builder pattern to create objects step-by-step.
> 3. **Refactor the Pizza class:** Refactor the Pizza class to support flexible customization without constructor bloat.
> 4. **See the Magic of Builder Pattern:** See how Builder promotes readability and avoids telescoping constructors.

5.1 Hook: What's the Pain?

"Adding just one new topping option forces us to modify the Pizza constructor and every place it's called. We're drowning in parameters like extraCheese, stuffedCrust, glutenFree — imagine adding 10 more options. This is a maintenance nightmare!"

5.2 The Problem in Our Pizza App

Look at the constructor in our Pizza.cs File. (Oops Moment: 1)

```
public Pizza(string name, decimal price, IEnumerable<string> toppings,
             bool extraCheese, bool stuffedCrust, bool glutenFree, bool doublePepperoni)
{
    // ... initialization
}
```

Why This Hurts:

- **Parameter explosion:** Constructors become unreadable.
- **Inflexibility:** Adding new options requires rewriting all existing calls.
- **Error-prone:** Boolean parameters are ambiguous (true for glutenFree? false for stuffedCrust?).

5.3 The Formal Pattern: Builder

Pattern Definition

*"**Builder** is a creational pattern that separates the construction of a complex object from its representation, allowing the same construction process to create different representations."*

In Simpler Terms: The Builder pattern is a way to create a complex object piece by piece. It separates the instructions for building an object from the actual object itself. This means you can use the same step-by-step process to create different types of objects.

5.4 Understanding the Pattern

The Real-World Analogy: The Pizza Order Form

Think of the Builder pattern as a **custom order form** for your pizza. You don't shout a long list of instructions to the chef all at once. Instead, you fill out a form, checking boxes for crust type, adding toppings one by one, and selecting extras. When you're done, you submit the form (*Build()*), and the kitchen delivers your perfectly crafted pizza.
The Builder is that digital form — it lets you specify exactly what you want, step by step, without ever confusing the chef with a messy jumble of options.

5.5 The Implementation Blueprint: Builder Pattern Steps

Before we refactor our pizza customization, let's break down the implementation into a simple, repeatable recipe. Whenever you need to create objects with many optional parameters or complex configuration, follow these steps:

1. **Define the Product Class:** Identify the complex object you need to create (e.g., *Pizza*). This class should have a large number of properties, many of which are optional.
2. **Create the Builder Class:** Create a separate class (e.g., *PizzaBuilder*) whose sole responsibility is to construct the Product. It should have methods to set each of the Product's configurable options.
3. **Implement Step-by-Step Methods:** For each configurable property of the Product, implement a method in the Builder class to set its value (e.g., *AddTopping()*, *SetCrustType()*). Each method should return Builder object itself (*return this;*) to enable method chaining.
4. **Implement the Build Method:** Add a *Build()* method to the Builder class. This method is responsible for constructing and returning the final, fully-configured Product object. It typically calls the Product's constructor, passing in all the values collected by the Builder.
5. **Write Client Code Using the Builder:** The client code creates an instance of the Builder and then calls the step-by-step methods to specify only the desired configuration options. It finishes by calling *Build()* to receive the final, immutable Product object.

    (For example: To build a pizza, the client code would call:
    new PizzaBuilder("Margherita").AddTopping("Cheese").SetExtraCheese(true).Build();)

5.6 Implementing the Builder Pattern

Step 1: Create a CustomPizza Class (if needed)

If your existing *Pizza* class doesn't support all these customizations, create a new class:

CustomPizza.cs

Scan to View Builder Pattern Code

```
public class CustomPizza : IPizza
{
  public string Name { get; }
  public decimal Price { get; }
  public List<string> Toppings { get; }
  public bool ExtraCheese { get; }
  public bool StuffedCrust { get; }
  public bool GlutenFree { get; }

  internal CustomPizza(string name, decimal price, List<string> toppings,
            bool extraCheese, bool stuffedCrust, bool glutenFree)
  {
    Name = name;
    Price = price;
    Toppings = toppings;
    ExtraCheese = extraCheese;
    StuffedCrust = stuffedCrust;
    GlutenFree = glutenFree;
  }

  public void Prepare() => Console.WriteLine($"Preparing {Name} with custom options...");
  public void Bake() => Console.WriteLine($"Baking {Name}...");
  public void Box() => Console.WriteLine($"Placing {Name} in a box.");
}
```

Step 2: Create a New *PizzaBuilder* Class

This class will handle the construction of customizable pizzas:

PizzaBuilder.cs

```
public class PizzaBuilder
{
  private string _name;
  private decimal _basePrice;
  private List<string> _toppings = new List<string>();
  private bool _extraCheese;
  private bool _stuffedCrust;
  private bool _glutenFree;
```

```
public PizzaBuilder(string name, decimal basePrice)
  {
    _name = name;
_basePrice = basePrice;
  }

  public PizzaBuilder AddTopping(string topping)
  {
    _toppings.Add(topping);
    return this; // Enables method chaining
  }

  public PizzaBuilder SetExtraCheese(bool extraCheese)
  {
    _extraCheese = extraCheese;
    return this;
  }

  public PizzaBuilder SetStuffedCrust(bool stuffedCrust)
  {
    _stuffedCrust = stuffedCrust;
    return this;
  }

  public PizzaBuilder SetGlutenFree(bool glutenFree)
  {
    _glutenFree = glutenFree;
    return this;
  }

  public IPizza Build()
  {
    // Calculate final price based on custom options
    decimal finalPrice = _basePrice;
    if (_extraCheese) finalPrice += 1.0m;
    if (_stuffedCrust) finalPrice += 1.5m;
    if (_glutenFree) finalPrice += 2.0m;
    finalPrice += _toppings.Count * 0.5m; // Charge for each topping

    // Create and return the fully constructed, immutable CustomPizza object.
    // This is the ONLY place where 'new CustomPizza()' is called.
    return new CustomPizza(_name, finalPrice, _toppings, _extraCheese, _stuffedCrust, _glutenFree);
  }
}
```

Step 3: Create a *BuildACustomPizza* Method

Now create a BuildACustomPizza Method in your Program.cs (for now), so that Users can input custom options to create their own custom pizza.

Program.cs

```
private static IPizza BuildACustomPizza()
{
    Console.WriteLine("Welcome to the Pizza Customizer!");

    // 1. Get the base details
    Console.Write("Enter a name for your custom pizza: ");
    string name = Console.ReadLine();

    Console.Write("Enter the base price for your pizza: $");
    decimal basePrice = decimal.Parse(Console.ReadLine());

    // 2. Initialize the Builder with the base details
    var pizzaBuilder = new PizzaBuilder(name, basePrice);

    // 3. Customize the pizza through a series of prompts
    Console.WriteLine("\nLet's add toppings. Type 'done' to finish.");
    string input;
    while (true)
    {
        Console.Write("Enter a topping: ");
        input = Console.ReadLine();
        if (input.ToLower() == "done") break;
        pizzaBuilder.AddTopping(input);
    }

    Console.Write("\nAdd extra cheese? (yes/no): ");
    pizzaBuilder.SetExtraCheese(Console.ReadLine().ToLower() == "yes");

    Console.Write("Make it stuffed crust? (yes/no): ");
    pizzaBuilder.SetStuffedCrust(Console.ReadLine().ToLower() == "yes");

    Console.Write("Make it gluten-free? (yes/no): ");
    pizzaBuilder.SetGlutenFree(Console.ReadLine().ToLower() == "yes");

    // 4. Finalize the construction process and return the pizza
    IPizza myCustomPizza = pizzaBuilder.Build();

    // 5. Display the details to the user
    Console.WriteLine("\n✅ Your custom pizza is ready!");
    Console.WriteLine($"--> Name: {myCustomPizza.Name}");
    Console.WriteLine($"--> Final Price: ${myCustomPizza.Price}");
```

```
// Since we know it's a CustomPizza, we can cast to show details
 var customPizza = myCustomPizza as CustomPizza;
 Console.WriteLine($"--> Toppings: {string.Join(", ", customPizza.Toppings)}");
 Console.WriteLine($"--> Extra Cheese: {customPizza.ExtraCheese}");
 Console.WriteLine($"--> Stuffed Crust: {customPizza.StuffedCrust}");
 Console.WriteLine($"--> Gluten-Free: {customPizza.GlutenFree}");

 // Return the created pizza
 return myCustomPizza;
}
```

Step 4: Usage in Client Code

Now you can use the builder through your factory:

Program.cs

```
// ... existing parsing code ...
if (choice.Equals("Combo1", StringComparison.OrdinalIgnoreCase))
{
   // ✅ ABSTRACT FACTORY IN ACTION: Get a family of products with one factory.
   IComboFactory comboFactory = new StandardComboFactory();
   chosenPizza = comboFactory.CreatePizza();
   chosenDrink = comboFactory.CreateDrink();
   chosenDessert = comboFactory.CreateDessert();

   Console.WriteLine($"Combo1 selected! You get:");
   Console.WriteLine($"  - {chosenPizza.Name} (${chosenPizza.Price})");
   Console.WriteLine($"  - {chosenDrink.Name} (${chosenDrink.Price})");
   Console.WriteLine($"  - {chosenDessert.Name} (${chosenDessert.Price})");

   decimal comboTotal = chosenPizza.Price + chosenDrink.Price + chosenDessert.Price;
   Console.WriteLine($"Total for combo: ${comboTotal}");
}
else if (choice.Equals("custom", StringComparison.OrdinalIgnoreCase))
{
   // ✅ BUILDER PATTERN IN ACTION: Let user build a custom pizza
   chosenPizza = BuildACustomPizza(); // This method returns an IPizza

   if (chosenPizza != null)
   {
      Console.WriteLine($"Your custom pizza created: {chosenPizza.Name} (${chosenPizza.Price})");
   }
   else
   {
      Console.WriteLine("Custom pizza creation was cancelled.");
      return;
   }
}
```

```
else
{
//☑ Not a combo or custom? Let the Pizza Factory handle it.
chosenPizza = _pizzaFactory.OrderPizza(choice);
if (chosenPizza != null)
{
Console.WriteLine($"You ordered: {chosenPizza.Name} (${chosenPizza.Price})");
}
}

// ... rest of your order processing code ...
```

You'll also need to update your initial message to inform users about the new "custom" option:

```
Console.WriteLine("Welcome to Delizioso Pizzeria!");
Console.WriteLine("Available options: Margherita, Pepperoni, Veggie, Combo1, or type 'custom' to build your own pizza");
Console.Write("What would you like? ");
```

Key Points:

- **Your Pizza Order Form:** Think of the *PizzaBuilder* as a digital order form. It guides you step-by-step (*AddTopping, SetExtraCheese*) to specify exactly what you want on your pizza.
- **The "Official Kitchen" Rule:** We made the *CustomPizza* constructor internal. This is a rule that says: *"Only classes in this 'kitchen' (our project) can bake a CustomPizza directly."* This prevents code in other projects from creating pizzas incorrectly.
- **The Builder is the Official Chef:** The *PizzaBuilder* lives in the same "kitchen" (project), so it has the special right to use the *CustomPizza* constructor. Its *Build()* method is the official way to create a pizza. It follows all the recipes and rules.
- **One-Stop Shop:** The *Build()* method doesn't just create the pizza; it also handles all the logic, like calculating the final price based on your choices, before serving you the finished product.
- **Consistency is Key:** Because everyone must use the *PizzaBuilder*, every pizza is created correctly. You can't accidentally forget to add the price for extra cheese or create a pizza with an invalid combination of toppings.
- **It Works with the Factory:** This Builder creates a single, complex object (a custom pizza). This is different from the Abstract Factory (Chapter 4), which created a whole family of related objects (a pizza, a drink, and a dessert). They solve different problems but work together beautifully.

Key Test Points: Put Your Builder to the Test

Once you've implemented the *PizzaBuilder*, verify it works correctly by running these tests:

1. **The Happy Path:** Use the builder to create a custom pizza with multiple toppings and options. Print its details to the console. Does it display the correct name, all the toppings, the extras you selected, and does the final price look right?
2. **The Power of Chaining:** Can you create a pizza by chaining the builder's methods together in a single, fluent statement? (e.g., *.AddTopping("X").SetExtraCheese(true).Build()*). This tests the core feature of a fluent interface.
3. **The Immutability Check:** After the pizza is built (*Build()* is called), try to change one of its properties (like Price). This should cause a compiler error. This proves your pizza object is truly immutable, which is a key benefit of the pattern.
4. **The Validation Test:** Try to build a pizza without a name or with a negative base price. Does your *Build()* method prevent this and throw a helpful error message? (This is where you'd add validation logic).

If all these tests pass, congratulations! You've successfully implemented the Builder pattern.

5.7 Why the Builder Matters

- **Eliminates constructor chaos:** No more parameter lists with 10+ arguments.
- **Promotes immutability:** The *Pizza* object is immutable(can't be changed) after *Build()*.
- **Enables method chaining:** Fluent syntax enhances code readability.

5.8 Mini Exercise: Add a New Feature

Your Task: Add a *SetSpicyLevel(int level)* option to the *PizzaBuilder*.
Hint: Add a private *_spicyLevel* field and a public *SetSpicyLevel* method.

5.9 When to Use the Builder

"Whenever you have a constructor with more than 4 parameters, or when you foresee future customization options, use the Builder pattern."

5.10 Transition to Chapter 5

"Now that we can build customized pizzas effortlessly, what if we want to clone a popular pizza configuration instead of building from scratch? Next, we'll explore the **Prototype** pattern for efficient object cloning."

> **Next Up: Chapter 6 — Prototype: The Art of the Perfect Copy**
> Ready to duplicate your best-selling pizzas without rebuilding them from scratch? Let's clone your masterpieces in a click.

Chapter 6

Prototype — The Art of the Perfect Copy

Setting The Stage

Your pizza app now creates customized masterpieces, but what if a customer wants to order "the same thing as last time"? Reconstructing complex pizzas from scratch is

> *In this chapter, you'll:*
> 1. **Identify the pitfalls:** ·*Identify the overhead of recreating complex objects.*
> 2. **Learn the Prototype pattern:** ·Learn the Prototype pattern to clone existing objects.
> 3. **Refactor the Pizza class:** ·Implement cloning for your pizzas and orders.
> 4. **Deep Vs. Shallow Copying:** Understand the difference between shallow and deep copying.

PROTOTYPE

6.1 Hook: What's the Pain?

"Reconstructing a complex pizza with 10 toppings through the Builder, every time someone wants a duplicate is like rewriting a document instead of hitting 'Copy-Paste'. It wastes resources and introduces potential errors."

6.2 The Problem in Our Pizza App

To duplicate a pizza, we must manually copy all properties: (Oops Moment: 4)(Oops Moment: 31)

```
//Original Pizza Object using Builder Pattern
Pizza original = new PizzaBuilder("Special", 12.99m)
    .AddTopping("Mushrooms")
    .AddTopping("Olives")
    .SetExtraCheese(true)
    .Build();
```

```
// Manual copying - error-prone and tedious!
Pizza duplicate = new Pizza(original.Name, original.Price,
    new List<string>(original.Toppings),
    original.ExtraCheese, original.StuffedCrust, original.GlutenFree);
```

Why This Hurts:

- **Boilerplate Code:** Duplicating complex objects requires repeating all construction logic.
- **Tight Coupling:** The duplication code must know all internal fields of the object.
- **Fragile:** Adding a new property to Pizza breaks all duplication code.

6.3 The Formal Pattern: Prototype

Pattern Definition

> *"**Prototype** is a creational pattern that lets you copy existing objects without making your code dependent on their classes."*

In Simpler Terms: Instead of reconstructing an object from scratch, you ask the object itself to give you a copy of itself. It's like a pizza that can create perfect duplicates of itself with all the same toppings and options.

6.4 Understanding the Pattern

The Real-World Analogy: The Pizza Press

Think of the Prortype pattern as **a pizza press** that can perfectly replicate any pizza placed into it. You don't need to know the original recipe - you just place a pizza in the press, and it creates an identical copy with all the same toppings, crust, and cheese distribution.

6.5 The Implementation Blueprint: Prototype Pattern Steps

Before we refactor our pizza to be clonable, let's break down the implementation into a clear, repeatable recipe. Whenever you need to add cloning capabilities to an object, follow these steps:

1. **Declare the Prototype Interface:** Create an interface that declares a *Clone()* method. This establishes a contract that all clonable objects will follow. Using a generic interface *ICloneable<T>* is preferred over the non-generic *ICloneable* in the .NET framework, as it provides type safety.
2. **Implement the Cloning Logic:** In each concrete class that needs to be cloned, implement the *Clone()* method. Inside this method, you are responsible for creating a new instance of the object and carefully copying all necessary data from the current instance to the new one.
3. **Choose the Copy Depth (Critical Decision):** This is the most important step. You must decide for each field whether you need a shallow copy or a deep copy.
    - Value types (e.g., int, decimal, bool, struct) can always be shallow copied.
    - Reference types (e.g., class, List<>, Array) require your attention. You must decide if you want to copy the reference (shallow) or create a new copy of the object the reference points to (deep).
4. **Client Code Uses Clone:** The client code can now create new copies of complex objects by simply calling the *Clone()* method on an existing instance. This completely decouples the client from the intricate details of the object's construction and internal data structure.

Deep Copy vs. Shallow Copy — What's the Difference?

Imagine you want to photocopy a document that has a sticky note on it.

- **A Shallow Copy** is like photocopying the document with the sticky note. The note itself isn't copied; the photocopy just shows a picture of the original note. If you write on the original sticky note, the change will be "seen" by the photocopy because it's the same physical note. In code, this means copying the reference to an object, so both the original and the copy share the same underlying data.
- **A Deep Copy** is like photocopying the document and then also writing the contents of the sticky note onto a new, separate sticky note and placing it on the photocopy. Now, if you change the original note, the photocopy's note remains untouched. In code, this means creating a brand new instance of a reference object and copying all its values, so the original and the copy are completely independent.

6.6 Implementing the Prototype Pattern

Step 1: Add Clone() to the IPizza Interface

The clone method can be created in your Pizza.cs class. But since now all our Pizzas are inheriting IPizza interface, we will add Clone method to our Pizza interface.

IPizza.cs

```
public interface IPizza
{
    string Name { get; }
    decimal Price { get; }
    void Prepare();
    void Bake();
    void Box();

    // Add this method
    IPizza Clone();
}
```

Step 2: Implement Clone() in All Pizza Classes

Now each concrete pizza class must implement the Clone() method:

For your specialized pizzas (MargheritaPizza, etc.):

MargheritaPizza.cs

```
public class MargheritaPizza : IPizza
{
    public string Name => "Margherita";
    public decimal Price => 5.00m;
```

```
    public void Prepare() => Console.WriteLine($"Preparing {Name} with fresh basil and mozzarella...");
    public void Bake() => Console.WriteLine($"Baking {Name} to perfection...");
    public void Box() => Console.WriteLine($"Placing {Name} in a classic box.");

    // Simple implementation for immutable pizzas
    public IPizza Clone()
    {
        return new MargheritaPizza();
    }
}
```

For your CustomPizza class:

CustomPizza.cs

```
public class CustomPizza : IPizza
{
    public string Name { get; private set; }
    public decimal Price { get; private set; }
    public List<string> Toppings { get; private set; }
    public bool ExtraCheese { get; private set; }
    public bool StuffedCrust { get; private set; }
    public bool GlutenFree { get; private set; }

    internal CustomPizza(string name, decimal price, List<string> toppings,
                bool extraCheese, bool stuffedCrust, bool glutenFree){
        Name = name;
        Price = price;
        Toppings = toppings;
        ExtraCheese = extraCheese;
        StuffedCrust = stuffedCrust;
        GlutenFree = glutenFree;
    }

    public void Prepare() => Console.WriteLine($"Preparing {Name} with custom options...");
    public void Bake() => Console.WriteLine($"Baking {Name}...");
    public void Box() => Console.WriteLine($"Placing {Name} in a box.");

    public IPizza Clone(){
        // Create a deep copy
        return new CustomPizza(
            Name,
            Price,
            new List<string>(Toppings), // Deep copy the list
            ExtraCheese,
            StuffedCrust,
            GlutenFree        );
    }
}
```

Step 3: Usage in Client Code

Now you can clone any pizza in your client code like below:

Config.cs

```
// AFTER the pizza is created, but BEFORE the for loop:
IPizza pizzaToClone = chosenPizza; // Store the original pizza

// Check if the user wants individual clones for each pizza in their quantity
// (This is especially useful for custom pizzas where each might need to be identical)
Console.Write("Do you want each pizza to be an identical copy? (yes/no): ");
bool cloneForEach = Console.ReadLine().Equals("yes", StringComparison.OrdinalIgnoreCase);


for (int i = 0; i < qty; i++)
{
  // ✅ PROTOTYPE PATTERN IN ACTION: Clone if requested, otherwise use original
  if (cloneForEach)
  {
    chosenPizza = pizzaToClone.Clone(); // Simple call directly on the interface
    Console.WriteLine($"Created identical copy #{i + 1} of your pizza.");
  }
  else
  {
    chosenPizza = pizzaToClone;
  }

  //.......... (other code continued for order Object creation)
}
```

Key Test Points: Validate Your Prototype

Once you've implemented the ICloneable<Pizza> interface, run these tests to ensure your cloning works correctly:

1. **The Basic Clone Test:** Create a complex pizza using the Builder. Call Clone() on it and store the result. Check that the original and the clone have the same values for all properties (Name, Price, Toppings, etc.). This verifies the clone was created successfully.
2. **The Independence Test (Most Important):** This test proves your clone is a deep copy, not just a shallow reference.
    - Create a pizza *originalPizza* with a list of toppings (e.g., "Cheese", "Tomato").
    - Clone it: *Pizza clonedPizza = originalPizza.Clone();*
    - Modify the clone's list: *clonedPizza.Toppings.Add("Olives");*
    - Check the original pizza's toppings. The original list should NOT contain "Olives". If it does, you performed a shallow copy, which is a bug.

3. **The Functionality Test:** Pass the cloned pizza to your existing order processing system *(e.g., PricingService.CalculateTotal(), inventory.ReserveIngredients())*. It should treat the clone exactly the same as it would any other pizza object. This validates that the clone is a fully functional, independent instance.

If all these tests pass, your Prototype pattern is working perfectly! You've successfully implemented efficient object copying.

6.7 Why the Prototype Matters

- **Performance:** Cloning is often faster than reconstruction through constructors, especially for complex objects with many parts or those that require expensive initialization (like fetching data).
- **Simplicity:** Client code doesn't need to know the intricate construction details of an object. It just asks for a copy.
- **Maintainability:** Adding new properties to a class doesn't break copying code. You only need to update the Clone() method in one place.
- **Encapsulation:** The object manages its own copying logic. The client doesn't need to know if it's a shallow or deep copy; it just gets a working clone.

6.8 Mini Exercise: Implement Order Cloning

Your Task: Make the *Order* class implement *ICloneable<Order>* and add a *Clone()* method.

6.9 When to Use the Prototype

"Use the Prototype pattern when the construction process is more expensive than copying, or when you need to create variations of complex objects without building them from scratch."

6.10 Transition to Chapter 7

"Now that we can efficiently duplicate our pizza creations, we need to ensure certain components exist only once throughout our application. Next, we'll explore the Singleton pattern for managing global state."

> **Next Up: Chapter 7 — Singleton: The One and Only**
> Ready to ensure there's just one menu, one configuration, one source of truth for your entire app? Let's give your pizza universe its single, unwavering constant.

Want to see this pattern in action? Scan me!

Singleton — One Menu to Rule Them All

Setting The Stage

Your pizza app has grown, with different services needing access to the same core information-like the menu, pricing configuration, or application settings. Having multiple copies of this data leads to inconsistency and chaos.

> In this chapter, you'll:
> 1. **Identify the Pitfalls:** Identify problems of multiple instances managing global state.
> 2. **Learn the Pattern:** Learn the Singleton pattern to ensure a class has only one instance.
> 3. **Implement Thread Safety:** Implement thread-safe Singleton initialization.
> 4. **Understand Proper Use:** Understand proper and improper use cases for Singletons.

SINGLETON

7.1 Hook: What's the Pain?

"Your menu is loaded from three different files. Your pricing configuration is cached in five different places. When you change a price, you have to update it in a dozen locations-and you still get mismatched totals. We need one source of truth for our entire application."

7.2 The Problem in Our Pizza App

1. No Single Source of Truth: (Oops Moment:5 & Oops Moment:6)

Any class could create its own Config or Logger object, leading to inconsistent state across the application.

```
// ❌ OLD: Multiple instances causing chaos.
var config1 = new Config(); // One set of rules
var config2 = new Config(); // Another set of rules? Who knows!
```

2. The Naive Static Approach: (Oops Moment:7 & Oops Moment:30)

Our *IdGenerator* and *Config* were implemented as simple static classes or were instantiated anywhere. This is not thread-safe and lacks flexibility.

```
// ❌ OLD: Thread-unsafe, cannot be reloaded or mocked.
public static class IdGenerator
{
    private static int _next = 1;
    public static int Next() => _next++; // Duplicate IDs in multi-threaded scenarios!
}
```

Why This Hurts:

- **Race Conditions:** The *IdGenerator* could hand out duplicate IDs under load, breaking order tracking.

- **Inconsistent State:** Different parts of the app use different config values, leading to unpredictable behavior.
- **Un-testable Code:** Static classes are difficult to mock and isolate in unit tests.
- **Wasted Resources:** Multiple instances load the same configuration, wasting memory and I/O operations.

7.3 The Formal Pattern: Singleton

Pattern Definition

> *"**Singleton** is a creational pattern that ensures a class has only one instance and provides a global point of access to it."*

In Simpler Terms: The Singleton pattern is like having a single, shared bulletin board in your pizza kitchen. Everyone reads from and posts to the same board-there aren't multiple copies floating around that might have different information.

7.4 Understanding the Pattern

The Real-World Analogy: The Restaurant Menu

A restaurant has only **one master menu.** All waitstaff refer to the same menu, and when the chef updates a dish or price, everyone sees the change immediately. There aren't multiple "versions" of the menu that might have different prices or items.

7.5 The Implementation Blueprint: Singleton Pattern Steps

Think of building a Singleton like building a secure, single-room fortress. Only one person can ever be in that room, and we need to control exactly how they get in.

1. **Make Constructor Private (Lock the Doors):** Change your class's constructor from public to private. This is the most important step. It prevents any other part of your code from using the *new* keyword to create a new instance of your class. If the doors are locked, no one can get in without your permission. In simple terms: "No one can bake a new config pizza except our official chef."
2. **Create Static Instance Field (Create the One-and-Only Room):** Inside the class, create a private static field whose type is the class itself (e.g., private static ApplicationConfig _instance;). This field will be the memory address where our single, precious object will live. It's static because it needs to belong to the class itself, not to any individual object (since we'll only have one!). In simple terms: "We're reserving a named room in the building for our one-and-only config object. The room is empty at first, but it's ready."
3. **Provide Public Static Accessor (Install a Single, Secure Entrance):** Create a public static property (*e.g., Instance*) that provides access to the instance field you created in Step 2. This property is the only way for the outside world to get the object. It controls the access. The first time someone asks for it, the property will create the object and put it in the room. Every subsequent time, it will just point to the already-created object.

4. **Implement Thread Safety (Post a Guard for Crowds):** This step protects against a specific problem: what if two people ask for the instance for the very first time at the exact same moment? Without a guard, they might both try to furnish the room, creating two objects and breaking the "single instance" rule. We solve this by using a special .NET tool called Lazy<T>. Lazy<T> is like a super-smart, thread-safe receptionist. It's built to handle crowds. It guarantees that the room is only furnished once, no matter how many people are lining up at the door. In simple terms: "We hire a professional receptionist (Lazy<T>) who is an expert at handling rushes. They ensure the room is only set up one time, ever."
5. **Seal the Class - Optional (Don't Build a Back Door):** Add the *sealed* keyword to your class definition *(e.g., public sealed class ApplicationConfig).* This prevents other developers from creating subclasses of your Singleton. A subclass could accidentally expose a public constructor or otherwise break the rules you've so carefully set up. It's a final safety measure. In simple terms: "We weld the windows shut so no one can try to sneak in through a back door or build a weird addition to our perfect single room."

SINGLETON

7.6 Implementing the Singleton Pattern

Part 1: The Core Concept — Simple Singleton

Step 1: Implement SIngleton in Config Class

Config.cs

```
public sealed class Config
{
    private static Config _instance; // 1. Store the single instance in a static field.

    private Config()    // 2. Make the constructor private so no one else can use `new`.
    {
        CurrencySymbol = "$";   // Load configuration settings
        TaxRate = 0.08m;
    }

    public static Config Instance  // 3. Provide a global access point to that single instance.
    {
        get
        {  // If the instance doesn't exist yet, create it.
            if (_instance == null)  _instance = new Config();
            return _instance;
        }
    }
    public string CurrencySymbol { get; private set; } // Application properties
    public decimal TaxRate { get; private set; }
}
```

Step 2: Usage in Client Code

```
// Anywhere in your code, you now get the same instance.
decimal tax = orderTotal * Config.Instance.TaxRate;
Config.Instance.CurrencySymbol = "€"; // Change is seen everywhere
```

What This Solves:

- Oops Moment 5 & Oops Moment 6 has been solved. We now have a Single Source of Truth. There is only one *Config* object in the entire application.
- The pattern's core goal is achieved: controlled access to a single instance.

The Remaining Problem:

- Oops Moment 7 & Oops Moment 30 are still remaining. This simple version is not thread-safe. If two threads call *Instance* at the same exact time when *_instance* is null, they might both pass the if check and create two separate instances, breaking the pattern.

Part 2: The Robust Implementation — Thread-Safe Singleton

Now that we understand the goal, let's solve the thread-safety problem for production-ready code.

Step 1: Introducing the Lazy<T> Class:

.NET provides a built-in class, Lazy<T>, whose sole purpose is to handle thread-safe, lazy initialization. It's the modern, recommended way to implement Singletons.

Config.cs (FInal)

```
public sealed class Config
{
  // 1. Use Lazy<T> to handle lazy, thread-safe initialization.
 //The lambda expression tells it how to create the instance when needed.
  private static readonly Lazy<Config> _lazyInstance =  new Lazy<Config>(() => new Config());

  // 2. The public accessor now returns the .Value of the Lazy object.
  public static Config Instance => _lazyInstance.Value;

  private Config()  // 3. Private constructor remains.
  {
    CurrencySymbol = "$";
    TaxRate = 0.08m;
  }
  public string CurrencySymbol { get; private set; }
  public decimal TaxRate { get; private set; }
  public void UpdateTaxRate(decimal newRate) => TaxRate = newRate;
}
```

We apply the same robust pattern to IdGenerator Class:

Config.cs (Final)

```
public sealed class IdGenerator
{
   private static readonly Lazy<IdGenerator> _lazyInstance =  new Lazy<IdGenerator>(() => new
IdGenerator());

   public static IdGenerator Instance => _lazyInstance.Value;

   private int _nextId = 1;
   private readonly object _lock = new object(); // Lock for thread-safe increment.

   private IdGenerator() { }

   public int GetNextId()
   {
      lock (_lock) // Ensure the increment operation is atomic.
      {
         return _nextId++;
      }
   }
}
```

The Problem: The Race Condition (Why we are using the lock keyword here?)

Imagine the _*nextId*_ variable is a piece of paper on a wall with the number 5 written on it. Two cooks (Thread 1 and Thread 2) need to read the number, add 1 to it, write down the new number, and take the old number for an order.

Without a lock, this can happen:

1. **Thread 1** reads the number: 5.
2. **Thread 2** also reads the number before Thread 1 can update it: 5.
3. **Thread 1** does its calculation: 5 + 1 = 6. It writes 6 on the paper and uses 5 for its order. ■
4. **Thread 2** does its calculation: 5 + 1 = 6. It writes 6 on the paper and uses 5 for its order. ✕

The Disaster: Both cooks used the same ID (5)! The number on the wall is now 6, meaning the next cook will get 7, but we've completely lost track of ID 6. This is a ***race condition.***

The Solution: The lock Keyword

The lock keyword is like **giving a single, unique kitchen buzzer** to the cooks. The rule is: you must have the buzzer to look at and change the number on the wall. *(continue on next page)*

```
private readonly object _lock = new object(); // This is the "kitchen buzzer"
private int _nextId = 1;

public int GetNextId()
{
    lock (_lock) // A cook grabs the buzzer. Others must wait.
    {
        return _nextId++; // They safely read, increment, and return the value.
    } // The cook puts the buzzer back, and someone else can grab it.
}
```

How it works with the lock:

1. **Thread 1** arrives, grabs the *_lock* buzzer, and enters the *lock* block.
2. **Thread 2** arrives and also tries to grab the buzzer. It sees Thread 1 has it, so Thread 2 is forced **to stop and wait.**
3. **Thread 1** safely executes the code inside the block:
    - It reads *_nextId* (e.g., **5**).
    - It increments it to **6**.
    - It returns the value **5** for its order.
4. **Thread 1** finishes the block and **releases the *_lock* buzzer.**
5. **Thread 2** can now grab the buzzer, enter the block, and safely read the new value **6**. It increments it to **7** and returns **6**.

The Result: Every ID is unique. **Thread 1 got 5, Thread 2 got 6**, and the next thread will get **7**. Disaster averted!

Key Points to Remember:

- **The _lock Object:** This is just a harmless, dummy object. Its only job is to be a unique token that threads fight over. It's *readonly* to ensure the token itself can never be changed.
- **What it Protects:** The *lock* protects the critical section of code inside its { } braces. It ensures only one thread can be executing that code at any given moment.
- **Atomic Operation:** The operation *return _nextId++;* is not a single step for the computer. It's actually three steps: (1) Read value, (2) Increment value, (3) Return the old value. The lock makes these three steps atomic — meaning they become an indivisible unit that cannot be interrupted.

Step 2: Usage in Client Code

Now you can use it in client code as follows:

Program.cs

```
for (int i = 0; i < qty; i++)
{
//■ SOLVED Oops Moment 30: Now using thread-safe Singleton ID generation
// This will never produce duplicate IDs, even under multi-threaded load

   int id = IdGenerator.Instance.GetNextId();
   var order = new Order
   {
      //..........order code
   };

   //■ Using the global config Singleton for currency instead of hardcoded "USD"
   if (!payment.Pay(total, ApplicationConfig.Instance.CurrencySymbol, "card-..."))
   {
      Console.WriteLine("Payment failed");
      continue;
   }
```

Key Test Points: Validate Your Singleton

1.Single Instance Test: Create the Singleton in multiple parts of your code and verify they all return the same instance using *ReferenceEquals()*.

2.Thread Safety Test: Access the Singleton simultaneously from multiple threads and verify no duplicate instances are created.

3.Configuration Change Test: Change a value through the Singleton in one service and verify other services immediately see the updated value.

4.Persistence Test: Verify that configuration changes persist appropriately (e.g., save to file when changed).

If all tests pass, your Singleton implementation is working correctly!

7.7 Why the Singleton Matters

- **Consistency:** All components use the same data and configuration.
- **Resource Efficiency:** Avoids duplicate loading of resources.
- **Centralized Control:** Configuration changes affect the entire application.
- **Access Control:** Can implement security around the single access point.

7.8 Mini Exercise: Create a Singleton Menu

Task: Convert the *Menu* class into a Singleton that loads menu items from a file.

Bonus: Implement lazy initialization so the menu only loads when first accessed.

7.9 When to Use the Singleton

"Use the Singleton pattern when you need exactly one instance of a class to coordinate actions across the system, such as configuration managers, logging services, or shared resource pools."

7.10 Transition to Chapter 8

"Now that we have a single source of truth for our application's configuration, we need to integrate with external systems that don't match our interface. Next, we'll explore the **Adapter** pattern to make incompatible interfaces work together seamlessly."

> **Next Up: Chapter 8 — Adapter: The Universal Translator**
> Ready to connect with third-party services that speak a different language? Let's build adapters that make awkward APIs work seamlessly with your elegant pizza app.

Want to see this pattern in action? Scan me!

🏗️PART 3: STRUCTURAL PATTERNS- ORGANIZING THE SYSTEM

Where Everything Fits Perfectly!

Meet "The Architects" - the master organizers who make sure all our code pieces work together beautifully. This is where we learn to build flexible, well-structured systems that don't collapse under pressure!

What We're Building:

- **Adapter:** The universal translator for incompatible interfaces
- **Bridge:** The flexible connector between layers
- **Composite:** The group organizer for menus and combos
- **Decorator:** The dynamic feature adder
- **Facade:** The simple front door to complex systems
- **Flyweight:** The memory-saving ingredient sharer
- **Proxy:** The smart access controller

You'll Master:

- Making incompatible components work together
- Adding features without changing core code
- Creating flexible, maintainable structures
- Optimizing memory with shared resources

Perfect if you've ever:

- Struggled with tangled object relationships
- Added too many features to one class
- Faced memory issues from duplicate objects
- Wanted to simplify complex subsystems

Get ready to become a code architect! 🏛️

Chapter 8

Adapter — The Universal Translator

Setting The Stage

Your pizza app needs to process payments, but the best payment gateway has a weird, incompatible API. Forcing your clean code to work with its awkward interface would create a mess.

> In this chapter, you'll:
> 1. **Identify the Pitfalls:** Identify the problem of incompatible interfaces between systems.
> 2. **Learn the Pattern:** Learn the Adapter pattern to translate between interfaces.
> 3. **Clean & Consistent Interface:** Wrap the third-party payment gateway in a clean, consistent interface.
> 4. **Protect Core Application:** Protect your core application from external changes.

8.1 Hook: What's the Pain?

"Integrating the payment gateway feels like trying to plug a US appliance into a European socket — the pins don't match, the voltage is wrong, and you might break something. We need an adapter that makes everything just work."

8.2 The Problem in Our Pizza App

We're forced to use the payment gateway's awkward API directly.
(Oops Moment 18) & (Oops Moment 24)

```
// ✗ OLD: Using the awkward third-party API directly
if (!payment.Pay(total, "USD", "card-..."))
{
    Console.WriteLine("Payment failed");
    continue;
}
```

Why This Hurts:

- **Brittle Integration:** Our core code is tightly coupled to the payment gateway's specific method signature.
- **Parameter Confusion:** What does *"card-..."* mean? What format should it be? The method doesn't tell us.
- **Change Intolerance:** If the gateway changes its API or we switch providers, we must find and update every call throughout our codebase.
- **Error Handling:** The gateway might return false on failure, but what kind of failure? We get no details.

8.3 The Formal Pattern: Adapter

Pattern Definition

> *"**Adapter** is a structural pattern that allows objects with incompatible interfaces to collaborate."*

In Simpler Terms: The Adapter pattern acts as a translator between two objects that speak different languages. It wraps the awkward object and exposes a clean, familiar interface that the rest of your code can use comfortably.

8.4 Understanding the Pattern

The Real-World Analogy: The Power Plug Adapter

When traveling abroad, you don't rewire your laptop to fit foreign outlets—you use **a small plug adapter.** The adapter understands both your laptop's plug (your application's interface) and the wall outlet's design (the third-party interface), making them work together seamlessly.

8.5 The Implementation Blueprint: Adapter Pattern Steps

Think of using the Adapter pattern like hiring a professional translator for an important business meeting. You speak English, your client speaks Japanese. The translator's job is to sit between you, listen to what you say, and repeat it in Japanese to the client, & vice-versa.

1. **Analyze the Incompatibility (Identify the Language Barrier):**
    - ***<u>What to do:</u>*** Take a close look at the awkward, third-party class. Write down the method name it expects you to call and all the parameters it requires. Then, write down what a simple, clear method name for your app would be and what parameters would make sense for you to pass.
    - ***<u>Why we do it:</u>*** You can't build a translator if you don't know the two languages that need to be translated. This step is about understanding the "language" of the external service and the "language" your application wants to speak.
    - ***<u>In simple terms:</u>*** "The payment gateway wants me to call *Pay(amount, currencyCode, rawCardToken)*. But I wish I could just call something like *ProcessPayment(amount, currency, card)* with my own *Card* object. I've found the language barrier!"
2. **Define Your Ideal Interface (Design Your Perfect Conversation):**
    - ***<u>What to do:</u>*** Create a new C# interface. Give it a method name that is perfect for your application. Define parameters that are easy for your app to provide and return a result object that gives you all the information you need.
    - ***<u>Why we do it:</u>*** This interface is your "rulebook" for how your application will talk about payments from now on. It defines the clean, simple language you want to use everywhere in your code.
    - ***<u>In simple terms:</u>*** "I'm going to define my perfect way to talk about payments. I'll create an *IPaymentProcessor* interface with a method *ProcessPayment(decimal amount, string currency, string cardToken)*. This is the English I want to speak."

3. **Create the Adapter Class (Hire the Translator):**
    - ***What to do:*** Create a new class that implements your perfect interface. In this class, you will create an instance of the awkward third-party class. Then, you will write the code for your interface's method. Inside that method, you will "translate" your perfect parameters into the weird parameters the third-party class expects, call its method, and then "translate" its weird response back into your perfect response.
    - ***Why we do it:*** This class is the translator. It implements the rules you defined and does all the dirty work of talking to the difficult external service so that the rest of your app doesn't have to.
    - ***In simple terms:*** "Now I create my translator, the *PaymentGatewayAdapter* class. It knows how to speak both languages. When my app says *ProcessPayment(10.0, "USD", "token_123"),* the translator turns that into *Pay(10.0, "USD", "token_123")* for the gateway. It's doing all the hard work!"
4. **Inject the Adapter (Introduce the Translator to Your Team):**
    - ***What to do:*** In your main application code *(like Program.Main)*, create an instance of your Adapter class. Then, pass this instance (via a constructor or method parameter) to any other class that needs to process payments. Those classes should only know about your perfect interface, not the specific adapter.
    - ***Why we do it:*** This ensures that every part of your application uses the translator instead of trying to speak the foreign language themselves. It also lets you easily swap translators later if you change payment gateways.
    - ***In simple terms:*** "I now tell everyone on my team: 'Hey, if you need to process a payment, don't call the gateway directly. Just talk to our translator, the *IPaymentProcessor*. It will handle everything for you.'"

By following these four steps, you build a clean, robust bridge between your application and the messy outside world, keeping your core code simple and maintainable.

8.6 Implementing the Adapter Pattern

Step 1: Define Your Clean Interface

IPaymentProcessor.cs

```
public interface IPaymentProcessor
{
   PaymentResult ProcessPayment(decimal amount, string
currency, string cardToken);
}
public class PaymentResult
{
   public bool IsSuccess { get; set; }
   public string ErrorMessage { get; set; }
   public string TransactionId { get; set; }
}
```

Scan to View Adapter Pattern Code

Step 2: Create the Adapter Class

PaymentGatewayAdapter.cs

```
public class PaymentGatewayAdapter : IPaymentProcessor
{
   private readonly PaymentGateway3rdParty _thirdPartyGateway;

   public PaymentGatewayAdapter()
   {
      _thirdPartyGateway = new PaymentGateway3rdParty();
   }

   public PaymentResult ProcessPayment(decimal amount, string currency, string cardToken)
   {
      // This is where the translation happens!
      // Convert our clean parameters to what the third-party expects
      bool isSuccess = _thirdPartyGateway.Pay(amount, currency, cardToken);

      // Convert the third-party's simple response to our rich response
      return new PaymentResult
      {
         IsSuccess = isSuccess,
         ErrorMessage = isSuccess ? null : "Payment processing failed",
         TransactionId = Guid.NewGuid().ToString() // In real life, get from gateway
      };
   }
}
```

Step 3: Use the Adapter in Your Code

Program.cs

```
// In Program.Main() or a service class:
IPaymentProcessor paymentProcessor = new PaymentGatewayAdapter();

// Later, in your order processing code:
var result = paymentProcessor.ProcessPayment(total, "USD", "card-token-123");

if (!result.IsSuccess){
   // ✅ Now we have rich error information!
   Console.WriteLine($"Payment failed: {result.ErrorMessage}");
   continue;
}
// ✅ Now we have a transaction ID for records!
Console.WriteLine($"Payment successful. Transaction ID: {result.TransactionId}");
```

Key Test Points: Validate Your Adapter

1. **Successful Payment Test:** Process a payment and verify the adapter returns a successful *PaymentResult* with a transaction ID.
2. **Failed Payment Test:** Simulate a payment failure and verify the adapter properly captures and returns error information.
3. **Parameter Translation Test:** Verify that the adapter correctly translates parameters between your interface and the third-party interface.
4. **Interface Consistency Test:** Ensure all code now uses only your clean *IPaymentProcessor* interface, with no direct calls to the third-party gateway.

If all tests pass, your Adapter pattern is working correctly! You've successfully integrated an incompatible system without polluting your core application logic.

8.7 Why the Adapter Matters

- **Clean Abstraction:** Your core application no longer depends on awkward third-party APIs.
- **Single Responsibility:** The adapter's only job is translation, keeping other classes focused.
- **Testability:** You can mock the *IPaymentProcessor* interface for testing.
- **Future-Proofing:** If you switch payment providers, you only need to update the adapter.

8.8 Mini Exercise: Create a Notification Adapter

Task: The *NotificationService* has a confusing method: *Send(string channel, string provider, string message)*. Create an adapter with a cleaner interface like *SendNotification(string message, NotificationType type)*.

8.9 When to Use the Adapter

"Use the Adapter pattern whenever you need to integrate with a class whose interface doesn't match what the rest of your application expects, particularly with third-party libraries, legacy code, or external APIs."

8.10 Transition to Chapter 9

"Now that we've seamlessly integrated external services, we need to handle another complexity: our notification system has become a tangled web of channels and providers. Next, we'll explore the **Bridge** pattern to separate these concerns cleanly."

> **Next Up: Chapter 9 — Bridge: Building Stable Connections**
> Ready to decouple your notification channels from their providers forever? Let's separate the what from the how and create a flexible messaging system that can evolve without breaking.

Chapter 9

Bridge — Separating Abstraction from Implementation

Setting The Stage

Your notification system has become a tangled web of channels and providers. Adding a new notification type means updating multiple classes, and the code is filled with if/else statements.

> In this chapter, you'll:
> 1. **Identify the Pitfalls:** ·Identify the problem of tightly coupled abstractions and implementations.
> 2. **Learn the Pattern:** Learn the Bridge pattern to separate notification channels from providers.
> 3. **Create a Flexible System:** Create a flexible system where channels and providers can vary independently.
> 4. **Protect Core Application:** Eliminate the explosion of classes that would occur from combining all options.

9.1 Hook: What's the Pain?

"Adding SMS notifications shouldn't require understanding how email works. Supporting Twilio shouldn't force us to modify push notification code. Our notification system is a classic example of 'cartesian product' complexity — every new channel multiplied by every new provider creates maintenance hell."

9.2 The Problem in Our Pizza App

The *NotificationService* has a deeply coupled interface:
(Oops Moment 20) & (Oops Moment 25)

```
// ❌ OLD: Tightly coupled channels and providers
notifier.Send("email", "smtp", $"Order #{orderId} delivered'
notifier.Send("sms", "twilio", $"Your pizza is here!");
```

Why This Hurts:

- **Combinatorial Explosion:** 3 channels × 3 providers = 9 possible combinations, each requiring special handling.
- **Tight Coupling:** Changing a provider implementation affects all channels using it.
- **Maintenance Nightmare:** Adding a new channel (like WhatsApp) requires modifying all provider code.
- **Rigid Architecture:** The system cannot evolve independently — channels and providers are locked together.

9.3 The Formal Pattern: Bridge

Pattern Definition

*"**Bridge** is a structural pattern that separates an abstraction from its implementation so that the two can vary independently."*

In Simpler Terms: The Bridge pattern is like having separate volume and source controls on your stereo. You can change the volume (abstraction) without affecting the input source (implementation), and vice versa. They work together but aren't tightly coupled.

9.4 Understanding the Pattern

The Real-World Analogy: The Remote Control and Device

Think of a **universal remote control** (abstraction) that works with different devices (implementations) — TV, stereo, DVD player. The remote has standard buttons (power, volume, menu), but each device implements these functions differently. You can replace the device without changing the remote, and vice versa.

BRIDGE

9.5 The Implementation Blueprint: Bridge Pattern Steps

Think of using the Bridge pattern like building a universal remote control system. You have different devices (TV, stereo, AC) and different remote types (basic, smart, voice-controlled). The Bridge pattern lets you mix and match any remote with any device without rewiring anything.

1. **Find the Dimensions of Variation (Identify What Changes Independently):**
   - ***What to do:*** Look at your system and find the aspects that can change for different reasons. In our case, we have:
     - Notification Channels: Email, SMS, Push (the "what" we're sending)
     - Delivery Providers: SMTP, Twilio, Firebase (the "how" we send it)
   - ***Why we do it:*** You can't build a flexible system until you understand what needs to be flexible. This step is about recognizing the two independent "axes of change" in your system.
   - ***In simple terms:*** "I realize that choosing between Email or SMS is a completely separate decision from choosing between Twilio or SendGrid. They change for different reasons, so they shouldn't be tangled together."
2. **Define the Implementation Interface (Create the Device Interface):**
   - ***What to do:*** Create a C# interface that represents the "implementation" side of the bridge — the providers. This interface should declare the methods that all providers must implement, like *SendMessage()*.
   - ***Why we do it:*** This interface defines the contract that all providers must follow. It's like defining the standard electrical plug that all devices must use to work with your remote control system.

- ***In simple terms:*** "I'll create an *IMessageSender* interface that says 'If you want to be a message provider, you must know how to SendMessage.' This way, I can plug in any provider that follows this rule."

3. **Create the Abstraction Base Class (Build the Universal Remote Base):**
   - ***What to do:*** Create an abstract class that represents the "abstraction" side of the bridge — the notification channels. This class should hold a reference to the implementation interface (from Step 2) and declare the high-level operations like *Send()*.
   - ***Why we do it:*** This class serves as the base that all channels will inherit from. It maintains the connection to the implementation but doesn't dictate which specific implementation to use.
   - ***In simple terms:*** "I'll create a *Notification* base class that has a slot for any *IMessageSender*. Think of it as a universal remote base that has a slot for any compatible device, but doesn't care which specific device you plug in."
4. **Create Refined Abstractions (Add Specific Remote Types):**
   - ***What to do:*** Create concrete subclasses of your abstraction base class for each variation on the abstraction side. For us, these are the specific notification channels: *EmailNotification, SmsNotification, PushNotification*.
   - ***Why we do it:*** Each refined abstraction can provide channel-specific behavior while still using the general implementation interface. The email notification might add subject lines, while SMS might handle character limits.
   - ***In simple terms:*** "Now I create specialized remotes: an 'Email Remote,' an 'SMS Remote,' and a 'Push Notification Remote.' Each knows its specific type of notification but still uses the standard device interface to actually send messages."
5. **Create Concrete Implementations (Build the Specific Devices):**
   - ***What to do:*** Create concrete classes that implement the implementation interface from Step 2. These are the specific providers: *SmtpEmailSender, TwilioSmsSender, FirebasePushSender*.
   - ***Why we do it:*** These classes contain the actual, provider-specific code. They know the nitty-gritty details of how to communicate with external services, but they don't need to know anything about the notification channels using them.
   - ***In simple terms:*** "Finally, I build the actual devices: an 'SMTP Box,' a 'Twilio Box,' and a 'Firebase Box.' Each knows exactly how to talk to its specific service, and they all have the standard plug (interface) so they can work with any of my remotes."

By following these five steps, you build a system where any of your channels and providers can vary completely independently. You can add a new provider without touching any channel code, and vice versa — exactly what the Bridge pattern is designed to achieve.

9.6 Implementing the Bridge Pattern

Step 1: Define the Implementation Interface

IMessageSender.cs

```
public interface IMessageSender
{
    void SendMessage(string message);
    string ProviderName { get; }
}
```

Step 2: Create Concrete Implementations (Providers)

SmtpEmailSender.cs

```
public class SmtpEmailSender : IMessageSender
{
    public string ProviderName => "SMTP";

    public void SendMessage(string message)
    {
        Console.WriteLine($"Sending email via {ProviderName}: {message}");
        // Actual SMTP implementation here
    }
}
```

TwilioSmsSender.cs

```
public class TwilioSmsSender : IMessageSender
{
    public string ProviderName => "Twilio";

    public void SendMessage(string message)
    {
        Console.WriteLine($"Sending SMS via {ProviderName}: {message}");
        // Actual Twilio API implementation here
    }
}
```

FirebasePushSender.cs

```
public class FirebasePushSender : IMessageSender
{
    public string ProviderName => "Firebase";
    public void SendMessage(string message)
    {
        Console.WriteLine($"Sending push notification via {ProviderName}: {message}");
        // Actual Firebase implementation here
    }
}
```

Step 3: Create the Abstraction Base Class

Notification.cs

```
public abstract class Notification
{
   protected IMessageSender _messageSender;

   protected Notification(IMessageSender messageSender)
   {
      _messageSender = messageSender;
   }

   public abstract void Send(string message);

   public void ChangeMessageSender(IMessageSender messageSender)
   {
      _messageSender = messageSender;
   }
}
```

Step 4: Create Refined Abstractions (Channels)

EmailNotification.cs

```
public class EmailNotification : Notification
{
   public EmailNotification(IMessageSender messageSender) : base(messageSender) {}

   public override void Send(string message)
   {
      Console.Write("Email notification: ");
      _messageSender.SendMessage(message);
   }
}
```

SmsNotification.cs

```
public class SmsNotification : Notification
{
   public SmsNotification(IMessageSender messageSender) : base(messageSender) {}

   public override void Send(string message)
   {
      Console.Write("SMS notification: ");
      _messageSender.SendMessage(message);
   }
}
```

PushNotification .cs

```
public class PushNotification : Notification
{
  public PushNotification(IMessageSender messageSender) : base(messageSender) {}

  public override void Send(string message)
  {
    Console.Write("Push notification: ");
    _messageSender.SendMessage(message);
  }
}
```

What does this line do?

```
public PushNotification(IMessageSender messageSender) : base(messageSender) {}
```

This line is the constructor for the *PushNotification* class. Here's what each part means:

- *public PushNotification(IMessageSender messageSender)* - This is declaring a constructor that takes an *IMessageSender* parameter called *messageSender*
- *: base(messageSender)* - This calls the constructor of the parent class (*Notification*) and passes the *messageSender* parameter to it
- *{}* - The empty braces mean this constructor doesn't need to do any additional work beyond what the parent constructor does

In simpler terms: "When creating a *PushNotification*, you must give it a message sender. We'll immediately pass that message sender up to our parent class (*Notification*) to handle it."

Why did we use the variable name with Underscore (_)? From where it came from?

```
_messageSender.SendMessage(message);
```

The underscore (_) prefix is a common naming convention in C# for private or protected fields (member variables) of a class. Here's why it's used:

- Immediate Recognition: The underscore makes it instantly clear that *_messageSender* is a field of the class, not a local variable or parameter.
- Avoids Naming Conflicts: Without this convention, you might have naming conflicts like:

```
public Notification(IMessageSender messageSender)
{
    // Without underscore, we'd have to use "this" to avoid confusion
    this.messageSender = messageSender;
}
```

- Visual Distinction: It provides visual distinction between parameters/local variables (messageSender) and class fields (_messageSender).
- Consistency: This is a widely adopted convention in the C# community, making code more readable to other developers.

In the Bridge pattern specifically, *_messageSender* is defined in the base *Notification* class as a protected field:

```
protected IMessageSender _messageSender;
```

This allows all derived notification classes (like *PushNotification*) to access and use the message sender that was provided to the base class constructor.

The pattern ensures that:

1. The abstraction (*Notification*) holds a reference to the implementation (*IMessageSender*)
2. All concrete notifications delegate the actual sending work to this implementation
3. We can easily swap implementations without changing the notification classes

This is the essence of the Bridge pattern - separating the abstraction (what we're doing) from the implementation (how we're doing it).

Step 5: Usage in Client Code

Program.cs

```
// In your order processing code:

// Set up different notification combinations
var emailNotifier = new EmailNotification(new SmtpEmailSender());
var smsNotifier = new SmsNotification(new TwilioSmsSender());
var pushNotifier = new PushNotification(new FirebasePushSender());

// Send notifications cleanly
emailNotifier.Send($"Order #{orderId} has been delivered");
smsNotifier.Send("Your pizza is out for delivery!");
pushNotifier.Send("Special offer: 20% off your next order!");

// Easily switch providers
emailNotifier.ChangeMessageSender(new SendGridEmailSender()); // New provider
emailNotifier.Send("Now using different email provider!");
```

Key Test Points: Validate Your Bridge

1.Channel-Provider Independence Test: Verify that you can create any channel with any provider without code changes.

2.Runtime Switching Test: Change a notification's provider at runtime and confirm it works correctly.

3.New Channel Test: Add a new notification channel (e.g., WhatsApp) without modifying any provider code.

4.New Provider Test: Add a new provider (e.g., SendGrid) without modifying any channel code.

If all tests pass, your Bridge pattern is working correctly! You've successfully decoupled your notification channels from their delivery providers.

9.7 Why the Bridge Matters

- **Decoupling:** Channels and providers can vary and evolve independently.
- **Extensibility:** Add new channels or providers without modifying existing code.
- **Single Responsibility:** Each class has one clear purpose.
- **Testability:** Easy to mock implementations for testing.
- **Runtime Changes:** Providers can be switched at runtime.

9.8 Mini Exercise: Add a New Provider

Task: Create a *SendGridEmailSender* class that implements *IMessageSender* and integrate it with the *EmailNotification* channel.
Bonus: Create a *WhatsAppNotification* channel that can use different providers.

9.9 When to Use the Bridge

"Use the Bridge pattern when you have multiple dimensions of variation in your system, when you want to avoid permanent binding between abstraction and implementation, or when you need to switch implementations at runtime."

9.10 Transition to Chapter 10

"Now that we've cleanly separated our notification channels from their providers, we need to address how we organize our menu items. Next, we'll explore the **Composite** pattern to handle individual items and meal combos uniformly."

> **Next Up: Chapter 10 — Composite: The Whole is Greater Than the Sum of Its Parts**
> Ready to treat individual pizzas and complex meal combos as equals? Let's build a unified menu system where single items and entire meal families work together seamlessly.

Scan to View Bridge Pattern In Action

Chapter 10

Composite — The Whole is Greater Than the Sum of Its Parts

Setting The Stage

Your menu system can only handle individual items, forcing you to create special handling for combos and meal deals. This leads to duplicated code and complex conditional logic.

> In this chapter, you'll:
> 1. **Identify the Pitfalls:** Identify the limitations of flat menu structures for handling combos and packages.
> 2. **Learn the Pattern:** Learn the Composite pattern to treat individual items and groups uniformly.
> 3. **Build a Flexible Menu:** Build a flexible menu hierarchy where single items and combos work interchangeably.
> 4. **Protect Core Application:** Eliminate special-case handling for grouped items throughout your application.

10.1 Hook: What's the Pain?

"Adding a 'Family Combo' to our menu shouldn't require rewriting our entire ordering system. We shouldn't need special 'if it's a combo then...' logic everywhere. Our menu should work the same whether it's handling a single pizza or a complete meal package with pizza, drinks, and desserts."

10.2 The Problem in Our Pizza App

The menu can only handle individual items, not groups:
(Oops Moment 8)

```
// ❌ OLD: Flat menu structure cannot represent combos
public class Menu
{
    public List<string> Categories = new() { "Pizzas", "Drinks", "Desserts" };
    public List<string> Items = new() { "Margherita", "Pepperoni", "Veggie", "Coke", "Brownie" };
    // No way to represent "Family Combo" containing pizza + drink + dessert
}
```

Why This Hurts:

- **Special Case Handling:** Combos require completely different logic from individual items.
- **Code Duplication:** Pricing, display, and ordering logic must be rewritten for combos.
- **Inflexible Structure:** Adding new combo types requires modifying multiple parts of the system.
- **No Uniform Interface:** You can't treat individual items and combos the same way in code.

10.3 The Formal Pattern: Composite

Pattern Definition

> *"**Composite** is a structural pattern that lets you compose objects into tree structures and then work with these structures as if they were individual objects."*

In Simpler Terms: The Composite pattern allows you to treat single items and groups of items uniformly. It's like being able to put a single book or an entire bookshelf into your shopping cart — the cart doesn't need to know the difference.

10.4 Understanding the Pattern

The Real-World Analogy: The Restaurant Menu

Think of a restaurant menu that has individual items (pizza, drinks) and combos (meal deals). With the Composite pattern, both individual items and combos implement the same interface. The cashier can ring up a single pizza or a complete combo meal using exactly the same process — the register doesn't need to know whether it's handling one item or multiple items bundled together.

10.5 The Implementation Blueprint: Composite Pattern Steps

Think of using the Composite pattern like organizing a restaurant menu with both à la carte items and combo meals. You want waitstaff to be able to ring up both types of orders using the exact same process, without needing special training for combos.

1. **Create the Component Interface (Define the Universal Menu Language):**
    - ***What to do:*** Create a C# interface (e.g., *IMenuComponent*) that declares operations that make sense for both single items and groups. These typically include *GetName(), GetPrice()*, and *Display()*.
    - ***Why we do it:*** This interface defines the "common language" that all menu items — whether single pizzas or multi-item combos — must speak. It's like creating a standard order form that works for both individual items and complete meals.
    - ***In simple terms:*** "I'm creating a rulebook that says: 'Whether you're a single pizza or a full combo meal, you must be able to tell me your name, your price, and show yourself on the menu.'"
2. **Create Leaf Classes (Create the Individual Items):**
    - ***What to do:*** Create concrete classes for individual, indivisible menu items like *PizzaMenuItem, DrinkMenuItem*, and *DessertMenuItem*. These will implement the component interface but represent the end points of the hierarchy — they can't contain other items.
    - ***Why we do it:*** These are the building blocks of your menu. They implement the interface but for single items only. When asked for their price, they return their fixed price. When asked to display, they show just themselves.

COMPOSITE

- ***In simple terms:*** "I'm creating the basic menu items: a Margherita pizza ($10), a Coke ($2), a Brownie ($5). Each is a standalone item that can't contain other items."

3. **Create Composite Class (Create the Container for Groupings):**
   - ***What to do:*** Create a class (e.g., *MenuComposite*) that also implements the component interface but represents a container that can hold multiple other components (both individual items and other composites).
   - ***Why we do it:*** This class acts as the "combo meal" or "category" that can contain multiple items. It implements the same interface but behaves differently: when asked for its price, it might calculate the sum of its children; when asked to display, it shows itself and all its children.
   - ***In simple terms:*** "I'm creating a 'Family Combo' container that can hold multiple items—a pizza, two drinks, and a dessert. When someone asks for its price, it will add up all the contained items' prices."
4. **Implement Child Management (Add Doors to the Container):**
   - ***What to do:*** In your composite class, add methods like *Add()*, *Remove()*, and *GetChild()* that allow you to manage the children contained within the composite.
   - ***Why we do it:*** These methods give you the ability to build and modify the tree structure dynamically. You can add items to combos, remove them, or rearrange combos without breaking the uniform interface.
   - ***In simple terms:*** "I'm adding doors to my combo container so I can put items in (*Add*), take items out (*Remove*), or see what's inside (*GetChild*). This lets me create different combo combinations easily."
5. **Implement Uniform Operations (Ensure Consistent Behavior):**
   - ***What to do:*** Implement the interface methods in both leaf and composite classes in a way that makes sense for each. The key is that from the outside, they should be indistinguishable in how they're used, even if their internal behavior is different.
   - ***Why we do it:*** This is the core magic of the Composite pattern. The composite delegates work to its children but presents the same interface as a single item. This allows client code to work with both individual items and complex structures interchangeably.
   - ***In simple terms:*** "I'm making sure that whether the cashier rings up a single pizza or a full combo meal, they use the exact same process: scan the item, get the price, add to total. The combo automatically handles calculating its total price internally."

By following these five steps, you create a system where individual items and groups of items can be treated uniformly. Your code becomes simpler because it doesn't need to know whether it's dealing with a single pizza or a complex combo meal—it uses the same interface for both.

10.6 Implementing the Composite Pattern

Step 1: Define the Component Interface

IMenuComponent.cs

```
public interface IMenuComponent
{
    string Name { get; }
    string Id { get; }
    decimal Price { get; }
    bool IsCombo { get; }
    void Print();
    void Add(IMenuComponent component);
    void Remove(IMenuComponent component);
    IMenuComponent GetChild(int index);
    int ChildCount { get; } // Added for easier traversal
}
```

Step 2: Create Leaf Classes (Individual Items)

MenuItem.cs

```
public class MenuItem : IMenuComponent
{
    public string Name { get; private set; }
    public string Id { get; private set; }
    public decimal Price { get; private set; }
    public bool IsCombo => false;
    public int ChildCount => 0;

    public MenuItem(string id, string name, decimal price)
    {
        Id = id;
        Name = name;
        Price = price;
    }

    public void Print() => Console.WriteLine($" {Id} :-  {Name} - ${Price:0.00}");
    public void Add(IMenuComponent component) => throw new
InvalidOperationException("Cannot add to a leaf item");
    public void Remove(IMenuComponent component) => throw new
InvalidOperationException("Cannot remove from a leaf item");
    public IMenuComponent GetChild(int index) => throw new InvalidOperationException("Leaf item
has no children");
}
```

COMPOSITE

Step 3: Create Composite Class (Combos)

Now define the class for combo items.

MenuComposite.cs

```
public class MenuComposite : IMenuComponent
{
    private List<IMenuComponent> _children = new List<IMenuComponent>();
    public string Name { get; private set; }
    public string Id { get; private set; }
    public bool IsCombo { get; private set; }
    public int ChildCount => _children.Count;

    public decimal Price => IsCombo ? Math.Round(_children.Sum(child => child.Price) * 0.9m, 2) : 0;

    public MenuComposite(string id, string name, bool isCombo = false)
    {
        Id = id;
        Name = name;
        IsCombo = isCombo;
    }

    public void Print()
    {
        if (IsCombo)
        {
            Console.WriteLine($"{Id} :- {Name} - ${Price:0.00} (Combo)");
            Console.WriteLine("  Includes:");
        }
        else
        {
            Console.WriteLine($"{Name}:");
        }

        foreach (var child in _children) child.Print();
        if (IsCombo) Console.WriteLine();
    }

    public void Add(IMenuComponent component) => _children.Add(component);
    public void Remove(IMenuComponent component) => _children.Remove(component);
    public IMenuComponent GetChild(int index) => _children[index];
}
```

Step 4: Build the Menu Structure

Now we create a class to build our menu structure with Ids so that user can select an item from the menu. This class builds the menu structure and provides lookup functionality

MenuBuilder.cs

```
public static class MenuBuilder
{
    private static Dictionary<string, IMenuComponent> _menuLookup;

    public static IMenuComponent BuildMenu()
    {
        _menuLookup = new Dictionary<string, IMenuComponent>();
        var menu = BuildMenuStructure();
        BuildLookupTable(menu);
        return menu;
    }

    private static void BuildLookupTable(IMenuComponent component)
    {
        _menuLookup[component.Id] = component;
        if (component is MenuComposite composite)
        {
            for (int i = 0; i < composite.ChildCount; i++)
                BuildLookupTable(composite.GetChild(i));
        }
    }

    public static IMenuComponent FindComponent(string id) =>
        _menuLookup.TryGetValue(id, out var component) ? component : null;

    private static IMenuComponent BuildMenuStructure()
    {
        // Individual items
        var margherita = new MenuItem("pizza_marg", "Margherita Pizza", 10.99m);
        var pepperoni = new MenuItem("pizza_pep", "Pepperoni Pizza", 12.99m);
        var veggie = new MenuItem("pizza_veg", "Veggie Pizza", 11.99m);
        var coke = new MenuItem("drink_coke", "Coke", 2.99m);
        var brownie = new MenuItem("dess_brownie", "Brownie", 4.99m);

        // Combos
        var familyCombo = new MenuComposite("combo_family", "Family Combo", true);
        familyCombo.Add(margherita);
        familyCombo.Add(pepperoni);
        familyCombo.Add(coke);
        familyCombo.Add(coke);
        familyCombo.Add(brownie);
```

COMPOSITE

```
    var dayNightCombo = new MenuComposite("combo_day", "Day Night Combo", true);
    dayNightCombo.Add(margherita);
    dayNightCombo.Add(coke);
    dayNightCombo.Add(brownie);

    // Menu structure
    var menu = new MenuComposite("menu_main", "Main Menu");
    var pizzas = new MenuComposite("cat_pizzas", "Pizzas");
    var drinks = new MenuComposite("cat_drinks", "Drinks");
    var desserts = new MenuComposite("cat_desserts", "Desserts");
    var combos = new MenuComposite("cat_combos", "Combos");

    pizzas.Add(margherita); pizzas.Add(pepperoni); pizzas.Add(veggie);
    drinks.Add(coke);
    desserts.Add(brownie);
    combos.Add(familyCombo); combos.Add(dayNightCombo);

    menu.Add(pizzas); menu.Add(drinks); menu.Add(desserts); menu.Add(combos);
    return menu;
  }
}
```

Step 5: Define OrderCart Class

This class represents a shopping cart that can hold any IMenuComponent (items or combos) and calculate the total price.

OrderCart.cs

```
public class OrderCart
{
  private List<IMenuComponent> _items = new List<IMenuComponent>();

  public void AddItem(IMenuComponent item){
    _items.Add(item);
  }
  public decimal CalculateTotal(){
    return _items.Sum(item => item.Price);
  }

  public void PrintOrder(){
    Console.WriteLine("Your Order:");
    foreach (var item in _items)
    {
      item.Print(); // Leverages the Print method of IMenuComponent
    }
    Console.WriteLine($"Total: ${CalculateTotal():0.00}");
  }
}
```

Step 6: Usage in Client Code

In your main program, you can use the MenuBuilder to build the menu, display it, and then create an order by adding items and combos to the OrderCart. This code is simple and only uses the Composite Pattern.

Program.cs

```
class Program
{
  static void Main()
  {
    // Build the menu using MenuBuilder
    var menu = MenuBuilder.BuildMenu();

    // Display the entire menu
    Console.WriteLine("Full Menu:");
    menu.Print();

    // Create an order cart
    var orderCart = new OrderCart();

    // Find individual items and combos by their ID (using MenuBuilder's lookup)
    var margherita = MenuBuilder.FindComponent("pizza_marg");
    var familyCombo = MenuBuilder.FindComponent("combo_family");

    // Add items to the order - works uniformly for both single items and combos
    if (margherita != null)
      orderCart.AddItem(margherita);
    if (familyCombo != null)
      orderCart.AddItem(familyCombo);

    // Display the order details and total
    orderCart.PrintOrder();
  }
}
```

- **Composite Pattern in Action:** The *OrderCart* treats individual items (*MenuItem*) and combos (*MenuComposite*) uniformly through the *IMenuComponent* interface. This allows you to add any menu component to the order and calculate the total price without knowing whether it's a single item or a combo.

COMPOSITE

Key Test Points for Composite Pattern Validation

1. **Uniform Interface Test:** Verify that both individual items (*MenuItem*) and combos (*MenuComposite*) implement the *IMenuComponent* interface correctly and respond uniformly to the *Price* property and *Print()* method.
    - **Test Action:** Create instances of *MenuItem* and *MenuComposite*, and call *Price* and *Print()* on each.
    - **Expected Result:** Both types should return their respective prices and display their details without errors. For *MenuComposite*, the price should be the sum of its children's prices (with discount if applied), and *Print()* should display the combo name and its items.
2. **Nested Combos Test:** Ensure that a combo (*MenuComposite*) can contain another combo, and that price calculation works recursively through multiple levels.
    - **Test Action:** Create a nested combo structure (e.g., a combo that includes another combo as a child). Check the *Price* property of the parent combo.
    - **Expected Result:** The total price should be calculated recursively, including all items in the nested combos, with discounts applied at each combo level if implemented.
3. **Display Test:** Validate that the menu display shows both individual items and combos with proper indentation and hierarchy when *Print()* is called.
    - **Test Action:** Build a menu structure with multiple levels (e.g., categories, items, and combos) and call *Print()* on the root menu.
    - **Expected Result:** The output should show a tree-like structure with correct indentation. Items should be listed under their respective categories, and combos should display their included items with indentation.
4. **Order Processing Test:** Confirm that the *OrderCart* class can handle both individual items and combos uniformly, and that the total calculation is correct.
    - **Test Action:** Add instances of *MenuItem* and *MenuComposite* to an *OrderCart* and call *CalculateTotal()*.
    - **Expected Result:** The total should be the sum of all items and combos added, with combos contributing their calculated prices (including discounts if applicable). The *PrintOrder()* method should display each item and combo correctly.

If all these tests pass, your Composite pattern implementation is working correctly.

10.7 Why the Composite Matters

- **Uniform Treatment:** Single items and combos can be handled identically in code.
- **Simplified Client Code:** No more "if it's a combo then..." special cases.
- **Flexible Structure:** Easy to add new combo types without changing existing code.
- **Recursive Processing:** Natural support for hierarchical structures (combos within combos).
- **Consistent Interface:** All menu components respond to the same set of operations.

10.8 Mini Exercise: Create a New Combo

Task: Create a "Lunch Special" combo that includes a personal pizza, drink, and cookie at a fixed price rather than a discounted sum.
Bonus: Add a method to calculate calories that works for individual items & combos.

10.9 When to Use the Composite

"Use the Composite pattern when you need to represent part-whole hierarchies and want clients to be able to ignore the difference between individual objects and compositions of objects."

10.10 Transition to Chapter 11

"Now that we can seamlessly handle both individual items and complex combos, we need to add flexibility to our pizzas themselves. Next, we'll explore the **Decorator** pattern to dynamically add toppings and extras to our pizzas without creating a subclass for every possible combination."

> **Next Up: Chapter 11 — Decorator: Dress Your Pizza Without Changing the Recipe**
> Ready to add extra cheese, spicy toppings, or premium sauces without creating endless pizza subclasses? Let's dynamically layer flavors at runtime and watch your pizza transform while keeping the core recipe untouched!

Scan to View Composite Pattern In Action

Integrating Composite Pattern with Factory and Abstract Factory Patterns

Now that we've learned how to implement the Composite Pattern for our menu structure, we need to integrate it with our existing Factory and Abstract Factory patterns. Currently, our menu is built using the Composite Pattern, but our ordering system still only handles individual pizzas. We need to:

1. Create an *IOrderItem* interface to represent any item that can be ordered
2. Refactor our *Order* class to handle all types of order items, not just pizzas
3. Create conversion logic to transform menu components into order items
4. Ensure price consistency across our menu and order systems

Let's implement these changes step by step.

Step 1: Create the IOrderItem Interface

We'll create a new interface that will represent any item that can be ordered, whether it's a single item or a combo.

IOrderItem.cs

```
public interface IOrderItem
{
    string Name { get; }
    decimal Price { get; }
}
```

Step 2: Update Existing Interfaces to Implement IOrderItem

We'll modify our existing product interfaces to implement the new *IOrderItem* interface.

IPizza.cs

```
public interface IPizza : IOrderItem
{
    // Pizza-specific properties and methods
}
```

IDrink.cs

```
public interface IDrink : IOrderItem
{
    // Drink-specific properties and methods
}
```

IDessert.cs

```
public interface IDessert : IOrderItem
{
    // Dessert-specific properties and methods
}
```

See how Composite Pattern works with Other Pattern

Step 3: Create the OrderComposite Class

This class will represent a combo in our ordering system, implementing the *IOrderItem* interface.

OrderComposite.cs

```
public class OrderComposite : IOrderItem
{
    private readonly List<IOrderItem> _items = new List<IOrderItem>();
    public string Name { get; }
    public decimal Price => _items.Sum(item => item.Price);

    public OrderComposite(string name)
    {
        Name = name;
    }

    public void AddItem(IOrderItem item)
    {
        _items.Add(item);
    }

    public IEnumerable<IOrderItem> GetItems()
    {
        return _items;
    }
}
```

Step 4: Refactor the Order Class

We'll modify the *Order* class to use *IOrderItem* instead of *IPizza*.

Order.cs

```
public class Order
{
    public int OrderId { get; set; }
    public string CustomerName { get; set; }
    public string Address { get; set; }
    public IOrderItem Item { get; set; }
    public string Status { get; set; }
    public DateTime TimeOrdered { get; set; }
}
```

Step 5: Modify Pizza, Drink & Dessert Classes to Accept Price

Update all pizza, Drink and Dessert classes to accept price as a parameter in their constructors and not hardcoded in the classes.

MargheritaPizza.cs

```
public class MargheritaPizza : IPizza
{
    public string Name { get; }
    public decimal Price { get; }
    public List<string> Toppings { get; }
    public bool ExtraCheese { get; private set; }
    public bool StuffedCrust { get; private set; }

    public MargheritaPizza(decimal price)
    {
        Name = "Margherita Pizza";
        Price = price;
        Toppings = new List<string> { "Tomato Sauce", "Mozzarella", "Basil" };
    }

    public void Prepare() => Console.WriteLine("Preparing Margherita Pizza");
    public void Bake() => Console.WriteLine("Baking Margherita Pizza");
    public void Box() => Console.WriteLine("Boxing Margherita Pizza");

    public IPizza Clone()
    {
        return new MargheritaPizza(Price)
        {
            ExtraCheese = this.ExtraCheese,
            StuffedCrust = this.StuffedCrust
        };
    }
}
```

Coke.cs

```
public class Coke : IDrink
{
    public string Name { get; }
    public decimal Price { get; }

    public Coke(decimal price)
    {
        Name = "Coke";
        Price = price;
    }
}
```

Brownie.cs

```
public class Brownie : IDessert
{
    public string Name { get; }
    public decimal Price { get; }

    public Brownie(decimal price)
    {
        Name = "Brownie";
        Price = price;
    }
}
```

Repeat similar changes for other pizza, drink and dessert classes

Step 6: Create a Unified MenuItemFactory

MenuItemFactory.cs

```
public static class MenuItemFactory
{
  public static IOrderItem CreateOrderItem(IMenuComponent component)
  {
    if (component is MenuItem menuItem){
      return CreateFromMenuItem(menuItem);
    }
    else if (component is MenuComposite menuComposite){
      if (menuComposite.IsCombo){
        return CreateFromMenuComposite(menuComposite);
      }
      else{
      // Handle category composites (like "Pizzas", "Drinks", etc.)
       throw new ArgumentException("Cannot order a category directly. Please select a specific
item.");
      }
    }

    throw new ArgumentException("Unsupported menu component type");
  }

  private static IOrderItem CreateFromMenuItem(MenuItem menuItem)
  {
    if (menuItem.Id.StartsWith("pizza_")){
      string pizzaType = menuItem.Id.Replace("pizza_", "");
      return CreatePizza(pizzaType, menuItem.Price);
    }
    else if (menuItem.Id.StartsWith("drink_")){
      string drinkType = menuItem.Id.Replace("drink_", "");
      return CreateDrink(drinkType, menuItem.Price);
    }
    else if (menuItem.Id.StartsWith("dess_")){
      string dessertType = menuItem.Id.Replace("dess_", "");
      return CreateDessert(dessertType, menuItem.Price);
    }
    else if (menuItem.Id.StartsWith("combo_")){
     // This shouldn't happen as combos are MenuComposite, not MenuItem
      throw new ArgumentException($"Combo {menuItem.Id} is not properly configured");
    }

    throw new ArgumentException($"Unknown item type: {menuItem.Id}");
  }
```

COMPOSITE

```
private static IPizza CreatePizza(string type, decimal price)
{
   switch (type.ToLower()) {
      case "marg": return new MargheritaPizza(price);
      case "pep": return new PepperoniPizza(price);
      case "veg": return new VeggiePizza(price);
      default: throw new ArgumentException($"Unknown pizza type: {type}");
   }
}

private static IDrink CreateDrink(string type, decimal price)
{
   switch (type.ToLower()) {
      case "coke": return new Coke(price) // Add other drink types
      default:  throw new ArgumentException($"Unknown drink type: {type}");
   }
}

private static IDessert CreateDessert(string type, decimal price)
{
   switch (type.ToLower()) {
      case "brownie": return new Brownie(price);
      // Add other dessert types
      default: throw new ArgumentException($"Unknown dessert type: {type}");
   }
}

private static IOrderItem CreateFromMenuComposite(MenuComposite menuComposite)
{
   if (!menuComposite.IsCombo)
   {
      throw new ArgumentException("Cannot create order item from a non-combo composite");
   }
   var orderComposite = new OrderComposite(menuComposite.Name);

   for (int i = 0; i < menuComposite.ChildCount; i++)
   {
      var child = menuComposite.GetChild(i);
      if (child is MenuItem childMenuItem){
         orderComposite.AddItem(CreateFromMenuItem(childMenuItem));
      }
      else if (child is MenuComposite childComposite && childComposite.IsCombo){
         // Handle nested combos (if supported)
         orderComposite.AddItem(CreateFromMenuComposite(childComposite));
      }
   }

   return orderComposite;
}
```

What does MenuItemFactory do?

The Problem:

In our previous implementation, we had separate factories:

- *StandardPizzaFactory* for creating individual pizzas
- *StandardComboFactory* for creating combo meals

While this separation worked, it created some challenges:

a. **Code Duplication:** Both factories had similar creation logic
b. **Maintenance Overhead:** Changes to menu items required updates in multiple places
c. **Inconsistency Risk:** Different factories might create items with different pricing or behavior

The Solution:

We've consolidated both factories into a single, unified *MenuItemFactory* that can create any type of order item - whether it's a single pizza, drink, dessert, or a complete combo meal.

The Beauty of This Integration:

This refactoring demonstrates the elegant synergy between three patterns:

a. **Composite Pattern:** Provides the hierarchical menu structure where combos contain individual items
b. **Factory Method Pattern:** Handles the creation of individual products through a unified interface
c. **Abstract Factory Pattern:** Inspired the creation of related product families (though we've now streamlined it)

How It Works:

The *MenuItemFactory* now serves as the single entry point for creating all order items:

- For individual items (pizza_margherita, drink_coke, dessert_brownie), it uses the appropriate creation method
- For combo items (combo_family, combo_date), it recursively creates all components of the combo and packages them in an *OrderComposite*
- All items get their pricing from the *MenuBuilder*, ensuring complete consistency

Benefits of This Approach:

- **Single Responsibility:** One factory handles all order item creation
- **Consistent Pricing:** All prices come from the centralized *MenuBuilder*
- **Simplified Client Code:** Order processing now uses a single method call regardless of item type
- **Future-Proof:** Easy to add new item types without changing the factory interface

Code Example:

```
// Before: Multiple factory calls
var pizza = _pizzaFactory.OrderPizza("margherita");
var comboFactory = new StandardComboFactory();
var comboPizza = comboFactory.CreatePizza();

// After: Single factory call
var pizza = MenuItemFactory.CreateOrderItem("pizza_margherita");
var combo = MenuItemFactory.CreateOrderItem("combo_family");
```

This refactoring represents a significant simplification of our architecture while maintaining all the benefits of our design patterns. The Composite Pattern allows us to treat individual items and combos uniformly, while the unified factory ensures consistent creation of all menu items.

COMPOSITE

Step 7: Update *MenuBuilder* to Ensure Consistent Prices

Make sure the MenuBuilder uses the same prices that will be passed to the order items:

MenuBuilder.cs

```
public static class MenuBuilder
{
    // Define prices in one place
    private const decimal MargheritaPrice = 10.99m;
    private const decimal PepperoniPrice = 12.99m;
    private const decimal VeggiePrice = 11.99m;
    private const decimal CokePrice = 2.99m;
    private const decimal BrowniePrice = 4.99m;

    public static IMenuComponent BuildMenu()
    {
        // Individual items with consistent prices
        var margherita = new MenuItem("pizza_marg", "Margherita Pizza", MargheritaPrice);
        var pepperoni = new MenuItem("pizza_pep", "Pepperoni Pizza", PepperoniPrice);
        var veggie = new MenuItem("pizza_veg", "Veggie Pizza", VeggiePrice);
        var coke = new MenuItem("drink_coke", "Coke", CokePrice);
        var brownie = new MenuItem("dessert_brownie", "Brownie", BrowniePrice);

        // ... rest of the menu building code
    }
}
```

Step 8: Update the Client Code

Now we'll update the main program to use the new ordering system.

Program.cs

```
static void Main()
{
    // ... existing setup code ...
    Console.WriteLine("Welcome to Delizioso Pizzeria!");
    Console.WriteLine("Full Menu:");
    var menu = MenuBuilder.BuildMenu();
    menu.Print();

    Console.Write("Enter item ID: ");
    string input = Console.ReadLine();

    // Parse quantity and choice
    var match = Regex.Match(input, @"^(?<qty>\d+)x\s*(?<item>.+)$", RegexOptions.IgnoreCase);
    int qty = match.Success ? int.Parse(match.Groups["qty"].Value) : 1;
    string choice = match.Success ? match.Groups["item"].Value : input;
```

```
    IOrderItem orderItem = null;
    bool isCustom = choice.Equals("custom", StringComparison.OrdinalIgnoreCase);

    if (isCustom){
      orderItem = BuildACustomPizza();
    }
    else{
      var selectedComponent = MenuBuilder.FindComponent(choice);
      if (selectedComponent == null){
        Console.WriteLine("Item not found."); return;
      }
      orderItem = MenuItemFactory.CreateOrderItem(selectedComponent);
    }

    // Process the order
    Console.WriteLine($"You ordered: {orderItem.Name} (${orderItem.Price})");
    if (orderItem is OrderComposite composite){
      Console.WriteLine("Includes:");
      foreach (var item in composite.GetItems()) {
        Console.WriteLine($"  - {item.Name} (${item.Price})");
      }
    }

    // Create and process the order
    int id = IdGenerator.Instance.GetNextId();
    var order = new Order
    {
      OrderId = id,
      CustomerName = "Walk-in",
      Address = "Counter",
      Item = orderItem,
      Status = "Received",
      TimeOrdered = DateTime.Now
    };

    // Additional order processing logic...
}
```

Conclusion

With these changes, we've successfully integrated the Composite Pattern with our existing Factory and Abstract Factory patterns. Our system now:

1. Uses a unified *IOrderItem* interface for all orderable items
2. Can handle both individual items and combos in orders
3. Maintains price consistency between the menu and the ordering system
4. Provides a clean separation between menu display and order processing

This sets a solid foundation for the upcoming patterns we'll implement in future chapters, starting with the Decorator Pattern in Chapter 11.

Chapter 11

Decorator — Dress Your Pizza Without Changing the Recipe

Setting The Stage

Your pizza class is exploding with boolean flags for every possible topping and add-on. Adding a new topping like "Spicy Oil" means breaking open the Pizza class, adding another property, and modifying the price calculation logic.

> In this chapter, you'll:
> 1. **Identify Pitfalls:** Identify the rigidity caused by using inheritance or flags for add-ons.
> 2. **Learn the Pattern:** Learn the Decorator pattern to dynamically add responsibilities to objects.
> 3. **Build a Runtime Pizza:** Wrap your base pizza with flavorful layers of toppings at runtime.
> 4. **Protect Core Application:** Eliminate the need for a subclass for every possible pizza combination.

11.1 Hook: What's the Pain?

"Our Pizza class is drowning in a sea of *bool ExtraCheese, bool StuffedCrust, bool DoublePepperoni*... This is a maintenance nightmare! Adding a new topping shouldn't require us to modify the core Pizza class and risk breaking existing code. We need a way to add features like toppings dynamically, just like a customer would order them — one at a time."

11.2 The Problem in Our Pizza App

Toppings and add-ons are implemented as primitive boolean flags within the Pizza class. (Oops Moment 2) & (Oops Moment 17)

Why This Hurts:

- **Class Explosion:** To avoid the boolean mess, you'd need a *ExtraCheesePizza, StuffedCrustPizza, ExtraCheeseStuffedCrustPizza* subclass for every combination. This is unsustainable.
- **Rigid Design:** The *Pizza* class is closed for modification but also closed for extension. Every change affects the entire class.

```
// ❌ OLD: Inflexible pizza class with too many flags (Oops Moment #2)
public class Pizza
{
    public string Name { get; set; }
    public decimal BasePrice { get; set; }
    public bool ExtraCheese { get; set; } // Topping as a flag
    public bool StuffedCrust { get; set; } // Add-on as a flag
    public bool GlutenFree { get; set; }
    // ... imagine adding 20 more of these...

    // ❌ Complex, brittle price calculation
    public decimal CalculatePrice()
    {
        decimal total = BasePrice;
        if (ExtraCheese) total += 1.0m;
        if (StuffedCrust) total += 2.0m;
        if (GlutenFree) total += 1.5m;
        // ... a new 'if' for every new flag
        return total;
    }
}
```

- **Single Responsibility Violation:** The *Pizza* class is now responsible for its own base price and the logic and price of every single add-on.
- **Brittle Calculations:** The *CalculatePrice* method becomes a tangled web of if statements that is hard to read and easy to break.

11.3 The Formal Pattern: Decorator

Pattern Definition

> ***"Decorator** is a structural pattern that lets you attach new behaviors to objects by placing these objects inside special wrapper objects that contain the behaviors.."*

In Simpler Terms: The Decorator pattern allows you to start with a basic object (a plain pizza) and then dynamically "wrap" it with new functionality (toppings) by placing it inside a "decorator" object. Each decorator adds its own cost and description before passing the call to the object it wraps. You can wrap an object with multiple decorators, building a chain of flavors.

11.4 Understanding the Pattern

The Real-World Analogy: The Pizza Box

Imagine you order a plain Margherita pizza. That's your core object. The cook then adds extra cheese — this is like putting the pizza box inside a bigger box labeled *"+$1.0 for Extra Cheese."* Then they add stuffed crust, putting that box inside another labeled *"+$2.0 for Stuffed Crust."* When you get the final box and open it, you find your fully customized pizza. The cashier just needs to add up the prices on all the boxes to get total. Each box "decorates" what's inside it.

DECORATOR

11.5 How the Decorator Solves It

Instead of this monolithic class:

```
var pizza = new Pizza("Margherita", 10.0m) { ExtraCheese = true, StuffedCrust = true };
var total = pizza.CalculatePrice(); // ❌ Messy
```

We'll create this flexible, dynamic assembly:

```
// ✅ NEW: Dynamically build a pizza by wrapping it
IPizza myPizza = new MargheritaPizza(); // Base pizza ($10)
myPizza = new ExtraCheeseDecorator(myPizza); // Wrap it (+$1)
myPizza = new StuffedCrustDecorator(myPizza); // Wrap it again (+$2)

var total = myPizza.GetPrice(); // Returns 13.0
var description = myPizza.GetDescription(); // Returns "Margherita + Extra Cheese + Stuffed Crust"
```

The Decorator pattern lets us build complex, customized objects by combining simple components at runtime.

11.6 The Implementation Blueprint: Decorator Pattern Steps

Think of using the Decorator pattern like building the perfect pizza at a gourmet counter. You start with a simple base—a classic Margherita. Then, you point to the ingredients behind the glass: "I'll add some extra cheese... oh, and stuffed crust... and make it gluten-free, please!" The chef doesn't need a separate recipe for your unique creation; they just start with the base and keep adding your chosen toppings, building it layer by layer. The Decorator pattern lets your code do exactly this: start with a base object and dynamically add "toppings" of functionality.

1. **Create the Component Interface (Define the Core Pizza Contract):**
   - ***What to do:*** Create a C# interface (e.g., *IPizza*) that declares the common operations for all pizzas and toppings, like *GetPrice()* and *GetDescription().*
   - ***Why we do it:*** This interface is the universal contract. Both the core pizzas and all decorators will implement it, allowing them to be used interchangeably.
2. **Create Concrete Components (Create the Base Pizzas):**
   - ***What to do:*** Create concrete classes (e.g., *MargheritaPizza, PepperoniPizza*) that implement the *IPizza* interface. These are the objects that will be decorated.
   - ***Why we do it:*** These are the foundational, non-decorated pizzas that customers can start with.
3. **Create the Base Decorator Class (The Wrapper Foundation):**
   - ***What to do:*** Create an abstract class (e.g., *PizzaDecorator*) that also implements the *IPizza* interface. It must have a field to store a reference to a wrapped *IPizza* object.
   - ***Why we do it:*** This class acts as the base for all concrete decorators. It delegates all calls (like *GetPrice()*) to the wrapped pizza, allowing concrete decorators to override only what they need to change.
4. **Create Concrete Decorators (Create the Toppings):**
   - ***What to do:*** Create a class for each topping/add-on (e.g., *ExtraCheeseDecorator*, *StuffedCrustDecorator*) that inherits from the base *PizzaDecorator* class.
   - ***Why we do it:*** Each concrete decorator adds its own cost and description to the pizza it wraps. It overrides *GetPrice()* to return *base.GetPrice() + this.Price* and *GetDescription()* to return *base.GetDescription() + " + Topping Name"*.
5. **Assemble Dynamically at Runtime:**
   - ***What to do:*** Client code can now start with a base component and wrap it with any number of decorators.
   - ***Why we do it:*** This provides ultimate flexibility. You can create any pizza combination without ever touching the original class code again.

By following these five steps, you create a system where a base object can be transparently wrapped with any number of new behaviors. Your code becomes more flexible and resilient because you can mix and match features at runtime without creating a rigid class hierarchy or a monstrous class full of flags.

11.7 Implementing the Decorator Pattern

Step 1: Remove the boolean properties from the IPizza interface and base classes

We see that *IPizza* already extends *IOrderItem*, which is perfect. Our base pizzas (like *MargheritaPizza*) are already implemented as *IOrderItems*. We just need to remove the boolean properties from the IPizza interface and base classes

IPizza.cs

```
public interface IPizza : IOrderItem
{
   string Name { get; }
   decimal Price { get; }
   List<string> Toppings { get;  }
   void Prepare();
   void Bake();
   void Box();

   IPizza Clone();
}
```

MargheritaPizza.cs

```
public class MargheritaPizza : IPizza
{
   public string Name { get; }
   public decimal Price { get; }
   public List<string> Toppings { get; }

   public MargheritaPizza(decimal price){
      Name = "Margherita Pizza";
      Price = price;
      Toppings = new List<string> { "Tomato Sauce",
"Mozzarella", "Basil" };
   }
    //All other methods
}
```

Step 2: Create decorator class that handle the add-on logic

PizzaDecorator.cs

```
public abstract class PizzaDecorator : IPizza
{
   protected IPizza _pizza;

   protected PizzaDecorator(IPizza pizza)
   {
      _pizza = pizza;
   }

   public virtual string Name => _pizza.Name;
   public virtual decimal Price => _pizza.Price;
   public virtual List<string> Toppings => _pizza.Toppings;
   public virtual void Prepare() => _pizza.Prepare();
   public virtual void Bake() => _pizza.Bake();
   public virtual void Box() => _pizza.Box();
   public virtual IPizza Clone() => _pizza.Clone();
}
```

DECORATOR

Step 3: Create Concrete Decorators (Toppings)

These now modify the properties defined by *IOrderItem* and *IPizza*.

ExtraCheeseDecorator.cs

```
public class ExtraCheeseDecorator : PizzaDecorator
{
   public ExtraCheeseDecorator(IPizza pizza) : base(pizza) { }

   public override decimal Price => _pizza.Price + 1.50m; // Add cost for extra cheese
   public override bool ExtraCheese => true; // Set the flag
   public override string Name => _pizza.Name + " + Extra Cheese"; // Modify the name

   // We override GetDescription by leveraging the existing Toppings list and flags.
   // This is more integrated than the previous example.
   public override List<string> Toppings
   {
      get
      {
         var toppings = new List<string>(_pizza.Toppings);
         toppings.Add("Extra Cheese");
         return toppings;
      }
   }
}
```

StuffedCrustDecorator.cs

```
public class StuffedCrustDecorator : PizzaDecorator
{
   public StuffedCrustDecorator(IPizza pizza) : base(pizza) { }

   public override decimal Price => _pizza.Price + 2.0m;
   public override string Name => _pizza.Name + " + Stuffed Crust";
}
```

GlutenFreeDecorator.cs

```
public class GlutenFreeDecorator : PizzaDecorator
{
   public GlutenFreeDecorator(IPizza pizza) : base(pizza) { }

   public override decimal Price => _pizza.Price + 1.5m;
   public override string Name => _pizza.Name + " (Gluten-Free)";
}
```

Step 4: Usage in Client Code

Program.cs

```
IOrderItem orderItem = null;
bool isCustom = choice.Equals("custom", StringComparison.OrdinalIgnoreCase);

if (isCustom){
   orderItem = BuildACustomPizza();
}
else{
   if (selectedComponent == null){
      Console.WriteLine("Item not found.");
      return;
   }
   orderItem = MenuItemFactory.CreateOrderItem(selectedComponent);
}

// Check if the order item is a pizza
if (orderItem is IPizza basePizza){
   // Apply decorators based on user input
   Console.Write("\nAdd extra cheese? (yes/no): ");
   if (Console.ReadLine().ToLower() == "yes"){
      basePizza = new ExtraCheeseDecorator(basePizza);
   }

   Console.Write("Make it stuffed crust? (yes/no): ");
   if (Console.ReadLine().ToLower() == "yes"){
      basePizza = new StuffedCrustDecorator(basePizza);
   }

   Console.Write("Make it gluten-free? (yes/no): ");
   if (Console.ReadLine().ToLower() == "yes"){
      basePizza = new GlutenFreeDecorator(basePizza);
   }
   // Update orderItem to the decorated pizza
   orderItem = basePizza;
}

// Process the order
Console.WriteLine($"You ordered: {orderItem.Name} (${orderItem.Price})");

// If you need to display toppings, check if it's a pizza
if (orderItem is IPizza pizza){
   Console.WriteLine($"Toppings: {string.Join(", ", pizza.Toppings)}");
}


//Composite order code continued
```

Key Test Points for Decorator Pattern Validation

1. **Uniform Interface Test:** Verify that both the base component (e.g., *MargheritaPizza*) and all decorators (e.g., *ExtraCheeseDecorator*) implement the *IPizza* interface correctly and can be used interchangeably.
   - **Test Action:** Create an instance of a base pizza. Call *GetPrice()* and *GetDescription()* (or equivalent methods). Then, wrap it with one or more decorators and call the same methods on the decorated object.
   - **Expected Result:** Both the base object and the decorated object should respond to the same method calls without errors. The client code should not need to know whether it's dealing with a base object or a decorated one.
2. **Single Responsibility & Price Accumulation Test:** Ensure each decorator adds its own cost and description without affecting the core behavior of the wrapped object, and that prices accumulate correctly through a chain of decorators.
   - **Test Action:** Create a base pizza with a known price. Wrap it with a decorator that adds a fixed cost (e.g., + $1.50). Then, wrap the result with another decorator that adds a different cost (e.g., + $2.00). Check the final price and description.
   - **Expected Result:** The final price should be the sum of the base price and all decorator additions. The description should clearly list all added features in the order they were applied. Example: Margherita Pizza ($10) + ExtraCheeseDecorator ($1.50) + StuffedCrustDecorator ($2.00) = $13.50 and a description like "Margherita Pizza + Extra Cheese + Stuffed Crust".
3. **Order of Decoration Test:** Validate that the pattern allows decorators to be applied in any order and that the result is consistent and correct. (This is crucial for systems where the order of add-ons might matter, though it may not for pizza).
   - **Test Action:** Create two identical base pizzas. Decorate Pizza A with *ExtraCheeseDecorator* then *StuffedCrustDecorator*. Decorate Pizza B with *StuffedCrustDecorator* then *ExtraCheeseDecorator*. Check the price and description of both.
   - **Expected Result:** The final price for both pizzas must be identical, as the cost of add-ons is additive. The description might differ in order but should contain all elements.
4. **Core Functionality Preservation Test:** Ensure that decorating an object does not break its core functionality and original properties.
   - **Test Action:** Decorate a base pizza with multiple add-ons. Then, call core methods like *Prepare(), Bake()*, and *Box()* on the heavily decorated object.
   - **Expected Result:** All core methods should execute successfully, delegating to the underlying base pizza object. The decoration should only enhance the object, not break its fundamental behavior.

5. **Isolation Test (Liskov Substitution Principle):** Confirm that a decorated object can be used anywhere a base object is expected, without the client knowing the difference.
    - **Test Action:** Create a method or service (like *PricingService.CalculateTotal*) that takes an *IPizza* parameter and uses its *Price* property. Pass it a heavily decorated pizza.
    - **Expected Result:** The method should work correctly, returning the total calculated price without any knowledge of the decorators or need for type checking. This demonstrates that decorators are truly transparent extensions.
6. **Dynamic Composition at Runtime Test:** Validate that decorators can be applied based on dynamic conditions (like user input) at runtime, not just at compile time.
    - **Test Action:** Simulate user input (e.g., "yes" to extra cheese, "no" to stuffed crust) and build the decoration chain based on that input. Check the result.
    - **Expected Result:** The final object should only be decorated with the add-ons the user selected, and the price should reflect only those choices. This test proves the pattern's flexibility.
7. **Integration with Existing Systems Test:** Ensure the decorated pizzas work correctly with other parts of the system, such as the Order Cart, Inventory, or Composite-based menus.
    - **Test Action:** Add a decorated pizza to an *OrderCart*. Call *CalculateTotal()* on the cart.
    - **Expected Result:** The cart should correctly sum the price of the decorated pizza alongside any other items (like drinks or combos). The decorated pizza should be treated as a single IOrderItem with its price already finalized.

If all these tests pass, your Decorator pattern implementation is working correctly. You have successfully created a system that allows responsibilities to be added to objects dynamically and transparently, providing a flexible alternative to subclassing.

11.8 Why the Decorator Matters

- **Open/Closed Principle:** You can extend object behavior (add new toppings) without modifying the original object's code.
- **Runtime Flexibility:** Assemble complex objects from simple parts dynamically, based on user input.
- **Eliminates Class Explosion:** No need for *ExtraCheese StuffedCrust GlutenFree PepperoniPizza* classes.
- **Single Responsibility:** Each decorator class has one job: add one specific feature and its cost.
- **Transparent:** The decorated object is still an *IPizza* and can be used anywhere a base pizza is expected.

11.9 Mini-Exercise: Create a New Topping

Task: Create a new *DoublePepperoniDecorator* that adds an extra $2.00 and the text "+ Double Pepperoni" to the pizza's description.
Bonus: Create a *DiscountDecorator* that applies a 10% discount. Think about where in the decoration chain it should be applied (before or after adding toppings?) to change the total discount amount.

11.10 When to Use the Decorator

"Use the Decorator pattern when you need to assign additional responsibilities to individual objects dynamically and transparently, without affecting other objects. It's a flexible alternative to subclassing for extending functionality."

11.10 Transition to Chapter 12

"Now that we can dynamically build incredibly complex pizza orders, our ordering system has become a series of intricate steps: validate the order, process payment, update inventory, notify the kitchen, and confirm with the customer. Next, we'll introduce the **Facade** pattern to provide a simple, one-click ordering interface that hides this overwhelming complexity."

> **Next Up: Chapter 12 — Facade: The Magic of One-Click Ordering**
> Ready to hide the complex dance of kitchen coordination, payment processing, and inventory management behind a single, simple *PlaceOrder()* method? Let's build a welcome simplification for our clients

Scan to View Decorator Pattern Code

🍕 Builder vs. Decorator: A Quick Guide for Pizza Lovers (and Coders!)

Now that we've learned how to implement both the Builder Pattern & Decorator Pattern, let's clear up the confusion between these two patterns. Both are about creating/customizing objects, but they solve different problems.

The Builder Pattern: The "From-Scratch" Custom Order

- **What it does:** It helps you build a complex object step-by-step. Think of it like filling out a custom pizza order form online.
- **The Pizza Analogy:** You start from nothing. You choose the name ("My Awesome Pizza"), set the base price, hand-pick every single topping, and select all your options (crust type, cheese, etc.). When you click "Order," the kitchen gets the complete blueprint and builds your unique pizza all at once.
- **The Code Result:** You get one, final, immutable *CustomPizza* object created in a single *Build()* step. The builder's job is done after that.
- **When to Use It:**
  - When you need to create an object that requires many steps or configurations.
  - When you want to avoid a constructor with a huge number of parameters.
  - When the construction process should be separated from the object's class.
  - **Use Case in Our App: BuildACustomPizza()** uses a builder to create a pizza that doesn't exist on the main menu.

The Decorator Pattern: The "Add-Ons" Counter

- **What it does:** It lets you add new functionality to an existing object dynamically. Think of it like standing at the pizza counter and asking the chef to add more toppings to a pre-made base pizza.
- **The Pizza Analogy:** You start with an existing base pizza from the menu (e.g., a standard Margherita). You then say: "Please add extra cheese to that one. Now add stuffed crust to that." The chef modifies the original pizza by adding layers to it.
- **The Code Result:** You don't create a new pizza class. Instead, you "wrap" the original *MargheritaPizza* object with an *ExtraCheeseDecorator* object, which is then wrapped by a *StuffedCrustDecorator* object. You end up with a chain of objects that together form your customized pizza.
- **When to Use It:**
  - When you need to add responsibilities to objects dynamically and transparently (without affecting other objects).
  - When extension by subclassing is impractical (e.g., too many possible combinations).
  - **Use Case in Our App:** Adding extra cheese, stuffed crust, or gluten-free options to any pizza that comes from the menu (*MenuItemFactory*).

DECORATOR

The Key Difference at a Glance

Feature	Builder Pattern	Decorator Pattern
Purpose	Construction	Extension
Starts With	Nothing (or basic parameters)	An already existing object
Result	A new object is created	The original object is wrapped/enhanced
Analogy	Filling out a custom order form	Asking a chef to add toppings to a ready-made pizza
In Our Code	PizzaBuilder.Build() → CustomPizza	new ExtraCheeseDecorator(myPizza)

Simple Rule of Thumb:

- Need to create something completely new and unique that doesn't already exist? Use the **Builder**.
- Need to add features or options to something that already exists? Use the **Decorator**.

Both patterns are awesome tools. You don't always have to choose one over the other — in fact, our app uses both, exactly for the different reasons described above!

Chapter 12

Facade — The Magic of One-Click Ordering

Setting The Stage

Your *Program.Main()* method has become a "God Object," directly coordinating inventory checks, payment processing, baking, packing, delivery, and notifications. This creates a tangled web of dependencies and makes the code brittle and hard to change.

> In this chapter, you'll:
> 1. **Identify Pitfalls:** Identify the pain of directly managing complex subsystem interactions.
> 2. **Learn the Pattern:** Learn the Facade pattern to provide a simple, unified interface to a complex subsystem.
> 3. **Build a One-Click Ordering System:** Build a one-click ordering system that hides the intricate steps of order processing.
> 4. **Protect Core Application:** Decouple your high-level client code from the low-level complexities of the kitchen, payment, and delivery services.

FACADE

12.1 Hook: What's the Pain?

"Our main ordering code is a mess! It has to talk to the inventory system, the payment gateway, the pizza service, the delivery service, and the notifier. Adding a new step — like a loyalty points system — would mean digging into this already complex code. We need a simple PlaceOrder() button that hides all this chaos behind the scenes!"

12.2 The Problem in Our Pizza App

The client code (Program.Main()) is tightly coupled to every single service in our application. (Oops Moment 33)

Why This Hurts:

- **Tight Coupling to Subsystem:** The main program depends on the concrete classes of all services. Changing a service (e.g., switching from Twilio to AWS for SMS) requires changing the main code.
- **Complexity:** The high-level policy (the order workflow) is mixed with low-level details. The code is hard to read and understand.

```
// ✗ OLD: The "God Object" anti-pattern (Oops Moment #33)
// Client code must know about and coordinate every single step
var inventory = new InventoryApi();
var payment = new PaymentGateway3rdParty();
var pizzaService = new PizzaService();
var deliveryService = new DeliveryService();
var notifier = new NotificationService();

// ... code to create order ...

// ✗ Client code orchestrates everything manually
if (!inventory.ReserveIngredients(order.Pizza))
    { Console.WriteLine("Out of stock"); return; }

var total = PricingService.CalculateTotal(order);
if (!payment.Pay(total, "USD", "card-..."))
    { Console.WriteLine("Payment failed"); return; }

pizzaService.BakePizza(order);
pizzaService.PackPizza(order);
deliveryService.Deliver(order);
notifier.Send("email", "smtp", $"Order #{order.OrderId} delivered");
```

- **Brittleness:** Any change to the order fulfillment process (e.g., adding a quality check step) forces us to modify this central, sensitive code in multiple places.
- **Violates Single Responsibility:** The *Main()* method is now responsible for knowing the entire order workflow, not just for starting the application.

12.3 The Formal Pattern: Facade

Pattern Definition

> *"**Facade** is a structural pattern that provides a simplified interface to a complex subsystem of classes, libraries, or frameworks."*

In Simpler Terms: The Facade pattern creates a "front desk" for a complex system. You don't need to talk to the chef, the cashier, the bartender, and the delivery driver separately. You just talk to the front desk, and they handle all the complex coordination behind the scenes.

12.4 Understanding the Pattern

The Real-World Analogy: The Restaurant Host

Imagine a busy restaurant. As a customer, you don't run around the kitchen cooking your food, mixing your drinks, and washing the dishes. You talk to one person: the host. You give them your order ("one pepperoni pizza"). The host then becomes your facade. They coordinate with the kitchen, the bar, and the serving staff, hiding all the complex interactions from you. You get a simple interface: order -> eat -> pay.

12.5 How the Facade Solves It

Instead of this complex orchestration:

```
// ❌ Client knows too much
inventory.Check();
payment.Process();
kitchen.Bake();
delivery.Dispatch();
notifier.Send();
```

We'll create this this simple interaction:

```
// ✅ Client knows only one thing: the Facade
var orderFacade = new OrderProcessingFacade();
orderFacade.PlaceOrder(myOrder); // That's it! Everything is handled inside.
```

The Facade pattern decouples the client from the subsystem, making the system easier to use and more resilient to change.

12.6 The Implementation Blueprint: Facade Pattern Steps

Think of implementing the Facade pattern like hiring a general manager for your pizza shop. Their job isn't to cook or deliver themselves, but to manage all the specialized staff so you, the owner, only have to give one command: "Make this order happen."

1. **Identify the Complex Subsystem (Identify all Departments):**
   - ***What to do:*** List all the components that are currently being called directly by the client code (e.g., *InventoryApi, PaymentGateway3rdParty, PizzaService, DeliveryService, NotificationService*).
   - ***Why we do it:*** This defines the scope of complexity that our facade will need to manage. It's like identifying all the departments the general manager will oversee.
2. **Design the Simplified Interface (Front Desk):**
   - ***What to do:*** Determine what simple operations the client truly needs (e.g., *PlaceOrder(Order order), CancelOrder(int orderId), CheckOrderStatus(int orderId)*).
   - ***Why we do it:*** The goal is to hide the complex workflow behind a few, easy-to-understand methods. This is the "front desk" API you're creating for clients.
3. **Implement the Facade Class (Front Desk Manager):**
   - ***What to do:*** Create a new class (e.g., *OrderProcessor*) that implements the simplified interface. This class will have references to all the subsystem components.
   - ***Why we do it:*** This class will contain the complex coordination logic that was previously scattered throughout the client code. It's where the "magic" of orchestration happens.
4. **Delegate to the Subsystem (Distribute Tasks to Appropriate Workers):**
   - ***What to do:*** Inside each facade method, translate the client's simple request into the appropriate sequence of calls to the subsystem objects.
   - ***Why we do it:*** The facade doesn't do the real work; it just knows who should do it and in what order. It delegates tasks to the appropriate specialists in the subsystem.
5. **Redirect Client Code:**
   - ***What to do:*** Modify the client code (*Program.Main*) to call the facade's simple methods instead of directly calling the subsystem components.
   - ***Why we do it:*** This achieves the decoupling. The client no longer depends on the complex subsystem, only on the simple facade interface.

By following these five steps, you create a clear separation of concerns. The client code becomes simple and focused on its high-level tasks, while the facade handles the intricate details of coordinating the underlying machinery of your application.

12.7 Implementing the Facade Pattern

Step 1: Identify Subsystems and Design Interface

IOrderProcessorFacade.cs

```
public interface IOrderProcessorFacade
{
    bool PlaceOrder(Order order);
    bool CancelOrder(int orderId);
    string CheckOrderStatus(int orderId);
}
```

Step 2: Implement the Facade Class

OrderProcessor.cs

```
public class OrderProcessor : IOrderProcessorFacade
{
    // References to all the complex subsystem components
    private readonly InventoryApi _inventory;
    private readonly PaymentGatewayAdapter _paymentAdapter;
    private readonly PizzaService _pizzaService;
    private readonly DeliveryService _deliveryService;
    private readonly EmailNotification _emailNotifier;
    private readonly SmsNotification _smsNotifier;
    private readonly PushNotification _pushNotifier;

    public OrderProcessor(InventoryApi inventory,
                PaymentGatewayAdapter paymentAdapter,
                PizzaService pizzaService,
                DeliveryService deliveryService,
                EmailNotification emailNotifier,
                SmsNotification smsNotifier,
                PushNotification pushNotifier)
    {
        _inventory = inventory;
        _paymentAdapter = paymentAdapter;
        _pizzaService = pizzaService;
        _deliveryService = deliveryService;
        _emailNotifier = emailNotifier;
        _smsNotifier = smsNotifier;
        _pushNotifier = pushNotifier;
    }
```

```
    // The simplified interface method that hides all complexity
    public bool PlaceOrder(Order order)
    {
        Console.WriteLine($" Processing Order #{order.OrderId}...");

        // 1. Check inventory
        if (!_inventory.ReserveIngredients(order.OrderItem)){
            Console.WriteLine("Order failed: Out of stock.");
            return false;
        }

        // 2. Process payment
        var total = PricingService.CalculateTotal(order);
        var paymentResult = _paymentAdapter.ProcessPayment(total,
Config.Instance.CurrencySymbol, "card-token-123");
        if (!paymentResult.IsSuccess)
        {
            Console.WriteLine($"Order failed: Payment declined. {paymentResult.ErrorMessage}");
            return false;
        }
        Console.WriteLine($"Payment successful. Transaction ID: {paymentResult.TransactionId}");

        // 3. Fulfill order
        _pizzaService.BakePizza(order);
        _pizzaService.PackPizza(order);
        _deliveryService.Deliver(order);

        // 4. Notify customer using the Bridge-based notification services
        _emailNotifier.Send($"Order #{order.OrderId} has been delivered");
        _smsNotifier.Send("Your pizza is out for delivery!");
        _pushNotifier.Send("Special offer: 20% off your next order!");

        Console.WriteLine($"Order #{order.OrderId} processed successfully!");
        return true;
    }

    public bool CancelOrder(int orderId)
    {
        // Implementation for canceling an order
        Console.WriteLine($"Cancelling order #{orderId}...");
        // ... logic involving inventory, payment refund, etc.
        return true;
    }

    public string CheckOrderStatus(int orderId)
    {
        // Implementation for checking status
        return "Delivered"; // Simplified for example
    }
}
```

FACADE

Step 3: Usage in Client Code

Now, in your *Main* method, you can create the *OrderProcessor* with all the required dependencies, including the notification services. This simplifies the main method significantly.

Program.cs

```
static void Main()
{
   // Initialize all services and notifiers
   var pizzaService = new PizzaService();
   var deliveryService = new DeliveryService();
   var inventory = new InventoryApi();
   var paymentAdapter = new PaymentGatewayAdapter();

   // Set up different notification combinations using Bridge pattern
   var emailNotifier = new EmailNotification(new SmtpEmailSender());
   var smsNotifier = new SmsNotification(new TwilioSmsSender());
   var pushNotifier = new PushNotification(new FirebasePushSender());

   // Create the facade
   var orderProcessor = new OrderProcessor(
      inventory,    paymentAdapter,    pizzaService,    deliveryService,    emailNotifier,
      smsNotifier,    pushNotifier
   );
   Console.WriteLine("Welcome to Delizioso Pizzeria!");
   Console.WriteLine("Full Menu:");

   // ... [Code for parsing input and creating orderItem] ...

   // Create an order object from the orderItem
   var order = new Order{
      OrderId = IdGenerator.Instance.GetNextId(),
      CustomerName = "Walk-in",
      Address = "Counter",
      OrderItem = orderItem,
      Status = "Received",
      TimeOrdered = DateTime.Now
   };

   // Place the order with ONE simple call!
   bool orderSuccess = orderProcessor.PlaceOrder(order);
   if (orderSuccess) {
      Console.WriteLine("\n Thank you for your order!");
   }
   else {
      Console.WriteLine("\n There was a problem with your order.");
   }
}
```

Key Test Points for Facade Pattern Validation

1. **Simplified Interface Test**
   - **Objective:** Verify that the Facade provides a dramatically simpler interface for the client, hiding the complexity of the subsystem.
   - **Test Action:** Compare the client code before and after introducing the Facade. Count the number of service interactions the client code must perform directly.
   - **Expected Result:** The client code should be reduced to 1-2 method calls on the Facade object, rather than 5-10+ direct calls to various subsystem components.
2. **Subsystem Delegation Test**
   - **Objective:** Ensure that the Facade correctly delegates client requests to the appropriate subsystem objects.
   - **Test Action:** Using mocking frameworks (like Moq), create mock objects for all subsystem components (Inventory, Payment, PizzaService, etc.). Inject these mocks into the Facade and call its main method (e.g., *PlaceOrder()*). Then, verify that the expected methods were called on the mock objects in the correct sequence.
   - **Expected Result:** The mocks should verify that each subsystem component received the correct calls in the proper order (e.g., *InventoryApi.ReserveIngredients()* was called before *PaymentGateway.ProcessPayment()*).
3. **Decoupling Test**
   - **Objective:** Confirm that the client code is now decoupled from the subsystem components and only depends on the Facade.
   - **Test Action:** Examine the client code (*Program.Main*). It should only contain references to and calls on the *OrderProcessor* Facade. It should have no direct *new()* calls or method invocations on *PizzaService*, *DeliveryService*, *PaymentGateway*, etc.
   - **Expected Result:** The client code is clean, simple, and free of knowledge about the complex subsystem. Changing a subsystem component (e.g., swapping a payment provider) should require no changes to the client code.
4. **Error Handling and Propagation Test**
   - **Objective:** Validate that the Facade properly handles errors from the subsystem and translates them into a simple result for the client.
   - **Test Action:** Mock subsystem components to throw exceptions or return failure states (e.g., mock *InventoryApi* to return false on *ReserveIngredients*). Call the Facade method and check its return value and output.
   - **Expected Result:** The Facade should catch subsystem errors, log or handle them appropriately, and return a simple, client-friendly result (e.g., false or a Result object) without exposing the client to the subsystem's complex error types.

FACADE

5. **Integration with Other Patterns Test**
    - **Objective:** Ensure the Facade works seamlessly with other implemented patterns like *Bridge* (Notifications) and *Adapter* (Payment).
    - **Test Action:** In a full integration test, run through a complete order circuit. Verify that the Facade correctly uses the *PaymentGatewayAdapter* and the Bridge-based notification services (*EmailNotification*, *SmsNotification*) without the client needing to know about them.
    - **Expected Result:** The order should be processed successfully, with payments going through the adapter and notifications being sent via the appropriate Bridge implementations, all coordinated by the Facade.
6. **Single Responsibility Validation**
    - **Objective:** Confirm that the Facade has a single responsibility: coordinating the subsystem.
    - **Test Action:** Review the *OrderProcessor* class. It should not contain business logic (like calculating prices) or implementation details (like how to send an SMS). It should only orchestrate calls to other objects that handle those responsibilities.
    - **Expected Result:** The Facade's methods are concise and read like a recipe or a workflow: "do this, then that, then return the result."

If all these tests pass, your Facade pattern implementation is working correctly. You have successfully provided a simple, robust interface to a complex subsystem, making your client code easier to write, read, and maintain.

12.8 Why the Facade Matters

- **Simplified Client Code:** Reduces complexity for the client, which now only needs to know about the facade.
- **Decoupling:** Decouples the client from the subsystem components, making the system more modular and resilient to change.
- **Single Responsibility:** The facade class has one job: coordinate the order workflow. The client has one job: initiate the order.
- **Easier Testing:** You can mock the facade for client tests, and test the complex workflow logic separately in the facade tests.
- **Provides a Context-Specific API:** The facade can offer an interface that is tailored to the client's specific needs, which might be simpler than the general-purpose API of the subsystem.

12.9 Mini-Exercise: Add a New Step

Task: The pizza shop now wants to add a "Loyalty Points" step after successful payment. Members get 10 points per dollar spent.

- Create a *LoyaltyService* class with an *AddPoints(int customerId, int points)* method.
- Modify the *OrderProcessor.PlaceOrder()* method to include this new step without changing the client code (*Program.Main*).

Bonus: What principle does this exercise demonstrate? (Answer: The Open/Closed Principle - the system is open for extension but closed for modification).

12.10 When to Use the Facade

"Use the Facade pattern when you need to provide a simple interface to a complex subsystem or when you want to decouple your client code from the intricate details of subsystem interactions."

12.10 Transition to Chapter 13

"Our ordering system is now much simpler to use, but we're still calling the *InventoryApi* directly. What if that service is slow, unreliable, or we need to add access control? Next, we'll introduce the Proxy pattern to act as a controlled gateway to this remote service, adding caching, security, and resilience without changing the original API."

> **Next Up: Chapter 13 — Proxy: The Guardian of the Inventory Gateway**
> Ready to add a protective layer between your app and external services? Let's build a smart proxy that controls access, improves performance, and handles failures gracefully!

See how Facade Pattern Works

Chapter 13

Proxy — The Guardian of the Inventory Gateway

Setting The Stage

Your application calls the *InventoryApi* directly every time an order is placed. This creates a brittle, slow, and potentially insecure system, as there's no caching, no retry mechanism, and no access control.

> In this chapter, you'll:
> 1. **Identify Pitfalls:** Identify the risks and inefficiencies of direct access to remote services.
> 2. **Learn the Pattern:** Learn the Proxy pattern to control access to another object.
> 3. **Build a Protective System:** Build a protective proxy that adds caching, retry logic, and security to the inventory system.
> 4. **Protect Core Application:** Learn how to enhance functionality without modifying the original object's code.

13.1 Hook: What's the Pain?

"Every time we place an order, our app calls the remote InventoryApi directly. If the network is slow, the whole app waits. If the API is down, orders fail. If we get a million requests, we'll bombard the API with a million calls! We need a smart guardian that stands between our app and the remote service — one that can cache results, retry failed calls, and control access."

13.2 The Problem in Our Pizza App

The code calls the *InventoryApi* directly, with no protective layer. (Oops Moment 26)

```
// ✗ OLD: Direct, unprotected call to remote service (Oops Moment #26)
var inventory = new InventoryApi(); // Direct dependency

// This call is made every single time, with no caching or retry logic
if (!inventory.ReserveIngredients(order.OrderItem))
{
    Console.WriteLine("Out of stock");
    continue;
}
```

Why This Hurts:

- **Performance:** No caching means identical requests (e.g., for a popular pizza) hit the slow network repeatedly.
- **Reliability:** Network glitches or temporary API downtime cause immediate order failures.
- **Security:** There's no layer to add authentication or rate-limiting before the request goes to the remote API.
- **Tight Coupling:** The application is tightly coupled to the specific API implementation, making it hard to swap or test.

13.3 The Formal Pattern: Proxy

Pattern Definition

> *"**Proxy** is a structural pattern that provides an object that acts as a substitute for a real service object. The proxy controls access to the original object, allowing you to perform something either before or after the request gets through to the real object."*

In Simpler Terms: The Proxy pattern puts a "stand-in" or a "bodyguard" in front of an object. You talk to the bodyguard, and they decide if, when, and how to pass your message to the real object. They can add extra duties like checking your ID (security), giving you a cached answer (caching), or trying again if the first attempt fails (retry logic).

13.4 Understanding the Pattern

The Real-World Analogy: The Restaurant Expediter

In a busy restaurant, the chefs in the kitchen are the "real object." They are busy and focused on cooking. You don't talk to them directly. Instead, you talk to the expediter — the person who stands between the waitstaff and the kitchen. The expediter controls access to the chefs, prioritizes orders, checks if an order is already being prepared (caching), and shouts at the chefs to remake a dish if it was wrong (retry). The expediter is the proxy for the kitchen.

PROXY

13.5 How the Proxy Solves It

Instead of this direct, fragile call:

```
// ❌ Client talks directly to the remote service
var result = new InventoryApi().ReserveIngredients(pizza);
```

We'll create this controlled, smart access:

```
// ✅ Client talks to a proxy
IInventoryService inventory = new InventoryApiProxy(new InventoryApi());

// The proxy handles caching, retries, and security internally
var result = inventory.ReserveIngredients(pizza);
```

The Proxy pattern lets us add new behaviors like caching and retries without changing the client code or the original *InventoryApi* class.

13.6 The Implementation Blueprint: Proxy Pattern Steps

Think of implementing the Proxy pattern like hiring a personal assistant for a busy executive. The assistant screens your calls, manages the executive's schedule (caching availability), and only bothers the executive for truly important matters.

1. **Identify the Real Subject:**
   - ***What to do:*** Identify the object that needs protection or enhancement (e.g., the *InventoryApi* class).
   - ***Why we do it:*** This is the object whose functionality we want to control access to.
2. **Define the Subject Interface:**
   - ***What to do:*** Ensure both the real object and the proxy implement a common interface (e.g., *IInventoryService*). This allows them to be used interchangeably.

- ***Why we do it:*** This adherence to a common interface is what makes the proxy a drop-in replacement for the real object, a key principle of the pattern.

3. **Create the Proxy Class:**
   - ***What to do:*** Create a new class (e.g., *InventoryApiProxy*) that implements the common interface. This class will hold a reference to the real *InventoryApi* object.
   - ***Why we do it*:** The proxy will stand in for the real object, intercepting all calls.
4. **Implement Enhanced Behavior in the Proxy:**
   - ***What to do:*** In each method of the proxy, add the new functionality (caching, retries, logging) before or after delegating the call to the real object.
   - ***Why we do it:*** This is where the magic happens. The proxy enhances the behavior transparently.
5. **Redirect Client Code to Use the Proxy:**
   - ***What to do:*** Modify the client code (or, better yet, use Dependency Injection) to create an instance of the proxy instead of the real object.
   - ***Why we do it:*** The client code remains unchanged in its calls but now benefits from the proxy's enhanced behavior.

13.7 Implementing the Proxy Pattern

Step 1: Define the Subject Interface

Get Full Code Here

IInventoryService.cs

```
public interface IInventoryService
{
    bool ReserveIngredients(IOrderItem item);
}
```

Step 2: Create the Proxy Class with Enhanced Behavior

InventoryApiProxy.cs

```
public class InventoryApiProxy : IInventoryService
{
    private readonly InventoryApi _inventoryApi;
    private readonly Dictionary<string, (bool Result, DateTime Expiry)> _cache;
    private readonly TimeSpan _cacheDuration = TimeSpan.FromMinutes(5); // Cache for 5 minutes

    public InventoryApiProxy(InventoryApi inventoryApi)
    {
        _inventoryApi = inventoryApi;
        _cache = new Dictionary<string, (bool, DateTime)>();
    }
```

```
    public bool ReserveIngredients(IOrderItem item)
    {
        string cacheKey = $"{item.Name}_{item.GetHashCode()}"; // Create a unique key for the request

        // 1. Check Cache First
        if (_cache.TryGetValue(cacheKey, out var cacheEntry) && DateTime.Now < cacheEntry.Expiry)
        {
            Console.WriteLine($"[Proxy] Serving from cache: {item.Name} - Available:
{cacheEntry.Result}");
            return cacheEntry.Result;
        }

        // 2. If not in cache (or expired), call the real API with retry logic
        int maxRetries = 3;
        for (int attempt = 1; attempt <= maxRetries; attempt++)
        {
            try
            {
                Console.WriteLine($"[Proxy] Calling InventoryAPI (Attempt {attempt}) for {item.Name}...");
                bool result = _inventoryApi.ReserveIngredients(item); // Delegate to the real object

                // 3. Cache the result for future requests
                _cache[cacheKey] = (result, DateTime.Now.Add(_cacheDuration));
                Console.WriteLine($"[Proxy] Success. Cached result: {result}");
                return result;
            }
            catch (Exception ex) // e.g., Network timeout
            {
                Console.WriteLine($"[Proxy] Attempt {attempt} failed: {ex.Message}");
                if (attempt == maxRetries)
                {
                    Console.WriteLine("[Proxy] All retry attempts failed. Assuming out of stock.");
                    _cache[cacheKey] = (false, DateTime.Now.Add(_cacheDuration)); // Cache failure
                    return false;
                }
                Task.Delay(500 * attempt).Wait(); // Wait before retrying (500ms, 1000ms, 1500ms)
            }
        }
        return false;
    }
}
```

What We Are Doing in *InventoryApiProxy*.cs (In Simple Words)
Imagine the *InventoryApiProxy* is a smart helper for our app. Its main job is to manage calls to the slow remote *InventoryApi* and make everything faster and more reliable.
Here's what it does:

1. **It Remembers Answers (Caching)**
   - **The Dictionary:** It has a notebook (a *Dictionary* in code) where it writes down questions it has already asked and the answers it got.
   - **What it Stores:** In this notebook, it stores:
     - **The Question:** "Do we have enough ingredients for a Margherita pizza?"
     - **The Answer:** "Yes" or "No".
     - **An Expiry Time:** It remembers that this answer is only valid for 5 minutes (because ingredients can change!). After 5 minutes, it will ask the remote API again to get a fresh answer.
2. **It Checks the Notebook First**
   - Before bothering the slow remote API, the smart helper **first checks its notebook.**
   - If it finds the question and the answer hasn't expired, it immediately gives us the answer from the notebook. This is super fast!
3. **It Tries Again if it Fails (Retry Logic)**
   - If it does need to call the remote API and the network is glitchy, the helper doesn't give up right away.
   - It tries again a few times (e.g., 3 times), waiting a little longer between each try. This makes our app much more reliable.
4. **It Protects the Remote API**
   - By remembering answers, the helper ensures we don't ask the remote API the same question over and over again. This reduces the load on the remote server and keeps our app running smoothly.

Step 3: Redirect Client Code (In the Facade)

OrderProcessor.cs

```
public class OrderProcessor : IOrderProcessorFacade
{
    private readonly IInventoryService _inventory; // Now depends on the interface
    // ... other fields ...

    public OrderProcessor(IInventoryService inventory, // Accepts any IInventoryService
                PaymentGatewayAdapter paymentAdapter,
                PizzaService pizzaService,
                DeliveryService deliveryService,
                EmailNotification emailNotifier,
                SmsNotification smsNotifier,
                PushNotification pushNotifier)
    {
        _inventory = inventory; // Could be the real API or the Proxy
        // ... other assignments ...
    }
```

```
    public bool PlaceOrder(Order order)
    {
        Console.WriteLine($"🚀 Processing Order #{order.OrderId}...");

        // 1. Check inventory (now goes through the proxy)
        if (!_inventory.ReserveIngredients(order.OrderItem)) // Client code unchanged!
        {
            Console.WriteLine("❌ Order failed: Out of stock.");
            return false;
        }
        // ... rest of the method unchanged ...
    }
}
```

Step 4: Client Code Setup (In Program.Main or a DI Container)

Program.cs

```
// In the composition root (e.g., Program.Main)
// Create the real subject
var realInventoryApi = new InventoryApi();

// Wrap it in a protective proxy
IInventoryService inventoryService = new InventoryApiProxy(realInventoryApi);

// Pass the proxy to the facade
var orderProcessor = new OrderProcessor(
    inventoryService, // Injected proxy
    new PaymentGatewayAdapter(),
    new PizzaService(),
    new DeliveryService(),
    new EmailNotification(new SmtpEmailSender()),
    new SmsNotification(new TwilioSmsSender()),
    new PushNotification(new FirebasePushSender())
);
```

Key Test Points for Proxy Pattern Validation

1. Functional Equivalence Test

- **Objective:** Verify that the Proxy produces the same results as the Real Subject for the same requests.
- **Test Action:** Call the same method (e.g., *ReserveIngredients*) on both the real *InventoryApi* and the *InventoryApiProxy* with the same input. Compare the results.
- **Expected Result:** The results should be identical. The proxy must be a transparent stand-in for the real object.

2. Caching Behavior Test

- **Objective:** Ensure the proxy correctly caches responses and serves subsequent identical requests from the cache without calling the real object.

PROXY

- **Test Action:** Call *ReserveIngredients* twice with the same pizza object. Monitor the console output or use a mock to track how many times the real API's method is called.
- **Expected Result:** The real API method should be called only on the first request. The second request should return the cached result instantly, indicated by a log message like "Serving from cache".

3. **Cache Expiration Test**
    - **Objective:** Validate that the cache does not serve stale data after the defined expiry time.
    - **Test Action:**
        1. Make a request to cache a result.
        2. Artificially set the system time forward to be beyond the cache expiry duration (or use a test-friendly cache that allows you to manipulate expiry).
        3. Make the same request again.
    - **Expected Result:** After the cache expires, the proxy should bypass the cache and call the real API method again to fetch a fresh result.
4. **Retry Mechanism Test**
    - **Objective:** Confirm that the proxy retries failed calls to the real object the specified number of times before finally failing.
    - **Test Action:** Use a mock *InventoryApi* that is configured to throw an exception *(e.g., a TimeoutException)* on the first few calls. Call the proxy and observe the behavior.
    - **Expected Result:** The proxy should log multiple retry attempts (e.g., "Attempt 1 failed," "Attempt 2 failed") before eventually returning a failure after the maximum number of retries is exceeded.
5. **Decoupling Test (Dependency Inversion)**
    - **Objective:** Ensure the client code (the *OrderProcessor* facade) depends on the *IInventoryService* abstraction, not the concrete *InventoryApi* or *InventoryApiProxy*.
    - **Test Action:** Examine the *OrderProcessor* class. Its constructor should accept a parameter of type *IInventoryService*, not a concrete class.
    - **Expected Result:** The *OrderProcessor* is unaware of whether it is using the real API or the proxy. This allows you to easily switch between them or use a mock for testing.
6. **Integration Test with Facade**
    - **Objective:** Validate that the entire system works seamlessly with the proxy integrated into the workflow.
    - **Test Action:** Execute a full order placement test using the *OrderProcessor.PlaceOrder* method, which now internally uses the *InventoryApiProxy*.

- **Expected Result:** The order process should complete successfully. The logs should show proxy behavior (caching, retries) working within the context of the full order flow, demonstrating that the proxy is a well-integrated part of the system.

If all these tests pass, your Proxy pattern implementation is working correctly. You have successfully added a layer of control, resilience, and performance optimization without altering the core logic of the real subject or the client that uses it.

13.8 Why the Proxy Matters

- **Control:** You gain fine-grained control over how and when the real object is accessed.
- **Performance:** Caching can dramatically reduce latency and load on the remote service.
- **Resilience:** Retry logic makes your application more robust against temporary failures.
- **Security:** The proxy is a perfect place to add authentication and authorization checks.
- **Loose Coupling:** The client depends on an abstraction (*IInventoryService*), not a concrete class, making the system more flexible and testable.

13.9 Mini-Exercise: Add a New Feature

Task: Add rate-limiting to the *InventoryApiProxy*. Allow a maximum of 10 calls per minute from a single client. If the limit is exceeded, return false (assuming out of stock) without calling the real API.

Bonus: Add logging to the proxy to record every API call, its result, and whether it was served from the cache.

13.10 When to Use the Proxy

"Use the Proxy pattern when you need to control access to an object. Common use cases include lazy initialization, logging, access control, caching, and enforcing strict communication with remote services."

13.10 Transition to Chapter 14

"Our inventory system is now protected and efficient, thanks to the Proxy. But as our menu grows, we need to be smarter about how we manage the data of our most common ingredients. Next, we'll use the Flyweight pattern to share data between thousands of pizza objects and save precious memory."

> **Next Up: Chapter 14 — Flyweight: The Memory Saver for Toppings**
> Ready to optimize memory by sharing data between objects? Let's learn how to serve thousands of pizzas without consuming gigabytes of RAM!

Chapter 14

Flyweight — The Memory Saver for Toppings

Setting The Stage

Your application creates thousands of pizza objects, each with identical topping information stored repeatedly in memory. This wastes significant resources and slows down performance as your pizza business grows.

> In this chapter, you'll:
> 1. **Identify Pitfalls:** Identify the memory waste caused by duplicating identical topping data across pizza objects.
> 2. **Learn the Pattern:** Learn the Flyweight pattern to share common data between objects.
> 3. **Create a Registry:** Create a smart topping registry that stores each unique topping only once.
> 4. **Protect Core Application:** Dramatically reduce your application's memory footprint while maintaining performance.

14.1 Hook: What's the Pain?

"Every time we create a pepperoni pizza, we're creating new 'pepperoni' topping objects with the same name, description, and price. With 1,000 pepperoni pizzas, we have 1,000 identical pepperoni objects wasting memory! We need a way to store common topping information just once and share it across all pizzas that use that topping."

14.2 The Problem in Our Pizza App

Each pizza contains its own complete topping objects, duplicating data across instances.
(Oops Moment 3)

```
// ❌ OLD: Each pizza has its own complete topping objects
public class Pizza
{
    public List<Topping> Toppings { get; set; }
    // Each Topping has Name, Description, Price, Calories, etc.
}

// Creating 1000 Pepperoni pizzas creates 1000 identical Pepperoni topping objects
```

Why This Hurts:

- **Memory Bloat:** Identical topping data is stored repeatedly, wasting significant memory.
- **GC Pressure:** The garbage collector has to work harder to clean up all the duplicate objects.
- **Poor Scalability:** As order volume grows, memory usage grows linearly, potentially crashing the app.
- **Cache Inefficiency:** CPU caches become less effective with duplicated data spread throughout memory.

14.3 The Formal Pattern: Flyweight

Pattern Definition

> *"**Flyweight** is a structural pattern that lets you fit more objects into the available amount of RAM by sharing common parts of state between multiple objects instead of keeping all of the data in each object."*

In Simpler Terms: The Flyweight pattern is like having a shared ingredient pantry. Instead of each pizza having its own jar of pepperoni, all pizzas reference the same shared pepperoni jar. This way, we only store each unique topping once, no matter how many pizzas use it.

14.4 Understanding the Pattern

The Real-World Analogy: The Shared Pantry

Imagine a pizza kitchen where each chef has their own complete set of ingredients. This would require enormous space and be incredibly wasteful. Instead, all chefs share from a central pantry. When a chef needs pepperoni, they take it from the shared pantry rather than having their personal pepperoni supply. The Flyweight pattern works the same way - it creates a shared "pantry" of topping objects that all pizzas can use.

14.5 How the Flyweight Solves It

Instead of this wasteful approach:

```
// ❌ Memory-inefficient: each pizza has its own topping instances
pizza1.Toppings.Add(new Topping("Pepperoni", "Spicy sausage", 1.5m, 250));
pizza2.Toppings.Add(new Topping("Pepperoni", "Spicy sausage", 1.5m, 250)); // Duplicate!
```

We'll implement this efficient approach:

```
// ❌ Memory-inefficient: each pizza has its own topping instances
pizza1.Toppings.Add(new Topping("Pepperoni", "Spicy sausage", 1.5m, 250));// ✅ Memory efficient: all
pizzas share the same topping instance
var pepperoni = ToppingFlyweightFactory.GetTopping("Pepperoni");
pizza1.Toppings.Add(pepperoni);
pizza2.Toppings.Add(pepperoni); // Same instance!

// The factory ensures we only have one Pepperoni object in memory

pizza2.Toppings.Add(new Topping("Pepperoni", "Spicy sausage", 1.5m, 250)); // Duplicate!
```

The Flyweight pattern separates intrinsic state (shared data like name and price) from extrinsic state (context-specific data). We share the intrinsic state across all objects.

14.6 The Implementation Blueprint: Flyweight Pattern Steps

Think of using the Flyweight pattern like organizing a super-efficient pizza kitchen with a central ingredient pantry. Instead of every chef having their own private stock of ingredients, they all share from one central pantry.

1. **Identify Intrinsic vs. Extrinsic State (Identify Shared vs. Unique Ingredients):**
   - ***What to do:*** Analyze your objects and separate the data that is shared (intrinsic state) from the data that is unique to each object (extrinsic state). For a topping, its *Name*, *BasePrice*, and *Calories* are shared. The *Quantity* on a specific pizza is unique.
   - ***Why we do it:*** This tells us what data to store just once (in the shared pantry) and what data each pizza must keep for itself.

FLYWEIGHT

   - ***In simple terms:*** "I'm figuring out that all 'Pepperoni' toppings are identical, so we can share one definition. But the fact that this pizza has double pepperoni is unique to that pizza."
2. **Create a Flyweight Class (Create the Shared Ingredient Jar):**
   - ***What to do:*** Create a class (e.g., *ToppingFlyweight*) that only contains the shared, intrinsic data (the properties that are the same for every instance of that topping).
   - ***Why we do it:*** This class represents the shared ingredient in the pantry. It will be stored in memory only once per unique topping.
   - ***In simple terms:*** "I'm creating the official, single jar of 'Pepperoni' for the entire kitchen. It has the name, price, and description on the label."
3. **Create a Flyweight Factory (Build the Central Pantry):**
   - ***What to do:*** Create a factory class (e.g., *ToppingFlyweightFactory*) with a static dictionary to store and manage all the unique *ToppingFlyweight* objects.
   - ***Why we do it:*** This factory acts as the pantry manager. When a chef needs an ingredient, they ask the pantry manager, who either gives them the existing jar or creates a new one for a new ingredient.
   - ***In simple terms:*** "I'm building the pantry and hiring a manager. Their job is to make sure we only ever have one jar of each ingredient."
4. **Create a Factory Method (Get Ingredients from the Pantry):**
   - ***What to do:*** Add a method like *GetTopping(string name)* to the factory. This method checks if the topping exists in the dictionary; if it does, it returns it. If not, it creates it, stores it, and then returns it.
   - ***Why we do it:*** This ensures that every part of the code gets the same shared instance of a topping, preventing duplicates.
   - ***In simple terms:*** "The rule is now: never *new Topping()* directly. Always ask the pantry manager for *GetTopping("Pepperoni")*."
5. **Modify Client Code (Update the Pizza Recipe):**
   - ***What to do:*** Modify the *Pizza* class to store a list of *ToppingFlyweight* references and their corresponding quantities (the extrinsic state) instead of full *Topping* objects.
   - ***Why we do it:*** The pizza now just has a slip of paper saying "2x Pepperoni (from the shared jar)" instead of carrying its own private pepperoni. This saves a huge amount of space.
   - ***In simple terms:*** "The chefs now write their orders as '2 scoops from the shared pepperoni jar' instead of 'use my personal pepperoni.'"

By following these five steps, you create a system where thousands of pizzas can reference the same handful of topping objects. Your application's memory footprint becomes much smaller and more efficient, just like a well-organized kitchen.

14.7 Implementing the Flyweight Pattern

Step 1: Create the Flyweight Class

ToppingFlyweight.cs

Get Full Code Here

```
public class ToppingFlyweight
{
    // Intrinsic state (immutable, shared across all pizzas)
    public string Name { get; }
    public string Description { get; }
    public decimal BasePrice { get; }
    public int Calories { get; }

    public ToppingFlyweight(string name, string description, decimal basePrice, int calories)
    {
        Name = name;
        Description = description;
        BasePrice = basePrice;
        Calories = calories;
    }

    // Method that uses both intrinsic and extrinsic state
    public void Display(int quantity)
    {
        decimal totalPrice = BasePrice * quantity;
        int totalCalories = Calories * quantity;
        Console.WriteLine($"{quantity}x {Name}: ${totalPrice} ({totalCalories} cal)");
    }
}
```

Step 2: Create the Flyweight Factory

ToppingFlyweightFactory.cs

```
public static class ToppingFlyweightFactory
{
    private static readonly Dictionary<string, ToppingFlyweight> _flyweights
        = new Dictionary<string, ToppingFlyweight>();

    // Get a flyweight by key (topping name)
    public static ToppingFlyweight GetTopping(string name)
    {
        if (_flyweights.TryGetValue(name, out var flyweight))
        {
            return flyweight;
        }
```

```
        // If not found, create it (in real app, this would load from database)
        flyweight = name switch
        {
            "Basil" => new ToppingFlyweight("Basil", "Fresh Basil", 0.20m, 250),
            "Tomato Sauce" => new ToppingFlyweight("Tomato Sauce", "Fresh Tomato Sauce", 0.20m, 250),
            "Veggie" => new ToppingFlyweight("Veggie", "Capsicum & Onions", 1.0m, 250),
            "Pepperoni" => new ToppingFlyweight("Pepperoni", "Spicy sausage", 1.5m, 250),
            "Mozzarella" => new ToppingFlyweight("Mozzarella", "Mozzarella Cheese", 1.5m, 250),
            "Mushrooms" => new ToppingFlyweight("Mushrooms", "Sliced mushrooms", 1.0m, 50),
            "Extra Cheese" => new ToppingFlyweight("Extra Cheese", "Additional cheese", 1.0m, 200),
            "Olives" => new ToppingFlyweight("Olives", "Sliced black olives", 0.75m, 30),
            _ => throw new ArgumentException($"Unknown topping: {name}")
        };

        _flyweights[name] = flyweight;
        return flyweight;
    }

    public static int Count => _flyweights.Count;
}
```

Step 3: Modify the Pizza Class to Use Flyweights

Since we're using the *IPizza* interface with specific pizza classes like *MargheritaPizza*, we need to modify those classes to use the Flyweight pattern for toppings. Here's how we would update the MargheritaPizza class and also IPizza interface:

IPizza.cs

```
public interface IPizza : IOrderItem
{
    string Name { get; }
    decimal Price { get; }
    List<(ToppingFlyweight Topping, int Quantity)> Toppings { get; }
    void Prepare();
    void Bake();
    void Box();

    IPizza Clone();
    List<string> GetToppingNames();
}
```

MargheritaPizza.cs

```
public class MargheritaPizza : IPizza
{
    public string Name { get; }
    public decimal Price { get; }
    public List<(ToppingFlyweight Topping, int Quantity)> Toppings { get; set; }

    public MargheritaPizza(decimal price)
    {
        Name = "Margherita Pizza";
        Price = price;

        // Use the Flyweight factory to get shared topping instances
        Toppings = new List<(ToppingFlyweight, int)>
    {
        (ToppingFlyweightFactory.GetTopping("Tomato Sauce"), 1),
        (ToppingFlyweightFactory.GetTopping("Mozzarella"), 1),
        (ToppingFlyweightFactory.GetTopping("Basil"), 1)
    };
    }

    public void Prepare() => Console.WriteLine("Preparing Margherita Pizza");
    public void Bake() => Console.WriteLine("Baking Margherita Pizza");
    public void Box() => Console.WriteLine("Boxing Margherita Pizza");

    public IPizza Clone()
    {
        var clonedPizza = new MargheritaPizza(Price);

        // Clone the toppings list with the same flyweight references
        clonedPizza.Toppings = new List<(ToppingFlyweight, int)>(this.Toppings);

        return clonedPizza;
    }

    // Helper method to get topping names as strings (for compatibility)
    public List<string> GetToppingNames()
    {
        return Toppings.Select(t => $"{t.Quantity}x {t.Topping.Name}").ToList();
    }
}
```

Similarly modify other Pizza classes.

Step 4: Update Any Code That Uses Toppings

Any code that previously accessed *pizza.Toppings* (expecting a *List<string>*) should now use the new *GetToppingNames()* method or be updated to work with the new tuple structure.

FLYWEIGHT

Step 5: Modify the Decorator and Builder in our Pizza App

PizzaDecorator.cs

```
public abstract class PizzaDecorator : IPizza
{
   // All other properties
   public virtual List<(ToppingFlyweight Topping, int Quantity)> Toppings => _pizza.Toppings;
   public virtual List<string> GetToppingNames() => _pizza.GetToppingNames();
}
```

PizzaBuilder.cs

```
public class PizzaBuilder
{
   private string _name;
   private decimal _basePrice;
   private List<(ToppingFlyweight Topping, int Quantity)> _toppings= new List<(ToppingFlyweight,
int)>();
   private bool _extraCheese;
   private bool _stuffedCrust;
   private bool _glutenFree;

  //....constructor

   public PizzaBuilder AddTopping(string toppingName, int quantity = 1)
   {
      var topping = ToppingFlyweightFactory.GetTopping(toppingName);
      _toppings.Add((topping, quantity));
      return this; // Enables method chaining
   }

   //.. other properties
   public IPizza Build()
   {
      // Calculate final price based on custom options
      decimal finalPrice = _basePrice;

      // Add price for each topping
      foreach (var (topping, quantity) in _toppings)
      {
         finalPrice += topping.BasePrice * quantity;
      }
      if (_extraCheese) finalPrice += 1.0m;        if (_stuffedCrust) finalPrice += 1.5m;
      if (_glutenFree) finalPrice += 2.0m;
      finalPrice += _toppings.Count * 0.5m; // Charge for each topping
      return new CustomPizza(_name, finalPrice, _toppings, _extraCheese, _stuffedCrust, _glutenFree);
   }
}
```

Step 6: Usage in Client Code

In our current implementation, there is no requirement to modify any client code as the Topping Flyweight is called by Pizza Classes themselves. A sample usage of Flyweight Pattern in client code is as follows:

Program.cs

```
// Client code
var pepperoni = ToppingFlyweightFactory.GetTopping("Pepperoni");
var extraCheese = ToppingFlyweightFactory.GetTopping("Extra Cheese");

// Create multiple pizzas that share the same topping instances
var pizza1 = new Pizza { Name = "Pepperoni Pizza", BasePrice = 8.99m };
pizza1.AddTopping(pepperoni, 2);
pizza1.AddTopping(extraCheese);

var pizza2 = new Pizza { Name = "Supreme Pizza", BasePrice = 10.99m };
pizza2.AddTopping(pepperoni); // Same instance as pizza1
pizza2.AddTopping(ToppingFlyweightFactory.GetTopping("Mushrooms"));
pizza2.AddTopping(ToppingFlyweightFactory.GetTopping("Olives"));

// Display pizzas
pizza1.Display();
pizza2.Display();

// Show memory savings
Console.WriteLine($"\nMemory saved: {4 - ToppingFlyweightFactory.Count} topping objects");
// Only 4 unique toppings stored, no matter how many pizzas we create
```

Key Test Points for Flyweight Pattern Validation

1. Shared Instance Test

- **Objective:** Verify that multiple requests for the same flyweight return the exact same object instance.
- **Test Action:** Call *ToppingFlyweightFactory.GetTopping("Pepperoni")* multiple times and compare the object references.
- **Expected Result:** All returned objects should be the same instance (ReferenceEquals should return true).

2. Memory Efficiency Test

- **Objective:** Confirm that the pattern actually reduces memory usage.
- **Test Action:** Create a large number of pizzas (e.g., 10,000) with the same toppings before and after implementing the Flyweight pattern. Measure memory usage in both cases.
- **Expected Result:** Significant memory reduction when using the Flyweight pattern, with minimal increase in memory as more pizzas are created.

3. **Factory Management Test**
   - **Objective:** Ensure the factory properly manages the flyweight pool.
   - **Test Action:** Request multiple different toppings and check that the factory count increases appropriately.
   - **Expected Result:** *ToppingFlyweightFactory.Count* should equal the number of unique toppings requested, not the total number of topping instances used.
4. **Immutability Test**
   - **Objective:** Verify that flyweight objects are immutable and cannot be accidentally modified.
   - **Test Action:** Attempt to modify properties of a retrieved flyweight object.
   - **Expected Result:** The code should not compile or should throw exceptions if modification is attempted (depending on implementation).
5. **Thread Safety Test (If applicable)**
   - **Objective:** Ensure the flyweight factory works correctly in multi-threaded environments.
   - **Test Action:** Create multiple threads that simultaneously request the same flyweight objects.
   - **Expected Result:** All threads should receive valid references to the same flyweight objects without exceptions or race conditions.
6. **Integration with Pizza Classes Test**
   - **Objective:** Confirm that pizza classes correctly use flyweight toppings instead of creating their own instances.
   - **Test Action:** Create multiple pizzas with the same toppings and verify they reference the same flyweight instances.
   - **Expected Result:** Different pizza objects should share references to the same topping flyweight objects.
7. **Extrinsic State Handling Test**
   - **Objective:** Verify that pizza-specific data (like quantity) is handled correctly separately from the shared intrinsic state.
   - **Test Action:** Create two pizzas with the same topping but different quantities.
   - **Expected Result:** Both pizzas should reference the same topping flyweight but maintain different quantity values.
8. **Cache Performance Test**
   - **Objective:** Measure the performance improvement from flyweight caching.
   - **Test Action:** Time how long it takes to create many pizzas with the same toppings before and after implementing the pattern.
   - **Expected Result:** Significant performance improvement when using flyweights due to reduced object creation overhead.

9. **Error Handling Test**
    - **Objective:** Ensure the factory handles requests for unknown toppings gracefully.
    - **Test Action:** Request a topping that doesn't exist in the factory.
    - **Expected Result:** The factory should throw a clear exception or return a appropriate default value.

If all these tests pass, your Flyweight pattern implementation is working correctly. You have successfully created a system that shares common data across multiple objects, significantly reducing memory usage while maintaining functionality and performance.

14.8 Why the Flyweight Matters

- **Memory Efficiency:** Reduces memory usage by sharing common data across objects.
- **Performance:** Improves cache utilization and reduces garbage collection overhead.
- **Scalability:** Allows the application to handle orders of magnitude more objects.
- **Consistency:** Ensures all instances of a topping have identical properties.
- **Maintainability:** Centralizes topping definitions in one place.

14.9 Mini-Exercise: Add a New Topping

Task: Add a new "Pineapple" topping to the system with a base price of $1.25 and 80 calories. Create a pizza that uses this topping.

Bonus: Modify the factory to load toppings from a configuration file or database instead of hardcoding them.

14.10 When to Use the Flyweight

"Use the Flyweight pattern when all of the following are true:

- Your application uses a large number of objects
- Storage costs are high due to the quantity of objects
- Most object state can be made extrinsic
- Many groups of objects may be replaced by relatively few shared objects
- The application doesn't depend on object identity"

14.11 Transition to Chapter 15

"Now that we've optimized our memory usage with the Flyweight pattern, let's turn our attention to how we process orders. Our current order handling has a rigid, hardcoded sequence of steps. Next, we'll use the **Chain of Responsibility** pattern to create a flexible and customizable order processing pipeline."

> **Next Up: Chapter 15 — Chain of Responsibility: The Order Processing Pipeline**
> Ready to create a flexible workflow where each order processing step is handled by a dedicated component? Let's chain together validators, processors, and notifiers in a customizable sequence!

FLYWEIGHT

PART 4: BEHAVIORAL PATTERNS - DEFINING BEHAVIOR

Where Objects Learn to Work Together! 🤝

Meet "The Strategists" - the brilliant coordinators who make our objects communicate and collaborate like a well-rehearsed orchestra!

What We're Coordinating:

- **Observer:** The notification superstar
- **Strategy**: The algorithm switcher
- **Command:** The action packager
- **State**: The mood manager
- **Chain**: The request passer
- **Iterator**: The collection tour guide
- **Mediator**: The communication hub
- **Memento**: The time traveler
- **Template**: The recipe master
- **Visitor**: The operation adder
- **Interpreter**: The language guru

You'll Master:

- Making objects communicate without tangles
- Switching behaviors on the fly
- Managing complex workflows
- Adding operations without changing classes

Perfect if you've ever:

- Had objects talking directly to too many others
- Written giant switch statements for different behaviors
- Struggled with undo/redo functionality
- Needed to add features without breaking existing code

Get ready to conduct the object orchestra! 🎶✨

Chapter 15

Chain of Responsibility — The Order Processing Pipeline

Setting The Stage

Our current order processing has a rigid, hardcoded sequence of steps that's difficult to modify or extend. Adding new processing steps requires modifying core logic, and we can't easily customize the workflow for different order types.

> In this chapter, you'll:
> 1. **Identify Pitfalls:** Identify the limitations of hardcoded processing sequences.
> 2. **Learn the Pattern:** Learn the Chain of Responsibility pattern to create a flexible processing pipeline.
> 3. **Build a chain of handlers:** Build a chain of handlers for order processing, where each handler can decide to process or forward an order.
> 4. **Protect Core Application:** Create a dynamic, configurable order processing system that can be easily extended.

15.1 Hook: What's the Pain?

"Right now, our order processing is a rigid sequence: validate → payment → bake → pack → deliver. If we want to add a new step — like a quality check or a loyalty points update — we have to break open the core processing logic. We need a way to easily add, remove, or rearrange processing steps without creating a maintenance nightmare! Additionally, our validation logic is a monolithic block that's hard to maintain and extend "

15.2 The Problem in Our Pizza App

The order processing has two distinct problems:

1. Monolithic validation logic that's hard to maintain and extend (Oops Moment #10)
2. A rigid, hardcoded sequence of processing steps (Oops Moment #35) (Template Pattern will solve it)

```
// ❌ OLD: Two separate problems
// 1. Monolithic validation (Oops Moment #10)
if (!Validation.Validate(order, out error)) { /* handle error */ }

// 2. Rigid, hardcoded sequence (Oops Moment #35)
if (!inventory.ReserveIngredients(order.OrderItem)) { /* handle error */ }
var total = PricingService.CalculateTotal(order);
if (!payment.Pay(total, "USD", "card-...")) { /* handle error */ }
pizzaService.BakePizza(order);     // Fixed sequence
pizzaService.PackPizza(order);     // Fixed sequence
deliveryService.Deliver(order);    // Fixed sequence
notifier.Send("email", "smtp", $"Order #{order.OrderId} delivered");
```

Why This Hurts:

- **Monolithic Validation (Oops #10):** All validation rules are crammed into one place, making it hard to add, remove, or reorder checks.
- **Rigid Sequence (Oops #35):** The processing steps are hardcoded in a fixed order that's difficult to modify.
- **No Flexibility:** Cannot easily customize the workflow for different order types.
- **Single Responsibility Violation:** The processing code knows about all possible steps.
- **Difficult Testing:** Hard to test individual components in isolation.

15.3 The Formal Pattern: Chain of Responsibility

Pattern Definition

> *"**Chain of Responsibility** is a behavioral design pattern that lets you pass requests along a chain of handlers. Upon receiving a request, each handler decides either to process the request or to pass it to the next handler in the chain."*

In Simpler Terms: The Chain of Responsibility pattern is like a assembly line in a factory. Each worker (handler) on the line has a specific job. If they can do the job, they do it and pass the product to the next worker. If they can't, they just pass it along. This way, the product gets processed by multiple specialists without any one worker knowing about all the others.

15.4 Understanding the Pattern

The Real-World Analogy: The Restaurant Order Fulfillment Line

Imagine a pizza order moving through different stations in a restaurant:

1. **Order Taker:** Receives the order and checks if it's complete.
2. **Cashier:** Processes payment for the order.
3. **Chef:** Prepares and cooks the pizza.
4. **Quality Checker:** Ensures the pizza meets standards.
5. **Packager:** Boxes the pizza for delivery.
6. **Delivery Person:** Takes the pizza to the customer.

Each station does its specific job and passes the order to the next station. If any station can't complete its task (e.g., payment fails), the order stops moving through the chain.

15.5 How the Chain of Responsibility Solves It

The Chain of Responsibility pattern specifically addresses monolithic validation (Oops Moment:10) by allowing us to break validation into separate, focused handlers:

```
// ✅ SOLVES OOPS MOMENT #10: Chain of Responsibility for validation
var validator = new OrderNotNullValidator();
validator.SetNext(new CustomerNameValidator())
         .SetNext(new OrderItemsValidator())
         .SetNext(new InventoryValidator(inventoryService));

bool isValid = validator.Validate(order);
```

15.6 The Implementation Blueprint: Chain of Responsibility Steps

Think of implementing the Chain of Responsibility like building a custom pizza assembly line where each station specializes in one task and passes the pizza to the next station.

1. **Define the Handler Interface:**

- ***What to do:*** Create a C# interface (e.g., *IOrderHandler*) that declares methods for handling requests and setting the next handler.
- ***Why we do it:*** This interface defines the contract that all handlers must follow, ensuring they can be linked together in a chain.
- ***In simple terms:*** "I'm creating a rulebook that says: 'Every station in our assembly line must be able to handle an order and know about the next station.'"

2. **Create an Abstract Base Handler:**

- ***What to do:*** Create an abstract class that provides default implementation for setting the next handler.
- ***Why we do it:*** This eliminates code duplication across concrete handlers and provides a common base for all handlers.
- ***In simple terms:*** "I'm building the conveyor belt that connects all stations. Each station just needs to focus on its specific task."

3. **Create Concrete Handlers:**

- ***What to do:*** Implement specific handlers for each processing step (e.g., *ValidationHandler*, *PaymentHandler*, *BakingHandler*).
- ***Why we do it:*** Each handler encapsulates one specific processing task, following the Single Responsibility Principle.
- ***In simple terms:*** "I'm hiring specialized workers for each station: a validator, a payment processor, a baker, etc."

4. **Build the Chain:**

- ***What to do:*** Connect the handlers in the desired order using the *SetNext* method.
- ***Why we do it:*** This creates the processing pipeline where orders will flow from one handler to the next.
- ***In simple terms:*** "I'm arranging the stations in correct order on our assembly line."

5. **Initiate the Processing:**

- ***What to do:*** Start the processing by calling *Handle()* on first handler in the chain.
- ***Why we do it:*** This kicks off the processing pipeline, with each handler deciding whether to process the request or pass it along.
- ***In simple terms:*** "I'm placing the pizza at the start of the assembly line and watching it move through each station."

By following these five steps, you create a flexible processing system where you can easily add, remove, or rearrange steps without affecting the overall structure.

15.7 Implementing the Chain of Responsibility Pattern

Step 1: Define the Handler Interface

IOrderHandler.cs

```
public interface IOrderHandler
{
   IOrderHandler SetNext(IOrderHandler handler);
   bool Handle(Order order);
}
```

Step 2: Create an Abstract Base Handler

AbstractOrderHandler.cs

```
public abstract class AbstractOrderHandler : IOrderHandler
{
   private IOrderHandler _nextHandler;

   public IOrderHandler SetNext(IOrderHandler handler)
   {
      _nextHandler = handler;
      return handler;
   }

   public virtual bool Handle(Order order)
   {
      if (_nextHandler != null)
      {
         return _nextHandler.Handle(order);
      }

      // Reached end of chain successfully
      return true;
   }
}
```

Step 3: Create Concrete Handlers

OrderValidationHandler.cs

```
public class OrderValidationHandler : AbstractOrderHandler
{
  public override bool Handle(Order order){
    Console.WriteLine("🔍 Validating order structure...");
   if (order == null){
      Console.WriteLine("❌ Order is null");
      return false;
   }
```

```
if (string.IsNullOrEmpty(order.CustomerName))
    {
        Console.WriteLine("❌ Customer name is required");
        return false;
    }

    if (order.OrderItem == null)
    {
        Console.WriteLine("❌ No items in order");
        return false;
    }

    Console.WriteLine("✅ Order structure validated");
    return base.Handle(order);
  }
}
```

InventoryValidationHandler.cs

```
public class InventoryValidationHandler : AbstractOrderHandler
{
  private readonly IInventoryService _inventoryService;

  public InventoryValidationHandler(IInventoryService inventoryService)
  {
    _inventoryService = inventoryService;
  }

  public override bool Handle(Order order)
  {
    Console.WriteLine("📦 Validating inventory...");

    if (!_inventoryService.ReserveIngredients(order.OrderItem))
    {
      Console.WriteLine("❌ Insufficient ingredients");
      return false;
    }

    Console.WriteLine("✅ Inventory validated");
    return base.Handle(order);
  }
}
```

CHAIN OF RESPONSIBILITY

PaymentValidationHandler.cs

```
public class PaymentValidationHandler : AbstractOrderHandler
{
  private readonly PaymentGatewayAdapter _paymentAdapter;

  public PaymentValidationHandler(PaymentGatewayAdapter paymentAdapter)
  {
    _paymentAdapter = paymentAdapter;
  }

  public override bool Handle(Order order)
  {
    Console.WriteLine("💳 Validating payment...");

    var total = PricingService.CalculateTotal(order);
    var result = _paymentAdapter.ProcessPayment(total, "USD", "card-token-123");

    if (!result.IsSuccess)
    {
      Console.WriteLine($"❌ Payment validation failed: {result.ErrorMessage}");
      return false;
    }

    Console.WriteLine($"✅ Payment validated. Transaction ID: {result.TransactionId}");
    return base.Handle(order);
  }
}
```

Step 4: Build the Chain and Use It

Since we have implemented Facade Pattern and now our client code is Order Processor class, we will modify it:

OrderProcessor.cs

```
// In your OrderProcessor or similar class

public class OrderProcessor : IOrderProcessorFacade
{
  // References to all the complex subsystem components
  private readonly IInventoryService _inventory;
  private readonly PaymentGatewayAdapter _paymentAdapter;
  private readonly PizzaService _pizzaService;
  private readonly DeliveryService _deliveryService;
  private readonly EmailNotification _emailNotifier;
  private readonly SmsNotification _smsNotifier;
  private readonly PushNotification _pushNotifier;
```

```
// Chain of Responsibility handlers
    private readonly IOrderHandler _validationChain;

    public OrderProcessor(IInventoryService inventory,
                PaymentGatewayAdapter paymentAdapter,
                PizzaService pizzaService,
                DeliveryService deliveryService,
                EmailNotification emailNotifier,
                SmsNotification smsNotifier,
                PushNotification pushNotifier){
        _inventory = inventory;
        _paymentAdapter = paymentAdapter;
        _pizzaService = pizzaService;
        _deliveryService = deliveryService;
        _emailNotifier = emailNotifier;
        _smsNotifier = smsNotifier;
        _pushNotifier = pushNotifier;

        // Build the validation chain
        _validationChain = BuildValidationChain();
    }

    // Build the validation chain of responsibility
    private IOrderHandler BuildValidationChain()
    {
        var orderValidationHandler = new OrderValidationHandler();
        var inventoryValidationHandler = new InventoryValidationHandler(_inventory);
        var paymentValidationHandler = new PaymentValidationHandler(_paymentAdapter);

        orderValidationHandler.SetNext(inventoryValidationHandler)
                .SetNext(paymentValidationHandler);

        return orderValidationHandler;
    }

    // The simplified interface method that now uses the validation chain
    public bool PlaceOrder(Order order)
    {
        Console.WriteLine($"🚀 Processing Order #{order.OrderId}...");

        // 1. Validate order using the chain of responsibility
        if (!_validationChain.Handle(order))
        {
            Console.WriteLine("❌ Order validation failed");
            return false;
        }
```

CHAIN OF RESPONSIBILITY

```
// 2. Fulfill order (these steps will be refactored with Template Method in Chapter 24)
    _pizzaService.BakePizza(order);
    _pizzaService.PackPizza(order);
    _deliveryService.Deliver(order);

    // 3. Notify customer using the Bridge-based notification services
    _emailNotifier.Send($"Order #{order.OrderId} has been delivered");
    _smsNotifier.Send("Your pizza is out for delivery!");
    _pushNotifier.Send("Special offer: 20% off your next order!");

    Console.WriteLine($"■ Order #{order.OrderId} processed successfully!");
    return true;
  }

  public bool CancelOrder(int orderId)
  {
    // Implementation for canceling an order
    Console.WriteLine($"Cancelling order #{orderId}...");
    // ... logic involving inventory, payment refund, etc.
    return true;
  }

  public string CheckOrderStatus(int orderId)
  {
    // Implementation for checking status
    return "Delivered"; // Simplified for example
  }
}
```

What We Are Doing in *OrderProcessor*.cs (In Simple Words)

Let me break them down for clear explanation:

1. The SetNext() Method Chain

What it does:

```
orderValidationHandler.SetNext(inventoryValidationHandler)
                      .SetNext(paymentValidationHandler);
```

This is called **method chaining** or **fluent interface**. Each *SetNext()* method returns the handler that was passed to it, allowing us to call *SetNext()* again on the returned handler.

How it works:

1. *orderValidationHandler.SetNext(inventoryValidationHandler)* sets the next handler for *orderValidationHandler* to be *inventoryValidationHandler*
2. This method returns *inventoryValidationHandler*
3. We then call *SetNext(paymentValidationHandler)* on *inventoryValidationHandler*
4. This sets the next handler for *inventoryValidationHandler* to be *paymentValidationHandler*

Visual representation:

```
orderValidaticnHandler → inventoryValidationHandler → paymentValidationHandler → (end of chain)
```

Why it matters: This creates the chain where each handler can pass the order to the next one in sequence.

2. The return base.Handle(order) Call

What it does:

In each concrete handler, after performing its specific validation, it calls *return base.Handle(order).*

How it works:

1. Each handler performs its specific validation check
2. If the validation fails, it returns false immediately (breaking the chain)
3. If the validation passes, it calls *base.Handle(order)* which:
   - Checks if there's a next handler in the chain
   - If there is, it passes the order to that handler
   - If there isn't, it returns true (indicating all validations passed)

Why it matters:

This is the mechanism that allows the order to "flow" through the chain. Each handler only needs to know about its immediate next handler, not the entire chain.

In the Chain of Responsibility pattern, we connect handlers using the *SetNext()* method, which allows us to create a sequence of validation steps. Each handler focuses on one specific validation task. After a handler completes its validation, it calls *base.Handle(order)* to pass the order to the next handler in the chain. This creates a pipeline where the order flows through each validation step sequentially, and if any validation fails, the entire chain fails immediately.

Key Test Points for Chain of Responsibility Pattern Validation

1. Chain Construction Test

- **Objective:** Verify that handlers correctly linked together in desired sequence.
- **Test Action:** Build a chain of handlers and verify that each handler's Next property points to the correct next handler.
- **Expected Result:** The chain should be properly linked: HandlerA → HandlerB → HandlerC.

2. Sequential Processing Test

- **Objective:** Ensure that requests flow through the entire chain in the correct order.
- **Test Action:** Pass a request through the chain and monitor the execution order using debug output or mock call tracking.
- **Expected Result:** Handlers should execute in the order they were added to the chain.

3. Early Termination Test

- **Objective:** Verify that the chain stops processing when a handler fails or cannot handle the request.
- **Test Action:** Create a chain where one handler in the middle is designed to fail. Process a request through this chain.
- **Expected Result:** Processing should stop at the failing handler, and subsequent handlers should not be called.

4. **Individual Handler Responsibility Test**
    - **Objective:** Confirm that each handler correctly performs its specific validation task.
    - **Test Action:** Test each handler in isolation with various valid and invalid inputs.
    - **Expected Result:** Each handler should return the correct result (true/false) based on its specific validation logic.
5. **End of Chain Test**
    - **Objective:** Ensure the chain properly completes when all handlers succeed.
    - **Test Action:** Process a valid request through a complete chain where all handlers should succeed.
    - **Expected Result:** The chain should return true and all handlers should have been called.
6. **Empty Chain Test**
    - **Objective:** Verify that the chain behaves correctly when no handlers are present.
    - **Test Action:** Create a chain with no handlers and process a request.
    - **Expected Result:** The chain should return true (or the appropriate default result).
7. **Handler Order Significance Test**
    - **Objective:** Confirm that handler order matters and affects the processing outcome.
    - **Test Action:** Create two chains with the same handlers but in different orders. Process identical requests through both chains.
    - **Expected Result:** The chains may produce different results based on handler order (e.g., if HandlerA fails, HandlerB won't execute).
8. **Integration with Existing Systems Test**
    - **Objective:** Ensure the validation chain works correctly within the broader order processing system.
    - **Test Action:** Use complete *OrderProcessor* with validation chain to process test orders.
    - **Expected Result:** The order processor should correctly use the validation chain and respond appropriately to both valid and invalid orders.
9. **Error Handling Test**
    - **Objective:** Verify that the chain handles exceptions gracefully.
    - **Test Action:** Create a handler that throws an exception and add it to a chain.
    - **Expected Result:** The exception should be caught and handled appropriately, either by terminating the chain or by implementing a fallback mechanism.
10. **Dynamic Chain Modification Test**
    - **Objective:** Test the ability to add or remove handlers from the chain at runtime.
    - **Test Action:** Build a chain, process a request, then modify the chain and process another request.
    - **Expected Result:** The chain should correctly incorporate the changes and process requests differently after modification.

If all these tests pass, your Chain of Responsibility implementation is working correctly.

15.8 Why the Chain of Responsibility Matters

- **Flexibility:** Easily add, remove, or rearrange processing steps without modifying existing code.
- **Single Responsibility:** Each handler focuses on one specific task.
- **Decoupling:** Handlers don't need to know about each other, only about the next handler.
- **Dynamic Configuration:** Can build different chains for different order types.
- **Reusability:** Handlers can be reused in different chains.
- **Testability:** Easy to test individual handlers in isolation.

15.9 Mini-Exercise: Add a New Handler

Task: Create a new *LoyaltyPointsHandler* that adds loyalty points to the customer's account after successful payment. Add it to the chain between the *PaymentProcessingHandler* and the *PizzaPreparationHandler*.
Bonus: Make the chain configurable based on order type (e.g., skip delivery for pickup orders).

15.10 When to Use the Chain of Responsibility

"Use the Chain of Responsibility pattern when you need to process requests through multiple handlers in a specific order, and you want to decouple the sender from the receivers. Common use cases include:

- Processing pipelines with multiple steps.
- Request validation and filtering.
- Event handling systems
- Middleware in web frameworks."

15.11 Transition to Chapter 16

"Now that we've created a flexible processing pipeline using the Chain of Responsibility, let's look at how we can encapsulate individual pizza-making steps as commands. Next, we'll explore the **Command** pattern to represent each step of pizza preparation as a command object that can be queued, logged, or undone."

> **Next Up: Chapter 16 — Command: Encapsulating Pizza-Making Steps**
> Ready to turn pizza preparation steps into command objects that can be queued, logged, and controlled? Let's build a robust command system for our kitchen operations!

Get Full Code Here

Command — Encapsulating Pizza-Making Steps

Setting The Stage

Our pizza preparation steps are implemented as direct method calls that block the main thread and provide no way to queue, retry, or undo operations. This makes our system inflexible and vulnerable to failures.

> In this chapter, you'll:
> 1. **Identify Pitfalls:** Identify the limitations of direct method calls for pizza preparation operations.
> 2. **Learn the Pattern:** Learn the Command pattern to encapsulate requests as objects.
> 3. **Build a command system:** Build a command system for pizza-making steps that can be queued, logged, and controlled.
> 4. **Protect Core Application:** Create a robust, fault-tolerant kitchen operations system.

16.1 Hook: What's the Pain?

"Right now, when our system calls *pizzaService.BakePizza()*, it blocks the main thread until the pizza is done baking! If multiple orders come in, everything slows down. Plus, if any step fails, we have no way to retry or undo previous steps. We need to turn these pizza-making steps into command objects that we can queue, retry, and manage properly!"

16.2 The Problem in Our Pizza App

Pizza preparation steps are implemented as blocking, direct method calls with no management capabilities. (Oops Moment:21) & (Oops Moment:36)

```
// ✗ OLD: Direct, blocking method calls (Oops Moment #21 & #36)
_pizzaService.BakePizza(order);     // Blocks thread for 500ms!
_pizzaService.PackPizza(order);
_deliveryService.Deliver(order);

// No queuing, no retry mechanism, no undo capability
```

Why This Hurts:

- **Performance Bottleneck:** Synchronous baking operation (Thread.Sleep) blocks the main thread, causing system freeze under load.
- **No Fault Tolerance:** If any step fails, there's no built-in retry mechanism.
- **No Recovery:** Cannot undo steps if a subsequent operation fails (e.g., can't "unbake" a pizza if delivery fails).
- **No Queueing:** Cannot efficiently manage multiple simultaneous orders.

- **Poor Scalability:** System cannot handle high order volumes efficiently.
- **No Logging/Auditing:** Difficult to track and monitor kitchen operations.

16.3 The Formal Pattern: Command

Pattern Definition

> *"**Command** is a behavioral design pattern that turns a request into a stand-alone object that contains all information about the request. This transformation lets you parameterize methods with different requests, delay or queue a request's execution, and support undoable operations."*

In Simpler Terms: The Command pattern is like giving your kitchen staff written recipe cards instead of shouting instructions. Each card contains a complete set of instructions for one specific task. You can queue these cards, prioritize them, save them for later, or even throw them away if needed. The chef doesn't need to know who gave the command — just how to execute it.

16.4 Understanding the Pattern

The Real-World Analogy: The Restaurant Order Fulfillment Line

Imagine a busy restaurant kitchen using order tickets instead of verbal commands:

1. **Order Created:** Waitstaff writes an order on a ticket and places it in the queue.
2. **Ticket Queue:** Tickets are organized by priority and preparation time.
3. **Chef Execution:** Chefs take tickets from the queue and execute them one by one.
4. **Special Instructions:** Tickets can include notes like "retry if failed" or "discard if not completed in 10 minutes."
5. **Undo Capability:** If an order is canceled, the kitchen can see what was already prepared.

This system allows the kitchen to manage multiple orders efficiently, prioritize tasks, and handle special cases.

16.5 How the Command Pattern Solves It

Instead of this direct, blocking approach:

```
// ❌ Direct method calls with no control
_pizzaService.BakePizza(order);  // Blocks thread
_pizzaService.PackPizza(order);
```

We'll create this flexible command-based approach:

```
// ✅ Command-based execution with full control
var bakeCommand = new BakePizzaCommand(_pizzaService, order);
var packCommand = new PackPizzaCommand(_pizzaService, order);
var deliverCommand = new DeliverPizzaCommand(_deliveryService, order);

// Add to queue for execution
_commandQueue.Add(bakeCommand);
_commandQueue.Add(packCommand);
_commandQueue.Add(deliverCommand);

// Execute asynchronously without blocking
await _commandProcessor.ProcessQueueAsync();
```

The Command pattern gives us fine-grained control over each operation, allowing for queuing, retrying, undoing, and logging.

COMMAND

16.6 The Implementation Blueprint: Command Steps

Think of implementing the Command pattern like creating a sophisticated kitchen management system where each cooking instruction becomes a ticket that can be managed, tracked, and controlled.

1. **Define the Command Interface:**
   - ***What to do:*** Create a C# interface (e.g., *IKitchenCommand*) that declares execution methods like *ExecuteAsync()*, *Undo()*, and *CanRetry()*.
   - ***Why we do it:*** This interface defines the contract that all commands must follow, ensuring they can be handled uniformly by the command processor.
   - ***In simple terms:*** "I'm creating a standard format for all kitchen instruction tickets so they can be processed the same way."
2. **Create Concrete Command Classes:**
   - ***What to do:*** Implement specific command classes for each pizza operation (e.g., *BakePizzaCommand*, *PackPizzaCommand*, *DeliverPizzaCommand*).
   - ***Why we do it:*** Each command encapsulates all information needed to perform an operation, including the target object and parameters.
   - ***In simple terms:*** "I'm creating specific instruction tickets for baking, packing, and delivering pizzas, each with all the details needed to complete the task."
3. **Create the Invoker/Command Processor:**
   - ***What to do:*** Build a class that manages command execution, queuing, retry logic, and undo functionality.
   - ***Why we do it:*** This component coordinates command execution, handles errors, and maintains the command history for undo operations.
   - ***In simple terms:*** "I'm hiring a kitchen manager who takes tickets from the queue, assigns them to chefs, handles problems, and keeps track of what's been done."
4. **Set Up the Command Queue:**
   - ***What to do:*** Implement a mechanism to queue commands for execution, potentially with prioritization and scheduling.
   - ***Why we do it:*** This allows asynchronous processing and better resource management under heavy load.
   - ***In simple terms:*** "I'm installing a ticket queue in the kitchen where orders wait their turn to be processed."
5. **Replace Direct Calls with Command Execution:**
   - ***What to do:*** Modify the order processing code to create and queue commands instead of making direct method calls.
   - ***Why we do it:*** This transforms the rigid, synchronous process into a flexible, asynchronous command-driven system.
   - ***In simple terms:*** "Instead of shouting instructions to the kitchen, waitstaff now write tickets and put them in the queue."

By following these five steps, you create a system where each pizza-making operation is encapsulated as a command object that can be queued, executed asynchronously, retried on failure, and even undone if necessary.

16.7 Implementing the Command Pattern

Step 1: Define the Command Interface

IKitchenCommand.cs

```
public interface IKitchenCommand
{
    Task<bool> ExecuteAsync();
    Task<bool> UndoAsync();
    bool CanRetry { get; }
    string CommandName { get; }
}
```

Step 2: Create Concrete Command Classes

BakePizzaCommand.cs

```
public class BakePizzaCommand : IKitchenCommand
{
    private readonly IPizzaService _pizzaService;
    private readonly Order _order;

    public string CommandName => "Bake Pizza";
    public bool CanRetry => true;

    public BakePizzaCommand(IPizzaService pizzaService, Order order){
        _pizzaService = pizzaService;
        _order = order;
    }

    public async Task<bool> ExecuteAsync()
    {
        try{
            Console.WriteLine($"🔥 Baking pizza for order #{_order.OrderId}");
            // Run the synchronous Bake method on a background thread
                await Task.Run(() => _pizzaService.Bake());
            _order.Status = "Baked";
            Console.WriteLine($"✅ Pizza baked for order #{_order.OrderId}");
            return true;
        }
        catch (Exception ex){
            Console.WriteLine($"❌ Failed to bake pizza for order #{_order.OrderId}: {ex.Message}");
            return false;
        }
    }
```


COMMAND

```
public Task<bool> UndoAsync()
   {
      // Cannot unbake a pizza, but we can mark it as wasted
      Console.WriteLine($"❗ Cannot undo baking, but pizza from order #{_order.OrderId} will be
marked as wasted");
      _order.Status = "Failed - Pizza Wasted";
      return Task.FromResult(true);
   }
}
```

PackPizzaCommand.cs

```
public class PackPizzaCommand : IKitchenCommand
{
   private readonly IPizzaService _pizzaService;
   private readonly Order _order;

   public string CommandName => "Pack Pizza";
   public bool CanRetry => true;

   public PackPizzaCommand(IPizzaService pizzaService, Order order)
   {
      _pizzaService = pizzaService;
      _order = order;
   }

   public async Task<bool> ExecuteAsync()
   {
      try
      {
         Console.WriteLine($"📦 Packing pizza for order #{_order.OrderId}");
         // Run the synchronous Box method on a background thread
          await Task.Run(() => _pizzaService.Box());
         _order.Status = "Packed";
         Console.WriteLine($"✅ Pizza packed for order #{_order.OrderId}");
         return true;
      }
      catch (Exception ex){
         Console.WriteLine($"❌ Failed to pack pizza for order #{_order.OrderId}: {ex.Message}");
         return false;
      }
   }

   public async Task<bool> UndoAsync(){
      // Can unpack a pizza (remove from box)
      Console.WriteLine($"↩ Unpacking pizza for order #{_order.OrderId}");
      _order.Status = "Baked"; // Revert to previous state
      return true;
   }
}
```

DeliverPizzaCommand.cs

```
public class DeliverPizzaCommand : IKitchenCommand
{
    private readonly DeliveryService _deliveryService;
    private readonly Order _order;

    public string CommandName => "Deliver Pizza";
    public bool CanRetry => true;

    public DeliverPizzaCommand(DeliveryService deliveryService, Order order){
        _deliveryService = deliveryService;
        _order = order;
    }

    public async Task<bool> ExecuteAsync()
    {
        try{
            Console.WriteLine($"🚚 Delivering pizza for order #{_order.OrderId}");
            await _deliveryService.DeliverAsync(_order);
            _order.Status = "Delivered";
            _order.TimeDelivered = DateTime.Now;
            Console.WriteLine($"✅ Pizza delivered for order #{_order.OrderId}");
            return true;
        }
        catch (Exception ex){
            Console.WriteLine($"❌ Failed to deliver pizza for order #{_order.OrderId}: {ex.Message}");
            return false;
        }
    }

    public Task<bool> UndoAsync(){
        // Cannot undeliver a pizza, but we can note the failure
        Console.WriteLine($"⚠ Cannot undo delivery for order #{_order.OrderId}");
        return Task.FromResult(false);
    }
}
```

Step 3: Update your Delivery Service

DeliveryService.cs

```
public class DeliveryService
{
    public async Task DeliverAsync(Order order){
        Console.WriteLine($"[Command] Delivering order #{order.OrderId} to {order.Address}");
        await Task.Delay(1000); // Simulate delivery time
        order.Status = "Delivered";
        order.TimeDelivered = DateTime.Now;
    }
}
```

Step 4: Create the Command Processor

KitchenCommandProcessor.cs

```
public class KitchenCommandProcessor
{
   private readonly Queue<IKitchenCommand> _commandQueue = new
Queue<IKitchenCommand>();
   private readonly Stack<IKitchenCommand> _executedCommands = new
Stack<IKitchenCommand>();
   private readonly int _maxRetries;

   public KitchenCommandProcessor(int maxRetries = 3)
   {
      _maxRetries = maxRetries;
   }
   public void AddCommand(IKitchenCommand command)
   {
      _commandQueue.Enqueue(command);
   }
   public async Task<bool> ProcessQueueAsync(){
      while (_commandQueue.Count > 0){
         var command = _commandQueue.Dequeue();
         int attempt = 0;
         bool success = false;

         while (attempt < _maxRetries && !success){
            attempt++;
            Console.WriteLine($"[Command]Executing {command.CommandName} (Attempt
{attempt})");

            success = await command.ExecuteAsync();
            if (success){
               _executedCommands.Push(command);
            }
            else if (attempt < _maxRetries && command.CanRetry){
               Console.WriteLine($"[Command] Waiting before retry...");
               await Task.Delay(1000 * attempt); // Exponential backoff
            }
         }
         if (!success){
            Console.WriteLine($"[Command] All attempts failed for {command.CommandName}.
Undoing previous steps...");
            await UndoPreviousCommandsAsync();
            return false;
         }
      }
      return true;
   }
```

```
private async Task UndoPreviousCommandsAsync()
{
while (_executedCommands.Count > 0)
{
var command = _executedCommands.Pop();
Console.WriteLine($"[Command] Undoing {command.CommandName}...");
await command.UndoAsync();
}
}
}
```

Step 5: Update OrderProcessor to Use Commands

Since all our Main Program code is now moved to OrderProcessor.cs after implementing Facade Pattern, we need to modify this class to use Commands

OrderProcessor.cs

```
// In OrderProcessor.PlaceOrder method
public async Task<bool> PlaceOrder(Order order)
{
    Console.WriteLine($"🚀 Processing Order #{order.OrderId}...");

    // 1. Validate order using the chain of responsibility
    if (!_validationChain.Handle(order))
    {
        Console.WriteLine("❌ Order validation failed");
        return false;
    }

    // 2. Get the pizza from the order
    if (order.OrderItem is not IPizza pizza) {
        Console.WriteLine("❌ Order does not contain a valid pizza");
        return false;
    }

    // 3. Create kitchen commands
    var bakeCommand = new BakePizzaCommand(pizza, order);
    var packCommand = new PackPizzaCommand(pizza, order);
    var deliverCommand = new DeliverPizzaCommand(new SimpleDeliveryService(), order);

    // 4. Add commands to processor
    var commandProcessor = new KitchenCommandProcessor(maxRetries: 3);
    commandProcessor.AddCommand(bakeCommand);
    commandProcessor.AddCommand(packCommand);
    commandProcessor.AddCommand(deliverCommand);

    // 5. Execute commands asynchronously
    bool success = await commandProcessor.ProcessQueueAsync();
```

```
    if (success) {
        // 6. Send notifications
        _emailNotifier.Send($"Order #{order.OrderId} has been delivered");
        _smsNotifier.Send("Your pizza is out for delivery!");
        _pushNotifier.Send("Special offer: 20% off your next order!");

        Console.WriteLine($"✅ Order #{order.OrderId} processed successfully!");
    }
    else{
        Console.WriteLine($"❌ Order #{order.OrderId} processing failed!");
    }

    return success;
}
```

Note: This requires updating the necessary methods to be asynchronous.

Key Test Points for Command Pattern Validation

1. Command Execution Test

- **Objective:** Verify that each command executes its intended operation correctly.
- **Test Action:** Create individual command objects (*BakePizzaCommand*, *PackPizzaCommand*, etc.) and call their *ExecuteAsync()* methods. Verify the state changes and output.
- **Expected Result:** Each command should perform its specific operation and return the correct success/failure status.

2. Command Queueing Test

- **Objective:** Ensure commands are processed in the correct order from the queue.
- **Test Action:** Add multiple commands to the *KitchenCommandProcessor* in a specific order. Monitor the execution order.
- **Expected Result:** Commands should be executed in the same order they were added to the queue (FIFO).

3. Retry Mechanism Test

- **Objective:** Verify that failed commands are retried the specified number of times.
- **Test Action:** Create a command that is designed to fail on the first few attempts. Add it to the processor with a specific max retry value.
- **Expected Result:** The command should be retried up to the maximum specified times before finally failing.

4. Undo Functionality Test

- **Objective:** Confirm that commands can properly undo their operations.
- **Test Action:** Execute a command successfully, then call its *UndoAsync()* method. Verify the state is properly reverted.
- **Expected Result:** The undo operation should revert the system to its previous state where possible.

5. **Error Handling and Rollback Test**
    - **Objective:** Ensure the processor properly handles complete failure scenarios by undoing previous commands.
    - **Test Action:** Create a sequence of commands where one command in the middle will fail after all retry attempts. Process the sequence.
    - **Expected Result:** When a command fails completely, the processor should call *UndoAsync()* on all previously executed commands in reverse order.
6. **Async Execution Test**
    - **Objective:** Verify that commands execute asynchronously without blocking the main thread.
    - **Test Action:** Create commands with simulated delays and process them while monitoring thread usage.
    - **Expected Result:** Commands should execute without blocking the main thread, allowing other operations to continue.
7. **Command Isolation Test**
    - **Objective:** Ensure commands are independent and don't interfere with each other.
    - **Test Action:** Execute multiple command sequences concurrently and verify they don't interfere with each other.
    - **Expected Result:** Each command sequence should execute independently without side effects on other sequences.
8. **Integration with Order Processing Test**
    - **Objective:** Verify the command pattern works correctly within the complete order processing flow.
    - **Test Action:** Use the *OrderProcessor* with the command pattern implementation to process complete orders.
    - **Expected Result:** Orders should be processed correctly using the command pattern, with proper success/failure handling.
9. **State Consistency Test**
    - **Objective:** Ensure that command execution maintains system state consistency.
    - **Test Action:** Execute various command sequences and verify the system state remains consistent throughout.
    - **Expected Result:** The system should maintain a consistent state regardless of command success or failure.
10. **Performance Under Load Test**
    - **Objective:** Verify the command pattern handles multiple simultaneous orders efficiently.
    - **Test Action:** Simulate high order volume by processing many orders concurrently.
    - **Expected Result:** The system should handle concurrent orders without significant performance degradation or resource conflicts.

If all these tests pass, your Command pattern implementation is working correctly.

16.8 Why the Command Pattern Matters

- **Async Processing:** Solves Oops Moment #21 by enabling non-blocking execution of time-consuming operations.
- **Fault Tolerance:** Solves Oops Moment#36 by providing retry mechanisms for failed operations.
- **Undo Capability:** Allows rolling back operations when subsequent steps fail.
- **Queue Management:** Enables efficient processing of multiple orders simultaneously.
- **Decoupling:** Separates the request creation from request execution.
- **Logging/Auditing:** Commands can be logged for monitoring and debugging purposes.

16.9 Mini-Exercise: Add a New Command

Task: Create a *AddToppingsCommand* that handles the topping application process. Integrate it into the command sequence between *BakePizzaCommand* and *PackPizzaCommand*.
Bonus: Implement a priority system where delivery commands have higher priority than preparation commands.

16.10 When to Use the Command Pattern

"Use the Command pattern when you need to:

- Parameterize objects with operations
- Queue operations, schedule their execution, or execute them remotely
- Implement undo/redo functionality
- Implement callback systems
- Structure systems to be fault-tolerant and retryable"

16.11 Transition to Chapter 17

"Now that we've encapsulated our pizza-making steps as commands that can be queued and managed, let's look at how we can interpret complex customer orders. Next, we'll explore the **Interpreter** pattern to parse and process special order strings like *'Large Veggie + Cheese, No Onion'*."

> **Next Up: Chapter 17 — Interpreter: Understanding Complex Pizza Orders**
> Ready to build a language interpreter for pizza orders? Let's create a system that can understand and process complex customer requests with custom toppings and special instructions!

Get Full Code Here

Chapter 17

Interpreter — Understanding Complex Pizza Orders

Setting The Stage

Our current order input system relies on brittle regular expressions that can't handle complex customer requests. Adding new menu items or special instructions requires modifying fragile parsing logic.

> In this chapter, you'll:
> 1. **Identify Pitfalls:** Identify the limitations of regex-based input parsing for pizza orders.
> 2. **Learn the Pattern:** Learn the Interpreter pattern to define a grammar for pizza orders.
> 3. **Build a Parser:** Build a parser that can understand complex orders like "2x Large Veggie + Cheese, No Onion".
> 4. **Protect Core Application:** Create an extensible system that can handle new menu items and special instructions.

17.1 Hook: What's the Pain?

"Customers want to order using natural language like '2x Large Veggie + Extra Cheese, No Onions' but our system can barely handle simple item names! Every time we add a new topping or menu item, we have to modify our fragile regex patterns. We need a robust way to parse and understand these complex orders without creating a maintenance nightmare!"

17.2 The Problem in Our Pizza App

The order input parsing uses brittle regular expressions that can't handle complex grammar. (Oops Moment:27)

```
// ✗ OLD: Brittle regex parsing (Oops Moment #27)
var match = Regex.Match(input, @"^(?<qty>\d+)x\s*(?<item>.+)$", RegexOptions.IgnoreCase);
int qty = match.Success ? int.Parse(match.Groups["qty"].Value) : 1;
string choice = match.Success ? match.Groups["item"].Value : input;

// This fails with:
// - "Large Veggie + Cheese, No Onion"
// - "2x Pepperoni with Extra Cheese"
// - "Margherita, add Mushrooms, hold Basil"
```

Why This Hurts:

- **Brittle Code:** Regular expressions become unreadable and unmaintainable as complexity grows.
- **Limited Expressiveness:** Cannot handle complex customer requests with modifiers, exclusions, or combinations.
- **Hard to Extend:** Adding new menu items or modifiers requires modifying complex regex patterns.
- **No Grammar Structure:** Cannot validate orders against a defined grammar ruleset.

INTERPRETER

17.3 The Formal Pattern: Interpreter

Pattern Definition

> *"**Interpreter** is a behavioral design pattern that defines a grammatical representation for a language and provides an interpreter to deal with this grammar."*

In Simpler Terms: The Interpreter pattern is like hiring a translator who understands the grammar of a language. Instead of trying to parse sentences with simple pattern matching, the translator understands nouns, verbs, adjectives, and how they relate to each other. For pizza orders, this means understanding quantities, items, modifiers, and exclusions as distinct grammatical elements.

17.4 Understanding the Pattern

The Real-World Analogy: The Pizza Order Translator

Imagine a customer speaking to a pizza chef who doesn't understand complex requests. You need a translator who:

1. Understands pizza terminology ("large", "extra cheese", "hold the onions")
2. Knows grammar rules ("2x" means two of something, "+" means add, "-" means remove)
3. Can build a complete order from scattered requests
4. Can ask clarifying questions when requests are ambiguous

The Interpreter pattern acts as this translator, converting natural language requests into structured orders.

17.5 How the Interpreter Pattern Solves It

Instead of this brittle approach:

```
// ❌ Fragile regex parsing
var match = Regex.Match(input, @"^(?<qty>\d+)x\s*(?<item>.+)$");
```

We'll create this structured approach:

```
// ✅ Grammar-based parsing
var parser = new PizzaOrderParser();
var orderExpression = parser.Parse("2x Large Veggie + Cheese, No Onion");

// The expression can be evaluated to get a structured order
var order = orderExpression.Interpret();
```

The Interpreter pattern lets us define a grammar for pizza orders and create a parser that understands that grammar.

17.6 The Implementation Blueprint: Interpreter Steps

Think of implementing the Interpreter pattern like building a language translator for pizza orders. You need to define the vocabulary and grammar rules that make up the "language" of pizza ordering.

1.Define the Grammar:

- ***<u>What to do:</u>*** Identify the grammatical elements of pizza orders (quantifiers, items, modifiers, exclusions).
- ***<u>Why we do it:</u>*** This defines the "language" your interpreter will understand.

- ***In simple terms:*** "I'm creating a dictionary of pizza terms and the grammar rules for how they can be combined."

2. Create the Abstract Expression:
- ***What to do:*** Define an interface or abstract class that all expressions will implement.
- ***Why we do it:*** This ensures all elements in our grammar can be interpreted consistently.
- ***In simple terms:*** "I'm creating a rule that says every pizza order component must be able to explain what it means."

3. Implement Terminal Expressions:
- ***What to do:*** Create classes for the basic elements of the grammar (items, quantities, modifiers).
- ***Why we do it:*** These represent the basic building blocks of pizza orders.
- ***In simple terms:*** "I'm creating the basic words of our pizza language: 'pepperoni', 'large', 'extra'."

4. Implement Non-Terminal Expressions:
- ***What to do:*** Create classes that combine other expressions (modifier expressions, compound orders).
- ***Why we do it:*** These represent the grammar rules for how basic elements can be combined.
- ***In simple terms:*** "I'm creating the grammar rules that let us build sentences like 'large pepperoni with extra cheese'."

5. Build the Parser:
- ***What to do:*** Create a class that converts text input into expression objects based on your grammar.
- ***Why we do it:*** This is the "translator" that converts text into structured expressions.
- ***In simple terms:*** "I'm hiring a translator who listens to customer requests and converts them into structured orders using our pizza grammar."

By following these five steps, you create a system that can understand complex pizza orders by breaking them down into grammatical components that can be systematically interpreted.

INTERPRETER

17.7 Implementing the Interpreter Pattern

Step 1: Define the Grammar

What we're doing: Creating rules for how customers can place orders using natural language.

```
// Grammar Rules:
// Order → Item (('+' Item)* | Modifier)* // Item → Quantity? ItemName
// Quantity → Number 'x' | Number
// Modifier → ('with' | 'extra') ModifierName | ('without' | 'no') ModifierName
// ItemName → 'margherita' | 'pepperoni' | 'coke' | 'brownie' | etc.
```

We're creating a special language for ordering pizza! Customers can say things like:

- "2x pepperoni pizza + coke" (2 pepperoni pizzas and a drink)
- "margherita with extra cheese" (pizza with modifications)
- "family combo + brownie" (combos and desserts)

The grammar defines the rules for these sentences so our program can understand them.

Step 2: Create the Abstract Expression

What we're doing: Creating rules for how customers can place orders using natural language.

IOrderExpression.cs

```
public interface IOrderExpression
{
    Order Interpret();
}
public class InterpretationException : Exception
{
    public InterpretationException(string message) : base(message) { }
}
```

This is like creating a universal remote control that works for all our pizza order commands. Every type of order instruction (like "add pizza" or "add extra cheese") must have an Interpret() button that tells the system what to do.

Step 3: Implement Terminal Expressions

What we're doing: Creating expressions for basic items like pizzas, drinks, and desserts.

ItemExpression.cs

```
public class ItemExpression : IOrderExpression
{
    private readonly string _itemName;
    private readonly int _quantity;

    public ItemExpression(string itemName, int quantity = 1)
    {
        _itemName = itemName;
        _quantity = quantity;
    }

    public Order Interpret()
    {
        // Map user-friendly names to actual menu IDs
        string menuId = MapInputToMenuId(_itemName);

        var item = MenuBuilder.FindComponent(menuId);
```

```
        if (item == null)
            throw new InterpretationException($"Unknown item: {_itemName}");

        var orderItem = MenuItemFactory.CreateOrderItem(item);

        var order = new Order { Items = new List<IOrderItem>() };

        // Add the item multiple times based on quantity
        for (int i = 0; i < _quantity; i++)
        {
            order.Items.Add(orderItem.Clone());
        }

        order.OrderItem = order.Items.Count > 0 ? order.Items[0] : null;
        order.Quantity = _quantity;

        return order;
    }

    private string MapInputToMenuId(string input)
    {
        // Converts "margherita" → "pizza_marg", "coke" → "drink_coke", etc.
        var nameToIdMap = new Dictionary<string, string>(StringComparer.OrdinalIgnoreCase)
        {
            { "margherita", "pizza_marg" }, { "pepperoni", "pizza_pep" },
            { "coke", "drink_coke" }, { "brownie", "dess_brownie" }
            // ... more mappings
        };

        return nameToIdMap.ContainsKey(input) ? nameToIdMap[input] : input;
    }
}
```

This is like having a smart translator that converts simple words like "margherita" into actual menu items. When you say "2x pepperoni", it:

1. Understands "pepperoni" means pepperoni pizza
2. Knows "2x" means you want two of them
3. Creates the actual pizza objects for your order

INTERPRETER

Step 4: Implement Non-Terminal Expressions

What we're doing: Creating expressions that combine multiple items or add modifications.

CompoundOrderExpression.cs

```
public class CompoundOrderExpression : IOrderExpression
{
  private readonly List<IOrderExpression> _expressions;

  public CompoundOrderExpression(List<IOrderExpression> expressions){
    _expressions = expressions;
  }

  public Order Interpret(){
    var order = new Order { Items = new List<IOrderItem>(), Modifiers = new List<Modifier>() };

    foreach (var expression in _expressions)
    {
      var interpreted = expression.Interpret();
      order.Items.AddRange(interpreted.Items);
      order.Modifiers.AddRange(interpreted.Modifiers);
    }

    // Create composite for multiple items
    if (order.Items.Count > 1) {
      var composite = new OrderComposite("Your Order");
      foreach (var item in order.Items) composite.AddItem(item);
      order.OrderItem = composite;
    }
    else if (order.Items.Count == 1){
      order.OrderItem = order.Items[0];
    }

    order.Quantity = order.Items.Count;
    return order;
  }
}
```

ModifierExpression.cs

```
public class ModifierExpression : IOrderExpression
{
  private readonly string _modifier;
  private readonly bool _isAddition;
  private readonly IOrderExpression _targetExpression;
```

```
public ModifierExpression(string modifier, bool isAddition, IOrderExpression targetExpression)
{
_modifier = modifier;
_isAddition = isAddition;
_targetExpression = targetExpression;
}

public Order Interpret()
{
var order = _targetExpression.Interpret();

if (order.Modifiers == null)
order.Modifiers = new List<Modifier>();

order.Modifiers.Add(new Modifier(_modifier, _isAddition));
return order;
}
}
```

These are like sentence combiners:

- CompoundOrderExpression: When you say "pizza + coke + brownie", it combines them into one order
- ModifierExpression: When you say "with extra cheese", it adds this special instruction to your pizza

Think of it as building a meal combo by putting together different food items!

Step 5: Build the Parser

What we're doing: Creating the brain that understands customer sentences and converts them into expressions.

PizzaOrderParser.cs

```
public class PizzaOrderParser
{
  public IOrderExpression Parse(string input)
  {
    input = input.ToLower().Trim();

    // Split by '+' to separate different items
    var itemParts = input.Split('+')
                   .Select(part => part.Trim())
                   .Where(part => !string.IsNullOrEmpty(part))
                   .ToList();

    var expressions = new List<IOrderExpression>();
```

INTERPRETER

```
    foreach (var part in itemParts)
    {
        expressions.Add(ParseItemWithModifiers(part));
    }

    return expressions.Count == 1 ? expressions[0] : new CompoundOrderExpression(expressions);
}

private IOrderExpression ParseItemWithModifiers(string itemInput)
{
    var tokens = Tokenize(itemInput);
    if (tokens.Count == 0) throw new InterpretationException("Empty item expression");

    // Handle quantity (like "2x" or "2")
    int quantity = 1;
    int startIndex = 0;

    if (tokens.Count > 0 && IsQuantityToken(tokens[0]))
    {
        quantity = ParseQuantity(tokens[0]);
        startIndex = 1;
    }
    else
    {
        var quantityMatch = Regex.Match(tokens[0], @"^(\d+)x(.+)$");
        if (quantityMatch.Success)
        {
            quantity = int.Parse(quantityMatch.Groups[1].Value);
            tokens[0] = quantityMatch.Groups[2].Value.Trim();
            startIndex = 0;
        }
    }

    // Extract item name
    var itemNameTokens = new List<string>();
    int i = startIndex;

    while (i < tokens.Count && !IsModifierToken(tokens[i]))
    {
        itemNameTokens.Add(tokens[i]);
        i++;
    }

    if (!itemNameTokens.Any()) throw new InterpretationException("No item name found");

    string itemName = string.Join(" ", itemNameTokens);
    IOrderExpression expression = new ItemExpression(itemName, quantity);
```

```
    // Process modifiers
    while (i < tokens.Count){
        if (IsModifierToken(tokens[i])){
            bool isAddition = tokens[i] == "with" || tokens[i] == "extra";
            i++;

            if (i < tokens.Count)
            {
                var modifierTokens = new List<string>();
                while (i < tokens.Count && !IsModifierToken(tokens[i])){
                    modifierTokens.Add(tokens[i]);
                    i++;
                }

                string modifierName = string.Join(" ", modifierTokens);
                expression = new ModifierExpression(modifierName, isAddition, expression);
            }
        }
        else i++;
    }
    return expression;
}

private List<string> Tokenize(string input){
    return input.Split(new[] { ' ' }, StringSplitOptions.RemoveEmptyEntries)
            .Select(token => token.Trim())
            .Where(token => !string.IsNullOrEmpty(token))
            .ToList();
}

private bool IsQuantityToken(string token) => Regex.IsMatch(token, @"^\d+x$") ||
Regex.IsMatch(token, @"^\d+$");
private bool IsModifierToken(string token) => token == "with" || token == "extra" || token ==
"without" || token == "no";
private int ParseQuantity(string token) => token.EndsWith("x") ? int.Parse(token.TrimEnd('x', 'X')) :
int.Parse(token);
}
```

This is the super-smart translator that:

1. Listens to what you type ("2x pepperoni pizza + coke")
2. Breaks it down into pieces: ["2x pepperoni pizza", "coke"]
3. Understands each piece:
    - "2x pepperoni pizza" = 2 pepperoni pizzas
    - "coke" = 1 coke
4. Builds the order by combining everything together

It's like having a friendly waiter who understands exactly what you want!

INTERPRETER

Step 6: Modifications in OrderProcessor

What we're doing: Updating the order processor to work with our new interpreter system.

OrderProcessor.cs

```
public class OrderProcessor : IOrderProcessorFacade
{
  // References to all the complex subsystem components
  ....
  // Chain of Responsibility handlers
  .........

  // Build the validation chain of responsibility
  ......

  // The simplified interface method that now uses the validation chain
  public async Task<bool> PlaceOrder(Order order){
    Console.WriteLine($"[Facade + Chain of Responsibility] Processing Order #{order.OrderId}...");

    // 1. Validate order using the chain of responsibility
    if (!_validationChain.Handle(order))
    {
      Console.WriteLine("❌ Order validation failed");
      return false;
    }

    // 2. Get ALL pizzas from the order (handle both single items and composites)
    var pizzas = ExtractPizzasFromOrder(order);

    if (!pizzas.Any())
    {
      Console.WriteLine("❌ Order does not contain any valid pizzas");
      return false;
    }

    // 3. Create kitchen commands
    var deliverCommand = new DeliverPizzaCommand(new DeliveryService(), order);

    // 4. Add commands to processor
    var commandProcessor = new KitchenCommandProcessor(maxRetries: 3);

    foreach (var pizza in pizzas)
    {
      var bakeCommand = new BakePizzaCommand(pizza, order);
      var packCommand = new PackPizzaCommand(pizza, order);
      commandProcessor.AddCommand(bakeCommand);
      commandProcessor.AddCommand(packCommand);
    }
    commandProcessor.AddCommand(deliverCommand);
```

```
    // 5. Execute commands asynchronously
    bool success = await commandProcessor.ProcessQueueAsync();

    if (success){
      // 6. Send notifications
      Console.WriteLine($"✅ Order #{order.OrderId} processed successfully!");
    }
    else{
      Console.WriteLine($"❌ Order #{order.OrderId} processing failed!");
    }
    return success;
}

private List<IPizza> ExtractPizzasFromOrder(Order order)
{
    var pizzas = new List<IPizza>();

    // Use the Items list which contains all the individual items
    if (order.Items != null)
    {
      foreach (var item in order.Items)
      {
        if (item is IPizza pizza)
        {
          pizzas.Add(pizza);
        }
        else if (item is OrderComposite composite)
        {
          // Handle nested composites
          pizzas.AddRange(ExtractPizzasFromComposite(composite));
        }
      }
    }
    // Fallback to OrderItem for backward compatibility
    else if (order.OrderItem != null)
    {
      if (order.OrderItem is IPizza pizza)
      {
        pizzas.Add(pizza);
      }
      else if (order.OrderItem is OrderComposite composite)
      {
        pizzas.AddRange(ExtractPizzasFromComposite(composite));
      }
    }

    Console.WriteLine($"[OrderProcessor] Found {pizzas.Count} pizza(s) in order #{order.OrderId}");
    return pizzas;
}
```

INTERPRETER

```
  private List<IPizza> ExtractPizzasFromComposite(OrderComposite composite)
  {
    var pizzas = new List<IPizza>();

    foreach (var item in composite.GetItems())
    {
      if (item is IPizza pizza)
      {
        pizzas.Add(pizza);
      }
      else if (item is OrderComposite nestedComposite)
      {
        pizzas.AddRange(ExtractPizzasFromComposite(nestedComposite));
      }
      // Skip non-pizza items (drinks, desserts, etc.)
    }

    return pizzas;
  }
}
```

We're teaching our kitchen staff to:

1. Look at the entire order
2. Find only the pizzas (not drinks or desserts)
3. Cook exactly the right number of pizzas

This prevents them from trying to "bake" your coke or "pack" your brownie!

Step 7: Usage in Program.cs

What we're doing: Putting everything together in the main program.

PizzaOrderParser.cs

```
static async Task Main()
{
  // Setup all our services (inventory, payment, delivery, etc.)
  // ... setup code ...

  Console.WriteLine("Welcome to Delizioso Pizzeria!");
  var menu = MenuBuilder.BuildMenu();
  menu.Print();

  Console.WriteLine("\n=== How to Order ===");
  Console.WriteLine("Examples: '2x pepperoni pizza + coke', 'margherita with extra cheese'");
  Console.Write("\nWhat would you like? ");

  string input = Console.ReadLine();
```

```
    try
    {
        // Use our smart interpreter to understand the order!
        var parser = new PizzaOrderParser();
        var orderExpression = parser.Parse(input);
        Order interpretedOrder = orderExpression.Interpret();

        // Show what we understood
    Console.WriteLine($"You ordered: {interpretedOrder.OrderItem.Name
 (${interpretedOrder.OrderItem.Price})");

        if (interpretedOrder.OrderItem is OrderComposite composite)
        {
            Console.WriteLine("Includes:");
            foreach (var item in composite.GetItems())
            {
                Console.WriteLine($"  - {item.Name} (${item.Price})");
            }
        }

        // Process the order
        var order = new Order
        {
            OrderId = IdGenerator.Instance.GetNextId(),
            CustomerName = "Walk-in",
            Address = "Counter",
            OrderItem = interpretedOrder.OrderItem,
            Items = interpretedOrder.Items,
            Status = "Received"
        };

        bool success = await orderProcessor.PlaceOrder(order);

        if (success) Console.WriteLine("\nThank you for your order!");
        else Console.WriteLine("\nThere was a problem with your order.");
    }
    catch (InterpretationException ex) {
        Console.WriteLine($"Sorry, I didn't understand: {ex.Message}");
    }
}
```

This is our main restaurant manager that:

1. Greets customers and shows the menu
2. Takes orders using our smart interpreter
3. Confirms what you ordered
4. Sends everything to the kitchen
5. Handles mistakes gracefully if it doesn't understand something

It's the friendly face that makes sure your pizza experience is perfect!

Key Test Points for Interpreter Pattern Validation

1. **Basic Item Recognition Test**
    - **Objective:** Verify that the interpreter can recognize and parse basic menu items.
    - **Test Action:** Input simple item names like "Margherita", "Pepperoni", "Coke".
    - **Expected Result:** The interpreter should correctly identify these as valid menu items and create appropriate order expressions.
2. **Quantity Parsing Test**
    - **Objective:** Ensure the interpreter correctly handles quantity specifications.
    - **Test Action:** Test inputs like "2x Margherita", "3 Pepperoni", "1x Coke".
    - **Expected Result:** The interpreter should extract the correct quantity and apply it to the order.
3. **Modifier Recognition Test**
    - **Objective:** Verify that addition and exclusion modifiers are properly parsed.
    - **Test Action:** Test inputs like "Margherita + Cheese", "Pepperoni -Onions", "Veggie add Mushrooms".
    - **Expected Result:** The interpreter should create modifier expressions with correct inclusion/exclusion flags.
4. **Complex Order Parsing Test**
    - **Objective:** Ensure the interpreter can handle complex, multi-part orders.
    - **Test Action:** Test inputs like "2x Large Veggie + Cheese, No Onions", "Margherita with Extra Cheese and Mushrooms".
    - **Expected Result:** The interpreter should break down the order into correct components with proper relationships.
5. **Error Handling Test**
    - **Objective:** Verify that invalid inputs produce meaningful error messages.
    - **Test Action:** Test with unknown items ("Moon Pizza"), malformed syntax ("Pizza with"), or invalid combinations.
    - **Expected Result:** The interpreter should throw InterpretationException with clear, helpful error messages.
6. **Grammar Extension Test**
    - **Objective:** Confirm that new vocabulary can be added to the grammar easily.
    - **Test Action:** Add a new menu item or modifier to the system and test parsing.
    - **Expected Result:** New terms should be recognized without breaking existing parsing functionality.
7. **Integration with Menu System Test**
    - **Objective:** Ensure the interpreter works seamlessly with the existing menu and factory systems.
    - **Test Action:** Parse orders that include both individual items and combos from the menu.
    - **Expected Result:** The interpreter should correctly use MenuBuilder and MenuItemFactory to create valid order items.

8. **Multiple Item Order Test**
   - **Objective:** Verify that orders containing multiple distinct items are handled correctly.
   - **Test Action:** Test inputs like "Margherita Pizza and Coke", "Pepperoni, Veggie, Brownie".
   - **Expected Result:** The interpreter should create compound orders with multiple items.
9. **Case Insensitivity Test**
   - **Objective:** Ensure the interpreter handles different letter cases consistently.
   - **Test Action:** Test the same order with different capitalizations ("margherita", "Margherita", "MARGHERITA").
   - **Expected Result:** All variations should produce the same parsed result.
10. **Whitespace Tolerance Test**
    - **Objective:** Verify that the interpreter handles various whitespace patterns.
    - **Test Action:** Test inputs with extra spaces, missing spaces, or unusual spacing.
    - **Expected Result:** The interpreter should be robust to different whitespace patterns and produce consistent results.
11. **Backward Compatibility Test**
    - **Objective:** Ensure the new interpreter maintains compatibility with existing order processing.
    - **Test Action:** Process orders through both the old regex system and new interpreter.
    - **Expected Result:** Both systems should produce functionally equivalent orders for simple inputs.
12. **Performance Test**
    - **Objective:** Verify that the interpreter performs well with typical order volumes.
    - **Test Action:** Process a large number of diverse orders and measure parsing time.
    - **Expected Result:** Parsing should complete quickly enough for interactive use.

If all these tests pass, your Interpreter pattern implementation is working correctly.

INTERPRETER

17.8 Why the Interpreter Pattern Matters

- **Natural Language Processing:** Allows customers to use natural, expressive language for orders.
- **Extensibility:** New menu items and modifiers can be added without breaking existing parsing logic.
- **Maintainability:** Clear separation between grammar rules and parsing logic.
- **Error Handling:** Provides structured error messages for invalid orders.
- **Grammar Validation:** Orders can be validated against a defined grammar ruleset.
- **Multilingual Support:** The pattern can be extended to support multiple languages.

17.9 Mini-Exercise: Add a New Grammar Rule

Task: Add support for size modifiers ("Large", "Medium", "Small") to the grammar. Create a *SizeExpression* class and update the parser to handle size tokens.
Bonus: Add support for combo meals using the word "combo" or "meal" (e.g., "Veggie Combo with Coke").

17.10 When to Use the Interpreter Pattern

"Use the Interpreter pattern when you need to:

- Implement a simple language with a well-defined grammar
- Process expressions or statements in a language
- Handle complex parsing tasks that would be messy with regular expressions
- Allow users to express operations in the language of their domain"

17.11 Transition to Chapter 18

"Now that we can parse complex pizza orders using the Interpreter pattern, we need an efficient way to process and iterate through these orders. Next, we'll explore the **Iterator** pattern to provide a standardized way to access order collections without exposing their internal structure."

> **Next Up: Chapter 18 — Iterator: Looping Through Orders Efficiently**
> Ready to learn how to efficiently traverse order collections without exposing their internal details? Let's build robust iteration capabilities for our pizza order management system!

Get Full Code Here

Chapter 18

Iterator — Looping Through Orders Efficiently

Setting The Stage

Your reporting system manually loops through every list of pizzas, drinks, and desserts using raw foreach loops. Adding new collection types requires rewriting the same looping logic repeatedly.

> In this chapter, you'll:
> 1. **Identify Pitfalls:** Identify the maintenance nightmare of raw list iteration across the codebase.
> 2. **Learn the Pattern:** Learn the Iterator pattern to provide uniform collection traversal.
> 3. **Build an Iterator:** Build iterators for your menu structures and order collections.
> 4. **Protect Core Application:** Create a flexible reporting system that works with any collection type.

18.1 Hook: What's the Pain?

"Every time we need to generate a report, we write the same foreach loops: one for pizzas, one for drinks, one for desserts. If we add combos or coupons, we have to hunt down every loop and add another one! We need a consistent way to iterate through any collection without knowing what's inside or how it's stored."

18.2 The Problem in Our Pizza App

Reports and analytics manually iterate through raw lists with direct foreach loops. *(Oops Moment:14)*

```
// ❌ OLD: Manual iteration everywhere (Oops Moment #14)
public static int CountDelivered(List<Order> orders)
{
    int count = 0;
    foreach (var order in orders)  // Raw list iteration
    {
        if (order.Status == "Delivered")
            count++;
    }
    return count;
}

public static decimal CalculateRevenue(List<Order> orders, List<Pizza> pizzas, List<Drink> drinks)
{
    decimal total = 0;
    foreach (var order in orders)   // Multiple loops for different types
        total += order.TotalPrice;
    foreach (var pizza in pizzas)   // Another loop
        total += pizza.Price;
    foreach (var drink in drinks)   // And another...
        total += drink.Price;
    return total;
}
```

Why This Hurts:

- **Code Duplication:** The same looping logic is repeated everywhere.
- **Tight Coupling:** Reports are tightly coupled to specific collection types.
- **Maintenance Nightmare:** Adding new collection types requires modifying every loop.
- **No Abstraction:** Client code knows too much about internal data structures.
- **Inflexible:** Cannot easily change how collections are stored or traversed.

ITERATOR

18.3 The Formal Pattern: Iterator

Pattern Definition

> *"**Iterator** is a behavioral design pattern that lets you traverse elements of a collection without exposing its underlying representation (list, stack, tree, etc.)."*

In Simpler Terms: The Iterator pattern is like having a universal remote control for all your collections. Whether you have a simple list, a complex tree, or a custom data structure, you can use the same "next" and "has next" buttons to go through all the items without knowing how they're stored internally.

18.4 Understanding the Pattern

The Real-World Analogy: The Restaurant Inventory Counter

Imagine a restaurant manager who needs to count inventory:

- **Without Iterator:** The manager goes to each storage area separately - checks the fridge for drinks, the pantry for ingredients, the freezer for pizzas. Each area has different organization methods.
- **With Iterator:** The manager gives a checklist to an assistant who knows how to navigate all storage areas. The assistant returns each item one by one, regardless of where it's stored.

The assistant is the iterator - they hide the complexity of different storage systems.

18.5 How the Iterator Pattern Solves It

Instead of this manual approach:

```
// ❌ Direct access to internal structure
foreach (var pizza in _pizzas) { ... }
foreach (var drink in _drinks) { ... }
foreach (var order in _orders) { ... }
```

We'll create this uniform approach:

```
// ✅ Uniform iteration regardless of collection type
var pizzaIterator = _pizzaCollection.GetIterator();
var drinkIterator = _drinkCollection.GetIterator();
var orderIterator = _orderCollection.GetIterator();

while (pizzaIterator.HasNext())
{
    var pizza = pizzaIterator.Next();
    // Process pizza...
}
```

The Iterator pattern decouples the iteration logic from the collection implementation.

18.6 The Implementation Blueprint: Iterator Steps

Think of implementing the Iterator pattern like training specialized tour guides for different parts of your pizza restaurant. Each guide knows their area perfectly and can show you everything in order, but you don't need to know the layout yourself.

1.Define the Iterator Interface:

- ***What to do:*** Create a C# interface (e.g., *IIterator<T>*) with methods like *HasNext()*, *Next()*, and *Reset()*.
- ***Why we do it:*** This defines the standard "remote control" that all iterators will implement.
- ***In simple terms:*** "I'm creating a standard set of buttons that every tour guide must have: 'Is there more to see?', 'Show me the next thing', 'Start over'."

2.Define the Collection Interface:

- ***What to do:*** Create an interface (e.g., *IIterableCollection<T>*) with a method to get an iterator.
- ***Why we do it:*** This ensures that any collection can provide an iterator when needed.
- ***In simple terms:*** "I'm making a rule that every storage area must be able to provide a trained tour guide."

3.Implement Concrete Iterators:

- ***What to do:*** Create iterator classes for each collection type (e.g., *ListIterator*, *CompositeIterator*, *OrderIterator*).
- ***Why we do it:*** Each iterator knows the specific way to traverse its particular collection.
- ***In simple terms:*** "I'm training specialized guides: one for the pizza counter, one for the drink fridge, one for the combo menu."

4.Update Collections to Be Iterable:

- ***What to do:*** Modify existing collection classes to implement *IIterableCollection<T>*.
- ***Why we do it:*** This makes our existing collections compatible with the iterator pattern.
- **In simple terms:** "I'm giving each storage area the ability to provide a tour guide when asked."

5.Refactor Client Code:

- ***What to do:*** Replace raw foreach loops with iterator-based iteration.
- ***Why we do it:*** This decouples the client code from specific collection implementations.
- ***In simple terms:*** "Instead of rummaging through storage areas myself, I'll always ask for a tour guide."

18.7 Implementing the Iterator Pattern

Step 1: Define the Iterator Interface

IIterator.cs

```
public interface IIterator<T>{
   bool HasNext();    T Next();
   void Reset();
}
```

Step 2: Define the Collection Interface

IIterableCollection.cs

```
public interface IIterableCollection<T>
{
    IIterator<T> GetIterator();
    int Count { get; }
}
```

Create a specialized interface for Order collections
Instead of forcing all *IIterableCollection<T>* instances to have *GetStatusIterator* (which wouldn't make sense for non-order collections), you create a specialized interface for order-specific iteration logic.
This keeps your interfaces clean and focused:

- *IIterableCollection<T>* → general iteration
- *IOrderCollection* → specialized iteration for orders

IOrderCollection.cs

```
public interface IOrderCollection : IIterableCollection<Order>
{
    IIterator<Order> GetStatusIterator(string status);
}
```

Step 3: Implement Concrete Iterators

ListIterator.cs

```
public class ListIterator<T> : IIterator<T>
{
    private readonly List<T> _collection;
    private int _position = 0;

    public ListIterator(List<T> collection) {
        _collection = collection;
    }

    public bool HasNext()
    {
        return _position < _collection.Count;
    }
```

```
    public T Next()
    {
        if (!HasNext())
            throw new InvalidOperationException("No more elements");

        return _collection[_position++];
    }

    public void Reset()
    {
        _position = 0;
    }
}
```

CompositeIterator .cs

```
public class CompositeIterator : IIterator<IOrderItem>
{
    private readonly OrderComposite _composite;
    private int _position = 0;

    public CompositeIterator(OrderComposite composite)
    {
        _composite = composite;
    }

    public bool HasNext()
    {
        return _position < _composite.GetItems().Count();
    }

    public IOrderItem Next()
    {
        if (!HasNext())
            throw new InvalidOperationException("No more elements");

        return _composite.GetItems().ElementAt(_position++);
    }

    public void Reset()
    {
        _position = 0;
    }
}
```

ITERATOR

Now create your specialized Iterators

OrderStatusIterator.cs

```
public class OrderStatusIterator : IIterator<Order>
{
    private readonly List<Order> _orders;
    private readonly string _targetStatus;
    private int _position = 0;

    public OrderStatusIterator(List<Order> orders, string targetStatus)
    {
        _orders = orders;
        _targetStatus = targetStatus;
    }

    public bool HasNext()
    {
        // Skip non-matching orders
        while (_position < _orders.Count && _orders[_position].Status != _targetStatus)
        {
            _position++;
        }
        return _position < _orders.Count;
    }

    public Order Next()
    {
        if (!HasNext())
            throw new InvalidOperationException("No more matching orders");

        return _orders[_position++];
    }

    public void Reset()
    {
        _position = 0;
    }
}
```

Step 4: Update Collections to Be Iterable

OrderCollection.cs

```
public class OrderCollection : IOrderCollection
{
    private readonly List<Order> _orders = new List<Order>();

    public IIterator<Order> GetIterator()
    {
        return new ListIterator<Order>(_orders);
    }

    public IIterator<Order> GetStatusIterator(string status)
    {
        return new OrderStatusIterator(_orders, status);
    }

    public void AddOrder(Order order)
    {
        _orders.Add(order);
    }

    public int Count => _orders.Count;
}
```

Step 5: Refactor Reports to Use Iterators

Reports.cs

```
public class Reports
{
    // Oops Moment #14: Raw list iteration everywhere
    // SOLUTION: Use Iterator pattern for uniform collection traversal

    public static int CountDelivered(IOrderCollection orders)
    {
        var iterator = orders.GetStatusIterator("Delivered");
        int count = 0;

        while (iterator.HasNext())
        {
            iterator.Next();
            count++;
        }
        return count;
    }
```

ITERATOR

```
    public static decimal CalculateTotalRevenue(params IIterableCollection<IOrderItem>[] collections)
    {
        decimal total = 0;

        foreach (var collection in collections)
        {
            var iterator = collection.GetIterator();
            while (iterator.HasNext())
            {
                var item = iterator.Next();
                total += item.Price;
            }
        }
        return total;
    }

    public static void PrintAllItems(IIterableCollection<IOrderItem> collection)
    {
        var iterator = collection.GetIterator();
        Console.WriteLine("All Items:");

        while (iterator.HasNext())
        {
            var item = iterator.Next();
            Console.WriteLine($"  - {item.Name}: ${item.Price}");
        }
    }
}
```

Step 6: Usage in Client Code

Program.cs

```
//After Order Processing

Console.WriteLine("=== Testing Iterator Pattern in Reports ===\n");

// 1. Create sample orders (using your existing Order class)
var orders = new OrderCollection();

// Create orders with your existing Order class structure
// We are hardcoding values here. As we are currently not using any database or memory
management
var order1 = new Order
{
    OrderId = 1,
    Status = "Delivered"
};
```

```
// Assuming your Order has OrderItem property (from your existing code)
order1.OrderItem = new SimpleMenuItem("Margherita Pizza", 25.50m);
orders.AddOrder(order1);

var order2 = new Order
{
    OrderId = 2,
    Status = "Pending"
};
order2.OrderItem = new SimpleMenuItem("Pepperoni Pizza", 28.75m);
orders.AddOrder(order2);

var order3 = new Order
{
    OrderId = 3,
    Status = "Delivered"
};
order3.OrderItem = new SimpleMenuItem("Veggie Pizza", 22.00m);
orders.AddOrder(order3);

// 2. Create simple menu items (avoiding complex Pizza constructors)
var menuItems = new SimpleOrderItemCollection();
menuItems.AddItem(new SimpleMenuItem("Margherita Pizza", 12.99m));
menuItems.AddItem(new SimpleMenuItem("Pepperoni Pizza", 14.99m));
menuItems.AddItem(new SimpleMenuItem("Coke", 2.50m));

// 3. TEST ITERATOR PATTERN IN REPORTS
Console.WriteLine("=== REPORTS OUTPUT ===\n");

// Test 1: Count delivered orders using iterator
int deliveredCount = Reports.CountDelivered(orders);
Console.WriteLine($"Delivered Orders Count: {deliveredCount}");

// Test 2: Calculate total revenue using iterator
decimal totalRevenue = Reports.CalculateTotalRevenue(menuItems);
Console.WriteLine($"Total Menu Revenue: ${totalRevenue:0.00}");

// Test 3: Print all items using iterator
Reports.PrintAllItems(menuItems);

Console.WriteLine("\n=== TEST COMPLETE ===");
```

ITERATOR

Step 7: Creating some Supporting Classes for Testing Only

SimpleMenuItem.cs

```
// Simple class that implements IOrderItem (minimal, for testing only)
public class SimpleMenuItem : IOrderItem
{
    public string Name { get; }
    public decimal Price { get; }

    public SimpleMenuItem(string name, decimal price)
    {
        Name = name;
        Price = price;
    }
    public IOrderItem Clone()
    {
        return new SimpleMenuItem(Name, Price);
    }
}
```

SimpleOrderItemCollection.cs

```
public class SimpleOrderItemCollection : IIterableCollection<IOrderItem>
{
    private readonly List<IOrderItem> _items = new List<IOrderItem>();

    public IIterator<IOrderItem> GetIterator()
    {
        return new ListIterator<IOrderItem>(_items);
    }

    public int Count => _items.Count;

    public void AddItem(IOrderItem item)
    {
        _items.Add(item);
    }
}
```

Key Test Points for Iterator Pattern Validation

1. **Basic Collection Iteration Test**
   - **Objective:** Verify that iterators can traverse basic collections correctly.
   - **Test Action:** Create a collection with known items and iterate through them.
   - **Expected Result:** Iterator should return all items in the correct order without skipping or repeating.
2. **Empty Collection Handling Test**
   - **Objective:** Ensure iterators behave correctly with empty collections.
   - **Test Action:** Create an empty collection and attempt iteration.
   - **Expected Result:** *HasNext()* should return false immediately, and *Next()* should throw appropriate exception.
3. **Reset Functionality Test**
   - **Objective:** Verify that *Reset()* method properly restarts iteration.
   - **Test Action:** Iterate partially through a collection, call *Reset()*, then iterate again.
   - **Expected Result:** Second iteration should return the same items in the same order as the first.
4. **Multiple Independent Iterators Test**
   - **Objective:** Ensure multiple iterators on the same collection don't interfere.
   - **Test Action:** Create two iterators from the same collection and use them concurrently.
   - **Expected Result:** Each iterator should maintain independent position and traverse all items.
5. **Specialized Iterator Filtering Test**
   - **Objective:** Verify that specialized iterators (like *OrderStatusIterator*) filter correctly.
   - **Test Action:** Create a mixed collection and use specialized iterator to filter specific items.
   - **Expected Result:** Iterator should only return items matching the filter criteria.
6. **Boundary Conditions Test**
   - **Objective:** Ensure proper behavior at collection boundaries.
   - **Test Action:** Test iteration exactly at the last element and beyond.
   - **Expected Result:** *HasNext()* should return *false* after last element, *Next()* should *throw* when no elements left.
7. **Collection Modification Test**
   - **Objective:** Verify iterator behavior when underlying collection changes.
   - **Test Action:** Modify collection during iteration and observe behavior.
   - **Expected Result:** Iterator behavior should be predictable
8. **Type Safety Test**
   - **Objective:** Ensure iterators return correct types and maintain type safety.
   - **Test Action:** Iterate through collections of specific types and verify returned objects.
   - **Expected Result:** All returned objects should be of expected type and safe to use.

9. **Performance Characteristics Test**
   - **Objective:** Verify that iteration performance is O(n) and scales appropriately.
   - **Test Action:** Iterate through large collections and measure performance.
   - **Expected Result:** Iteration time should scale linearly with collection size.
10. **Integration with Reports Test**
   - **Objective:** Ensure iterator pattern works seamlessly with reporting system.
   - **Test Action:** Use *Reports* class methods with various collection types.
   - **Expected Result:** All reports should generate correct results using iterator pattern.
11. **Composite Structure Iteration Test**
   - **Objective:** Verify iterators work correctly with composite structures.
   - **Test Action:** Create nested menu composites and iterate through them.
   - **Expected Result:** Iterator should traverse all leaf nodes in the composite structure.
12. **Custom Iterator Implementation Test**
   - **Objective:** Ensure custom iterators (reverse, filtered, etc.) work as expected.
   - **Test Action:** Create and use custom iterator implementations.
   - **Expected Result:** Custom iterators should follow the iterator contract and provide specialized traversal.

If all these tests pass, your Iterator pattern implementation successfully solves Oops Moment #14 by providing uniform, decoupled collection traversal across your pizza ordering system!

18.8 Why the Iterator Pattern Matters

- **Decoupling:** Client code doesn't depend on collection implementation details.
- **Uniform Access:** Same iteration code works for lists, composites, trees, etc.
- **Multiple Iteration Strategies:** Different iterators can traverse the same collection in different ways.
- **Simplified Client Code:** No more complex foreach loops with conditional logic.
- **Extensibility:** Easy to add new collection types without changing client code.
- **Parallel Iteration:** Multiple iterators can traverse the same collection independently.

18.9 Mini-Exercise: Create a New Iterator

Task: Create a *HighValueOrderIterator* that only returns orders with a total price above $20. Update the reports to use this iterator for premium customer analysis.
Bonus: Create a reverse iterator that traverses collections from end to beginning.

18.10 When to Use the Iterator Pattern

"Use the Iterator pattern when:

- You need to access elements of a collection without exposing its internal structure.
- You want to support multiple traversal algorithms for the same collection.
- You want to provide a uniform interface for traversing different collections.
- Your collection has a complex data structure, but you want to hide its complexity from clients."

18.11 Transition to Chapter 19

"Now that we can efficiently iterate through our collections using the Iterator pattern, let's address how our services communicate with each other. Next, we'll explore the **Mediator** pattern to manage the complex web of dependencies between our kitchen, delivery, and notification services."

> **Next Up: Chapter 19 — Mediator: The Kitchen Communication Hub**
> Ready to simplify service communication and reduce dependencies? Let's build a central mediator to coordinate all our pizza services efficiently!

Scan to see Iterator Pattern in Action

Chapter 19

Mediator — The Kitchen Communication Hub

Setting The Stage

Your pizza services (PizzaService, DeliveryService, NotificationService, Inventory, Payment) are all talking directly to each other, creating a tangled web of dependencies.

> In this chapter, you'll:
> 1. **Identify Pitfalls:** Identify the spaghetti communication between services.
> 2. **Learn the Pattern:** Learn the Mediator pattern to centralize communication.
> 3. **Build an Kitchen Manager:** Build a kitchen manager that coordinates all services.
> 4. **Protect Core Application:** Reduce coupling and make the system more maintainable.

19.1 Hook: What's the Pain?

"Every time we add a new service (LoyaltyPoints, KitchenDisplay, Analytics), we have to modify all the existing services to know about it! Our services are like chefs shouting across a noisy kitchen instead of having a head chef who coordinates everything."

19.2 The Problem in Our Pizza App

OrderProcessor.cs is already solving Oops Moment #37 by acting as a mediator, but we can make it more explicit and powerful.

Why This Needs Enhancement:

- **Hidden Pattern:** The mediator role isn't explicit.
- **Limited Event Handling:** Hard to add new events without modifying the core logic.
- **Tight Coupling:** Still some direct service dependencies.
- **Missing Flexibility:** Can't easily add new services dynamically.

```
// ✅ OrderProcessor is ALREADY acting as a Mediator, but let's formalize it!
public async Task<bool> PlaceOrder(Order order)
{
    // Mediator coordinates: Validation → Inventory → Payment → Kitchen Commands → Notifications

    // 1. Validate order using chain of responsibility
    if (!_validationChain.Handle(order)) return false;

    // 2. Get pizzas and create kitchen commands
    var pizzas = ExtractPizzasFromOrder(order);

    // 3. Create and execute commands
    var commandProcessor = new KitchenCommandProcessor(maxRetries: 3);
    foreach (var pizza in pizzas)
    {
        commandProcessor.AddCommand(new BakePizzaCommand(pizza, order));
        commandProcessor.AddCommand(new PackPizzaCommand(pizza, order));
    }
    commandProcessor.AddCommand(new DeliverPizzaCommand(new DeliveryService(), order));

    // 4. Execute and coordinate notifications
    bool success = await commandProcessor.ProcessQueueAsync();
    if (success)
    {
        _emailNotifier.Send($"Order #{order.OrderId} delivered");
        _smsNotifier.Send("Your pizza is out for delivery!");
        _pushNotifier.Send("Special offer: 20% off your next order!");
    }

    return success;
}
```

19.3 The Formal Pattern: Mediator

Pattern Definition

> *"**Mediator** is a behavioral pattern that reduces coupling between components by making them communicate indirectly, through a central mediator object.."*

In Simpler Terms: The Mediator is like a restaurant manager who coordinates the kitchen, waitstaff, and delivery drivers. Instead of everyone shouting across the room, they all report to the manager who tells each person what to do next.

19.4 Understanding the Pattern

The Real-World Analogy: The Restaurant Inventory Counter

Imagine a busy pizza restaurant:

- **Without Mediator:** Cooks yell when pizzas are ready, delivery drivers shout when they're back, waitstaff interrupt cooks for updates
- **With Mediator:** Everyone reports to the manager. The manager tracks order status, tells cooks what to make, assigns drivers, and updates customers

19.5 How the Mediator Pattern Solves It

Instead of this hidden mediation:

```
// ✗ Implicit mediation (hard to extend)
pizzaService.BakePizza(order);
deliveryService.Deliver(order);
// Notifications scattered throughout
```

We'll create this explicit, event-driven approach:

```
//Explicit mediation with event system
_mediator.Notify("OrderValidated", order);
_mediator.Notify("PaymentProcessed", order);
_mediator.Notify("PizzaBaked", order, pizza);
//Mediator coordinates all responses
```

19.6 The Implementation Blueprint: Mediator Steps

Think of implementing the Mediator pattern like promoting your most organized chef to head chef. They don't cook themselves, but they make sure every station knows what to do and when.

1. Define the Mediator Interface:

- ***What to do:*** Create *IKitchenMediator* with methods for events and service registration
- ***Why we do it:*** This defines the contract for all kitchen coordination
- ***In simple terms:*** "I'm creating a job description for the head chef position".

2. Implement the Concrete Mediator:

- ***What to do:*** Create *KitchenMediator* that handles all event routing
- ***Why we do it:*** This centralizes all communication logic in one place
- ***In simple terms:*** "I'm hiring and training the head chef who knows every station".

3. Define Event Types:
- ***What to do:*** Create standard event names that services can publish.
- ***Why we do it:*** This creates a common language for service communication
- ***In simple terms:*** "I'm creating standard kitchen tickets that everyone understands".

4. Refactor Services to Use Mediator:
- ***What to do:*** Update services to publish events instead of calling other services directly.
- ***Why we do it:*** This decouples services from each other.
- ***In simple terms:*** "I'm telling all kitchen staff to report to the head chef instead of yelling across the kitchen".

5. Refactor Client Code:
- ***What to do:*** Make *OrderProcessor* use the mediator instead of direct coordination
- ***Why we do it:*** This separates the facade pattern from mediation responsibilities
- ***In simple terms:*** "I'm letting the head chef manage the kitchen while I focus on customer interface".

19.7 Implementing the Mediator Pattern

Mediator Place in our Pizza Application Architecture

```
Client Code
    ↓ (calls facade)
IOrderProcessorFacade ← OrderProcessor (Facade)
    ↓ (delegates to mediator)
IKitchenMediator ← KitchenMediator (Mediator)
    ↓ (coordinates services)
Validation → Inventory → Payment → Kitchen Commands → Notifications
```

Step 1: Define the Mediator Interface

Mediator.cs

```
public interface IIterator<T>{
   bool HasNext();
   T Next();
   void Reset();
}
```

Step 2: Implement the Concrete Mediator

KitchenMediator.cs

```
public class KitchenMediator : IKitchenMediator
{
  private readonly Dictionary<string, object> _services = new Dictionary<string, object>();
  private readonly EmailNotification _emailNotifier;
  private readonly SmsNotification _smsNotifier;
  private readonly PushNotification _pushNotifier;
```

```
public KitchenMediator(
    EmailNotification emailNotifier,
    SmsNotification smsNotifier,
    PushNotification pushNotifier)
{
    _emailNotifier = emailNotifier;
    _smsNotifier = smsNotifier;
    _pushNotifier = pushNotifier;

    // Only register notification services that mediator actually coordinates
    RegisterService("EmailNotifier", emailNotifier);
    RegisterService("SmsNotifier", smsNotifier);
    RegisterService("PushNotifier", pushNotifier);
}

public async Task<bool> ProcessOrder(Order order)
{
    Console.WriteLine($"[Mediator] Coordinating kitchen operations for #{order.OrderId}...");

    try
    {
        var pizzas = ExtractPizzasFromOrder(order);

        // Pure coordination: Execute kitchen workflow
        var success = await ExecuteKitchenOperations(order, pizzas);

        if (success)
        {
            Notify("OrderCompleted", order);
            return true;
        }
        else
        {
            Notify("OrderFailed", order, "Kitchen operations failed");
            return false;
        }
    }
    catch (Exception ex)
    {
        Notify("OrderFailed", order, ex.Message);
        return false;
    }
}

private async Task<bool> ExecuteKitchenOperations(Order order, List<IPizza> pizzas)
{
    // This is the core coordination that demonstrates mediator pattern
    var commandProcessor = new KitchenCommandProcessor(maxRetries: 3);
```

MEDIATOR

```
    foreach (var pizza in pizzas)
    {
        commandProcessor.AddCommand(new BakePizzaCommand(pizza, order));
        commandProcessor.AddCommand(new PackPizzaCommand(pizza, order));
    }
    commandProcessor.AddCommand(new DeliverPizzaCommand(new DeliveryService(), order));

    return await commandProcessor.ProcessQueueAsync();
}

// Event handlers for coordination
public void Notify(string eventType, Order order, object data = null)
{
    Console.WriteLine($"[Mediator] Event: {eventType} for Order #{order.OrderId}");

    switch (eventType)
    {
        case "OrderCompleted":
            HandleOrderCompleted(order);
            break;
        case "OrderFailed":
            HandleOrderFailed(order, data as string);
            break;
            // Kitchen events can be added here if needed
    }
}

private void HandleOrderCompleted(Order order)
{
    // Coordinate multiple notifications
    _emailNotifier.Send($"Order #{order.OrderId} completed!");
    _smsNotifier.Send("Your order is ready!");
    _pushNotifier.Send("Thanks for your order!");

    Console.WriteLine($"[Mediator] Order #{order.OrderId} - All notifications sent");
}

private void HandleOrderFailed(Order order, string reason)
{
    _emailNotifier.Send($"Order #{order.OrderId} failed: {reason}");
    _smsNotifier.Send("We're sorry, your order failed");

    Console.WriteLine($"[Mediator] Order #{order.OrderId} failed: {reason}");
}

public void RegisterService(string serviceName, object service)
{
    _services[serviceName] = service;
}
```

```
    public T GetService<T>(string serviceName) where T : class
    {
        return _services[serviceName] as T;
    }

    private List<IPizza> ExtractPizzasFromOrder(Order order)
    {
        // Your existing extraction logic
        var pizzas = new List<IPizza>();
        if (order.OrderItem is IPizza pizza)
            pizzas.Add(pizza);
        return pizzas;
    }
  }
}
```

Step 3: Refactor OrderProcessor to Use Mediator

OrderProcessor.cs

```
public class OrderProcessor : IOrderProcessorFacade
{
    private readonly IOrderHandler _validationChain; // Chain of Responsibility
    private readonly IKitchenMediator _mediator;     // Mediator Pattern

    private readonly IInventoryService _inventory;
    private readonly PaymentGatewayAdapter _paymentAdapter;

    private readonly List<Order> _orders = new List<Order>(); // Simple list for now

    public OrderProcessor(
        IInventoryService inventory,
        PaymentGatewayAdapter paymentAdapter,
        IKitchenMediator mediator
        )
    {
        _inventory = inventory;
        _paymentAdapter = paymentAdapter;
        // Build the validation chain
        _validationChain = BuildValidationChain();
        _mediator = mediator;
    }

    public async Task<bool> PlaceOrder(Order order)
    {
        Console.WriteLine($"[OrderProcessor] Processing order #{order.OrderId}...");

        _orders.Add(order);
```

MEDIATOR

```
    // 1. Chain of Responsibility: Validation (Order → Inventory → Payment)
    if (!_validationChain.Handle(order))
    {
        Console.WriteLine("❌ Order validation failed");
        order.Status = "Validation Failed";
        return false;
    }

    // 2. Mediator Pattern: Kitchen Operations Coordination
    bool success = await _mediator.ProcessOrder(order);

    order.Status = success ? "Completed" : "Kitchen Failed";
    return success;
}


// Build the validation chain of responsibility
private IOrderHandler BuildValidationChain()
{
    var orderValidationHandler = new OrderValidationHandler();
    var inventoryValidationHandler = new InventoryValidationHandler(_inventory);
    var paymentValidationHandler = new PaymentValidationHandler(_paymentAdapter);

    orderValidationHandler.SetNext(inventoryValidationHandler)
                 .SetNext(paymentValidationHandler);

    return orderValidationHandler;
}

public bool CancelOrder(int orderId)
{
    Console.WriteLine($"[OrderProcessor Facade] Cancelling order #{orderId}...");

    var order = _orders.FirstOrDefault(o => o.OrderId == orderId);
    if (order != null)
    {
        _mediator.Notify("OrderCancelled", order);
        return true;
    }
    return false;

}

public string CheckOrderStatus(int orderId)
{
    var order = _orders.FirstOrDefault(o => o.OrderId == orderId);
    return order?.Status ?? "Not Found";
}
}
```

Step 4: Usage in Client Code

Program.cs

```
// Create mediator (only for kitchen coordination)
var mediator = new KitchenMediator(emailNotifier, smsNotifier, pushNotifier);

// Create order processor that uses both patterns
var orderProcessor = new OrderProcessor(
    inventoryService,
    paymentProcessor,
    mediator);
```

Pattern Roles in Our Pizza Ordering System

- ***Facade Pattern (OrderProcessor):***
  - Provides Simple Client Interface - Single entry point for order operations
  - Hides Subsystem Complexity - Clients don't see validation chains or mediators
  - Unified API - Consistent methods for place, cancel, and status check
  - Decouples Clients - Client code doesn't depend on internal patterns
  - Orchestrates Pattern Collaboration - Coordinates Chain of Responsibility + Mediator
- ***Chain of Responsibility Pattern:***
  - Handles Validation Pipeline - Sequential order validation (Order → Inventory → Payment)
  - Single Responsibility per Handler - Each validator focuses on one concern
  - Easy to Extend Validation - Add new validation steps without modifying existing code
  - Flexible Order Processing - Dynamic validation chain configuration
  - Early Failure Detection - Stops processing at first validation failure
- ***Mediator Pattern:***
  - Coordinates Kitchen Workflow - Manages baking → packing → delivery sequence
  - Manages Complex Notification Routing - Coordinates multiple notification channels
  - Decouples Kitchen Services - Services communicate through mediator, not directly
  - Centralized Event Handling - Single point for kitchen operation events
  - Easy Service Integration - New services can be added without affecting existing ones

How They Work Together:

- **Chain of Responsibility:** "Can this order proceed?" *(Validation)*
- **Mediator:** "How do we execute this order?" *(Coordination)*
- **OrderProcessor:** "Let me manage the overall process" *(Facade)*

The facade provides the "what" (simple interface) while the mediator handles the "how" (complex coordination).

```
Client
    ↓ (Simple facade interface)
OrderProcessor (Facade)
    ↓ (Delegates validation)
Chain of Responsibility (Validation Pipeline)
    ↓ (Delegates execution)
KitchenMediator (Coordination Center)
    ↓ (Orchestrates services)
Individual Services (Baking, Packing, Delivery, Notifications)
```

Key Test Points for Mediator Pattern Validation

1. **Central Coordination Test**
   - **Objective:** Verify mediator coordinates all services without direct service communication.
   - **Test Action:** Process an order and verify mediator receives all events in correct sequence.
   - **Expected Result:** Mediator should receive and handle events in order: OrderReceived → KitchenOperations → OrderCompleted
2. **Service Decoupling Test**
   - **Objective:** Ensure services don't communicate directly.
   - **Test Action:** Modify one service implementation and verify others aren't affected.
   - **Expected Result:** Changes to one service (e.g., *EmailNotification*) don't require changes to other services.
3. **Event Routing Test**
   - **Objective:** Verify mediator correctly routes events to appropriate handlers.
   - **Test Action:** Trigger different events and verify correct handlers are called.
   - **Expected Result:** Each event type should trigger the correct handler method.
4. **Multiple Service Registration Test**
   - **Objective:** Ensure mediator can dynamically register and use new services.
   - **Test Action:** Register new services at runtime and verify they're used.
   - **Expected Result:** Newly registered services should be available for mediator coordination.
5. **Error Handling Coordination Test**
   - **Objective:** Verify mediator coordinates proper error handling across services.
   - **Test Action:** Simulate failures at different stages and verify coordinated response.
   - **Expected Result:** Mediator should notify all relevant services about failures.
6. **Kitchen Workflow Coordination Test**
   - **Objective:** Verify mediator coordinates the entire kitchen workflow.
   - **Test Action:** Process order, verify kitchen commands execute in correct sequence.
   - **Expected Result:** Bake → Pack → Deliver sequence maintained with proper timing.
7. **Notification Coordination Test**
   - **Objective:** Ensure mediator coordinates multiple notification channels correctly.
   - **Test Action:** Process order and verify all notification types are sent.
   - **Expected Result:** All registered notification services should receive appropriate messages.
8. **Extensibility Test**
   - **Objective:** Verify new event types can be added without breaking existing functionality.
   - **Test Action:** Add new event type and handler to mediator.
   - **Expected Result:** New events should be handled without modifying existing event logic.

9. **Performance Under Load Test**
    - **Objective:** Verify mediator handles multiple concurrent orders efficiently.
    - **Test Action:** Process multiple orders simultaneously.
    - **Expected Result:** Mediator should coordinate all orders without deadlocks or performance degradation.
10. **Integration with Other Patterns Test**
    - **Objective:** Verify mediator works correctly with Chain of Responsibility and Facade.
    - **Test Action:** Use full order processing pipeline.
    - **Expected Result:** All patterns should work together seamlessly.
11. **State Consistency Test**
    - **Objective:** Ensure mediator maintains consistent state during coordination.
    - **Test Action:** Process complex orders with multiple items and modifications.
    - **Expected Result:** All order items should be processed correctly with proper state tracking.
12. **Failure Recovery Test**
    - **Objective:** Verify mediator handles partial failures gracefully.
    - **Test Action:** Simulate service failures during order processing.
    - **Expected Result:** Mediator should coordinate recovery actions and proper error reporting.

If all these tests pass, your Mediator pattern successfully solves Oops Moment #37 by providing centralized, decoupled service coordination!

19.8 Why the Mediator Pattern Matters

- **Centralized Control:** All coordination logic in one place
- **Loose Coupling:** Services don't know about each other
- **Easy Extensibility:** Add new services without modifying existing ones
- **Better Testability:** Test mediator in isolation with mock services
- **Clear Responsibility:** Mediator's only job is coordination
- **Event-Driven Architecture:** Natural foundation for future enhancements

19.9 Mini-Exercise: Add a New Service

Task: Create an *AnalyticsService* that tracks order completion times and register it with the mediator. Modify the mediator to notify this service when orders are delivered.

Bonus: Create a *LoyaltyPointsService* that awards points when orders are completed successfully.

19.10 When to Use the Mediator Pattern

"Use the Mediator pattern when:

- You have a complex web of object relationships that's hard to understand
- Reusing an object is difficult because it references many other objects
- You want to customize behavior distributed between several classes without subclassing
- Communication between objects is complex and well-defined but complex"

19.11 Transition to Chapter 20

"Now that we have a clean, centralized communication system with our Kitchen Mediator, let's tackle another common problem: what happens when a customer wants to modify their pizza customization? Next, we'll explore the **Memento** pattern to implement undo functionality for pizza modifications."

> **Next Up: Chapter 20 — Memento: Undo Pizza Customization**
> Ready to implement rollback functionality for pizza modifications? Let's build a system that remembers previous states so customers can undo their changes!

Scan to see Mediator Pattern in Action

Chapter 20

Memento — Undo Pizza Customization

Setting The Stage

Your pizza customization system has no way to undo changes. Once a customer adds extra cheese or changes crust type, they're stuck with those choices.

> In this chapter, you'll:
> 1. **Identify Pitfalls:** Identify the need for rollback functionality in pizza customization
> 2. **Learn the Pattern:** Learn the Memento pattern to capture and restore object states
> 3. **Build an Undo System:** Build an undo system for pizza modifications
> 4. **Manage Modification History:** Create a caretake to manage modification history

20.1 Hook: What's the Pain?

"Customers keep saying 'I wish I could undo that last topping' or 'Can I go back to how my pizza was before?' Right now, we have to start over from scratch. We need a way to remember previous pizza states so customers can undo changes."

20.2 The Problem in Our Pizza App

No way to undo pizza modifications (Oops Moment #12)

```
// ✗ OLD: No undo capability
var pizza = new Pizza("Margherita", 10.00m, toppings, false, false);
pizza = new ExtraCheeseDecorator(pizza); // Committed - no going back!
pizza = new StuffedCrustDecorator(pizza); // Another permanent change

// Customer says: "Actually, remove the extra cheese"
// ✗ We have to recreate the entire pizza from scratch
```

Why This Hurts:

- **Customer Frustration:** No trial-and-error customization
- **Data Loss:** Previous states are overwritten
- **Complex Recreation:** Have to track all modifications manually
- **No History:** Can't see what changes were made

MEMENTO

20.3 The Formal Pattern: Memento

Pattern Definition

> *"**Memento** is a behavioral pattern that lets you save and restore the previous state of an object without revealing the details of its implementation."*

In Simpler Terms: The Memento pattern is like having a "time machine" for your pizza. You can take snapshots of your pizza at any point during customization and go back to any previous version with a single click.

20.4 Understanding the Pattern

The Real-World Analogy: Pizza Customization History

Imagine building your perfect pizza:

- **Without Memento:** You add toppings one by one. If you add too many mushrooms, you have to remove everything and start over.
- **With Memento:** The system remembers each step. You can click "undo" to go back to before the mushrooms, or even back to your original cheese pizza.

20.5 How the Memento Pattern Solves It

Instead of this irreversible process:

```
// ❌ One-way customization
pizza = new ExtraCheeseDecorator(pizza);
pizza = new StuffedCrustDecorator(pizza);
// No going back!
```

We'll create this reversible system:

```
// ✅ Reversible customization with history
_caretaker.SaveState(pizza); // Save before changes
pizza = new ExtraCheeseDecorator(pizza);
_caretaker.SaveState(pizza); // Save after cheese
pizza = new StuffedCrustDecorator(pizza);

// Customer wants to undo extra cheese:
pizza = _caretaker.Undo(); // Back to pre-cheese state
```

20.6 The Implementation Blueprint: Memento Steps

Think of implementing the Memento pattern like giving your pizza chef a photographic memory. They remember exactly how your pizza looked at every step of customization.

1. Define the Memento Interface:

- ***What to do:*** Create *IPizzaMemento* that can capture and restore pizza state.
- ***Why we do it:*** This defines the contract for saving/restoring pizza states.
- ***In simple terms:*** "I'm creating a pizza photo album that can remember exact pizza configurations".

2. **Create the Originator (Pizza):**
   - ***What to do:*** Enhance your *Pizza* class to create and restore from mementos
   - ***Why we do it:*** The pizza needs to be able to save its current state and restore previous ones
   - ***In simple terms:*** "I'm teaching the pizza how to pose for photos and how to recreate itself from those photos".
3. **Implement Concrete Memento:**
   - ***What to do:*** Create *PizzaMemento* that stores pizza state internally
   - ***Why we do it:*** This object holds the snapshot without exposing pizza internals.
   - ***In simple terms:*** "I'm creating the actual photos that store the pizza's appearance at specific moments"
4. **Create the Caretaker:**
   - ***What to do:*** Build *PizzaCaretaker* that manages the history stack
   - ***Why we do it:*** This object controls when to save states and handles undo/redo operations
   - ***In simple terms:*** "I'm hiring an assistant who manages the photo album and knows which photo to show when you say 'undo'"
5. **Integrate with User Interface:**
   - ***What to do:*** Add undo/redo buttons to your pizza customization flow
   - ***Why we do it:*** Users need a way to trigger the memento functionality
   - ***In simple terms:*** "I'm adding 'Undo' and 'Redo' buttons to the pizza builder so customers can easily go back and forth"

20.7 Implementing the Memento Pattern

Step 1: Define the Memento Interface

Get Full Code Here

IPizzaMemento.cs

```
public interface IPizzaMemento
{
    string GetDescription();
    DateTime GetSnapshotTime();
}
```

Step 2: Define the Originator Interface

IOriginator.cs

```
public interface IOriginator
{
    IPizzaMemento SaveState();
    void RestoreState(IPizzaMemento memento);
}
```

Step 3: Make CustomPizza Originator (Can Save/Restore State)

CustomPizza.cs

```
public class CustomPizza : IPizza, IOriginator
{
  public string Name { get; private set; }
  public decimal Price { get; private set; }
  public List<(ToppingFlyweight Topping, int Quantity)> Toppings { get; private set; }
  public bool ExtraCheese { get; private set; }
  public bool StuffedCrust { get; private set; }
  public bool GlutenFree { get; private set; }

  internal CustomPizza(string name, decimal price, List<(ToppingFlyweight Topping, int Quantity)>
toppings, bool extraCheese, bool stuffedCrust, bool glutenFree)
  {
    Name = name;
    Price = price;
    Toppings = toppings ?? new List<(ToppingFlyweight, int)>();
    ExtraCheese = extraCheese;
    StuffedCrust = stuffedCrust;
    GlutenFree = glutenFree;
  }

  public IPizzaMemento SaveState(){
    return new PizzaMemento(
      this.Name,
      this.Price,
      new List<(ToppingFlyweight Topping, int Quantity)>(this.Toppings), // Deep copy
      this.ExtraCheese,
      this.StuffedCrust,
      this.GlutenFree
    );
  }

  public void RestoreState(IPizzaMemento memento)
  {
    if (memento is PizzaMemento pizzaMemento){
      this.Name = pizzaMemento.Name;
      this.Price = pizzaMemento.Price;
      this.Toppings = new List<(ToppingFlyweight Topping, int Quantity)>(pizzaMemento.Toppings);
      this.ExtraCheese = pizzaMemento.ExtraCheese;
      this.StuffedCrust = pizzaMemento.StuffedCrust;
      this.GlutenFree = pizzaMemento.GlutenFree;
    }
  }
  //... existing methods (Prepare, Bake, Box, GetToppingNames, Clone) ..
}
```

Step 4: Implement Concrete Memento

PizzaMemento.cs

```
public class PizzaMemento : IPizzaMemento
{
    public string Name { get; }
    public decimal Price { get; }
    public List<(ToppingFlyweight Topping, int Quantity)> Toppings { get; }
    public bool ExtraCheese { get; }
    public bool StuffedCrust { get; }
    public bool GlutenFree { get; }
    public DateTime SnapshotTime { get; }

    public PizzaMemento(string name, decimal price,
                List<(ToppingFlyweight Topping, int Quantity)> toppings,
                bool extraCheese, bool stuffedCrust, bool glutenFree)
    {
        Name = name;
        Price = price;
        Toppings = new List<(ToppingFlyweight Topping, int Quantity)>(toppings); // Deep copy
        ExtraCheese = extraCheese;
        StuffedCrust = stuffedCrust;
        GlutenFree = glutenFree;
        SnapshotTime = DateTime.Now;
    }

    public string GetDescription()
    {
        var toppingsDesc = string.Join(", ", Toppings.Select(t => $"{t.Quantity}x {t.Topping.Name}"));
        return $"{Name} (${Price}) - Toppings: {toppingsDesc} - {SnapshotTime:HH:mm:ss}";
    }

    public DateTime GetSnapshotTime() => SnapshotTime;
}
```

Step 5: Create the Caretaker (Manages History)

PizzaCaretaker.cs

```
public class PizzaCaretaker
{
    private readonly Stack<IPizzaMemento> _undoStack = new Stack<IPizzaMemento>();
    private readonly Stack<IPizzaMemento> _redoStack = new Stack<IPizzaMemento>();
    private readonly int _maxHistorySize;

    public PizzaCaretaker(int maxHistorySize = 10)
    {
        _maxHistorySize = maxHistorySize;
    }
```

MEMENTO

```
public void SaveState(IOriginator originator)
{
    // Clear redo stack when new action is performed
    _redoStack.Clear();

    var memento = originator.SaveState();
    _undoStack.Push(memento);

    // Limit history size
    if (_undoStack.Count > _maxHistorySize)
    {
        // Remove oldest memento (bottom of stack)
        var tempStack = new Stack<IPizzaMemento>();
        while (_undoStack.Count > 1) // Keep one extra to remove the oldest
        {
            tempStack.Push(_undoStack.Pop());
        }
        _undoStack.Clear();
        while (tempStack.Count > 0)
        {
            _undoStack.Push(tempStack.Pop());
        }
    }

    Console.WriteLine($"[Memento] Saved state: {memento.GetDescription()}");
}

public bool Undo(IOriginator originator)
{
    if (_undoStack.Count <= 1) // Need at least 2 states to undo (current + previous)
        return false;

    var currentState = _undoStack.Pop();
    var previousState = _undoStack.Peek(); // Keep it for potential redo

    _redoStack.Push(currentState);
    originator.RestoreState(previousState);

    Console.WriteLine($"[Memento] Undo to: {previousState.GetDescription()}");
    return true;
}

public bool Redo(IOriginator originator)
{
    if (_redoStack.Count == 0)
        return false;

    var nextState = _redoStack.Pop();
    _undoStack.Push(nextState);
    originator.RestoreState(nextState);
```

```
        Console.WriteLine($"[Memento] Redo to: {nextState.GetDescription()}");
        return true;
    }

    public void ClearHistory()
    {
        _undoStack.Clear();
        _redoStack.Clear();
    }

    public bool CanUndo => _undoStack.Count > 1;
    public bool CanRedo => _redoStack.Count > 0;
    public int HistorySize => _undoStack.Count;

    public IEnumerable<string> GetHistory()
    {
        return _undoStack.Select(m => m.GetDescription()).Reverse();
    }
}
```

Step 6: Enhanced PizzaBuilder with Memento Support

PizzaBuilder.cs

```
public class PizzaBuilder
{
    private string _name;
    private decimal _basePrice;
    private List<(ToppingFlyweight Topping, int Quantity)> _toppings =
        new List<(ToppingFlyweight, int)>();
    private bool _extraCheese;
    private bool _stuffedCrust;
    private bool _glutenFree;

    private readonly PizzaCaretaker _caretaker = new PizzaCaretaker();
    private CustomPizza _currentPizza;

    public PizzaBuilder(string name, decimal basePrice)
    {
        _name = name;
        _basePrice = basePrice;
        // Create initial pizza state
        _currentPizza = CreatePizzaFromCurrentState();
        _caretaker.SaveState(_currentPizza);
    }
```

MEMENTO

```
    public PizzaBuilder AddTopping(string toppingName, int quantity = 1)
    {
        SaveCurrentState();
        var topping = ToppingFlyweightFactory.GetTopping(toppingName);
        _toppings.Add((topping, quantity));
        UpdateCurrentPizza();
        return this;
    }

    public PizzaBuilder RemoveTopping(string toppingName)
    {
        SaveCurrentState();
        var topping = _toppings.FirstOrDefault(t => t.Topping.Name.Equals(toppingName,
StringComparison.OrdinalIgnoreCase));
        if (topping.Topping != null)
        {
            _toppings.Remove(topping);
            UpdateCurrentPizza();
        }
        return this;
    }

    public PizzaBuilder SetExtraCheese(bool extraCheese)
    {
        SaveCurrentState();
        _extraCheese = extraCheese;
        UpdateCurrentPizza();
        return this;
    }

    public PizzaBuilder SetStuffedCrust(bool stuffedCrust)
    {
        SaveCurrentState();
        _stuffedCrust = stuffedCrust;
        UpdateCurrentPizza();
        return this;
    }

    public PizzaBuilder SetGlutenFree(bool glutenFree)
    {
        SaveCurrentState();
        _glutenFree = glutenFree;
        UpdateCurrentPizza();
        return this;
    }
```

```
public bool Undo()
{
    if (_caretaker.Undo(_currentPizza))
    {
        // Update builder state from restored pizza
        UpdateBuilderFromPizza(_currentPizza);
        Console.WriteLine("✓ Undone last change");
        return true;
    }
    return false;
}

public bool Redo()
{
    if (_caretaker.Redo(_currentPizza))
    {
        // Update builder state from restored pizza
        UpdateBuilderFromPizza(_currentPizza);
        Console.WriteLine("✓ Redone last change");
        return true;
    }
    return false;
}

public IPizza Build()
{
    // Return a clone of the current pizza (immutable)
    return _currentPizza.Clone() as IPizza;
}

public IPizza GetCurrentPizza() => _currentPizza;

// Helper methods
private void SaveCurrentState()
{
    _caretaker.SaveState(_currentPizza);
}

private void UpdateCurrentPizza()
{
    _currentPizza = CreatePizzaFromCurrentState();
}

private CustomPizza CreatePizzaFromCurrentState()
{
    decimal finalPrice = CalculateFinalPrice();
    return new CustomPizza(_name, finalPrice, _toppings, _extraCheese, _stuffedCrust,
_glutenFree);
}
```

MEMENTO

```
    private void UpdateBuilderFromPizza(CustomPizza pizza)
    {
        _name = pizza.Name;
        _basePrice = pizza.Price;
        _toppings = new List<(ToppingFlyweight Topping, int Quantity)>(pizza.Toppings);
        _extraCheese = pizza.ExtraCheese;
        _stuffedCrust = pizza.StuffedCrust;
        _glutenFree = pizza.GlutenFree;
    }

    private decimal CalculateFinalPrice()
    {
        decimal finalPrice = _basePrice;

        foreach (var (topping, quantity) in _toppings)
        {
            finalPrice += topping.BasePrice * quantity;
        }

        if (_extraCheese) finalPrice += 1.0m;
        if (_stuffedCrust) finalPrice += 1.5m;
        if (_glutenFree) finalPrice += 2.0m;

        return finalPrice;
    }

    public void DisplayCurrentState()
    {
        Console.WriteLine($"Current: {_currentPizza.Name} - ${_currentPizza.Price}");
        Console.WriteLine($"Toppings: {string.Join(", ", _currentPizza.GetToppingNames())}");
        Console.WriteLine($"Extra Cheese: {_extraCheese}, Stuffed Crust: {_stuffedCrust}, Gluten Free:
{_glutenFree}");
        Console.WriteLine($"Undo available: {_caretaker.CanUndo}, Redo available:
{_caretaker.CanRedo}");
    }

    public void DisplayHistory()
    {
        Console.WriteLine("Pizza Customization History:");
        foreach (var state in _caretaker.GetHistory())
        {
            Console.WriteLine($"  - {state}");
        }
    }

    public bool CanUndo => _caretaker.CanUndo;
    public bool CanRedo => _caretaker.CanRedo;
}
```

Step 7: Usage in Client Code

Program.cs

```
private static IPizza BuildACustomPizza()
{
   Console.WriteLine("Welcome to the Pizza Customizer!");

   // 1. Get the base details
   Console.Write("Enter a name for your custom pizza: ");
   string name = Console.ReadLine();

   Console.Write("Enter the base price for your pizza: $");
   decimal basePrice = decimal.Parse(Console.ReadLine());

   // 2. Initialize the Builder with the base details
   var pizzaBuilder = new PizzaBuilder(name, basePrice);

   // 3. Customize the pizza through a series of prompts
   Console.WriteLine("Building your custom pizza...");
   Console.WriteLine("Commands: add [topping], remove [topping], cheese [true/false], crust
[true/false], gluten [true/false], undo, redo, history, done");

   while (true)
   {
      pizzaBuilder.DisplayCurrentState();
      Console.Write("\nEnter command: ");

      var input = Console.ReadLine().ToLower().Split(' ');
      var command = input[0];
      var parameter = input.Length > 1 ? input[1] : null;

      switch (command)
      {
         case "add":
            if (!string.IsNullOrEmpty(parameter))
            {
               pizzaBuilder.AddTopping(parameter);
               Console.WriteLine($"✓ Added {parameter}");
            }
            break;

         case "remove":
            if (!string.IsNullOrEmpty(parameter))
            {
               pizzaBuilder.RemoveTopping(parameter);
               Console.WriteLine($"✓ Removed {parameter}");
            }
            break;
```

MEMENTO

```
            case "cheese":
                if (bool.TryParse(parameter, out bool cheese))
                {
                    pizzaBuilder.SetExtraCheese(cheese);
                    Console.WriteLine($"✓ Extra cheese: {cheese}");
                }
                break;

            case "crust":
                if (bool.TryParse(parameter, out bool crust))
                {
                    pizzaBuilder.SetStuffedCrust(crust);
                    Console.WriteLine($"✓ Stuffed crust: {crust}");
                }
                break;

            case "gluten":
                if (bool.TryParse(parameter, out bool gluten))
                {
                    pizzaBuilder.SetGlutenFree(gluten);
                    Console.WriteLine($"✓ Gluten free: {gluten}");
                }
                break;

            case "undo":
                if (!pizzaBuilder.Undo())
                    Console.WriteLine("✗ Nothing to undo");
                break;

            case "redo":
                if (!pizzaBuilder.Redo())
                    Console.WriteLine("✗ Nothing to redo");
                break;

            case "history":
                pizzaBuilder.DisplayHistory();
                break;

            case "done":
                goto finish;

            default:
                Console.WriteLine("Unknown command. Available: add, remove, cheese, crust, gluten, undo,
redo, history, done");
                break;
        }
    }
```

```
finish:
    var finalPizza = pizzaBuilder.Build();
    // 5. Display the details to the user
    Console.WriteLine("\n✅ Your custom pizza is ready!");
    Console.WriteLine($"\n🎉 Final Pizza: {finalPizza.Name}");
    Console.WriteLine($"💲 Price: ${finalPizza.Price}");
    Console.WriteLine($"🍕 Toppings: {string.Join(", ", finalPizza.GetToppingNames())}");

    return finalPizza;
}
```

Key Test Points for Memento Pattern Validation

1. Basic Undo/Redo Functionality Test
- **Objective:** Verify basic undo/redo operations work.
- **Test Action:** Make changes, undo, then redo.
- **Expected Result:** State should restore correctly after undo/redo.

2. Multiple Sequential Operations Test
- **Objective:** Verify multiple undo/redo operations in sequence.
- **Test Action:** Make multiple changes, undo several times, redo several times.
- **Expected Result:** Should traverse history correctly.

3. History Limit Test
- **Objective:** Verify history size limits work.
- **Test Action:** Make more changes than history limit.
- **Expected Result:** Oldest states should be discarded when limit exceeded.

4. State Integrity Test
- **Objective:** Verify restored states are complete and accurate.
- **Test Action:** Save state, modify, then restore and verify all properties.
- **Expected Result:** All pizza properties should restore exactly.

5. Boundary Conditions Test
- **Objective:** Verify behavior at history boundaries.
- **Test Action:** Try to undo when no history, redo when nothing to redo.
- **Expected Result:** Should handle gracefully without errors.

6. Complex Modification Sequence Test
- **Objective:** Verify pattern handles complex modification sequences.
- **Test Action:** Mix different types of modifications with undo/redo.
- **Expected Result:** All modification types should undo/redo correctly.

7. Integration with Builder Pattern Test
- **Objective:** Verify memento works seamlessly with builder pattern.
- **Test Action:** Use builder fluent interface with undo/redo.
- **Expected Result:** Builder should maintain state consistency.

8. **Memory Efficiency Test**
   - **Objective:** Verify mementos don't cause memory bloat (with flyweights).
   - **Test Action:** Create many pizzas with shared toppings.
   - **Expected Result:** Memory usage should be reasonable due to flyweights.
9. **Real User Workflow Test**
   - **Objective:** Test common user customization workflows.
   - **Test Action:** Simulate typical user pizza building behavior.
   - **Expected Result:** Should handle realistic usage patterns.

If these tests pass, your Memento pattern successfully solves Oops Moment #12 and provides robust undo/redo functionality for pizza customization!

20.8 Why the Memento Pattern Matters

- **User Experience:** Customers can experiment without fear
- **Data Integrity:** No accidental data loss during customization
- **Flexible Workflow:** Support for complex editing scenarios
- **State Management:** Clean separation of state storage from business logic
- **Audit Trail:** Complete history of changes for debugging

20.9 Mini-Exercise: Enhanced Memento Features

Task: Add a "Save Favorite" feature that lets customers save specific pizza configurations and restore them later.

Bonus: Implement a "Compare with Previous" feature that shows the differences between current and previous pizza states.

20.10 When to Use the Memento Pattern

"Use the Memento pattern when:

- You need to implement undo/redo functionality in your application
- You want to save snapshots of an object's state without exposing its internal structure
- Direct access to an object's fields/getters/setters would break encapsulation
- You need to maintain a history of state changes for audit purposes."

20.11 Transition to Chapter 21

"Now that customers can freely customize their pizzas with full undo/redo capabilities using our Memento implementation, let's tackle another communication challenge. Next, we'll explore the **Observer** pattern to automatically notify customers and kitchen staff when order status changes."

> **Next Up: Chapter 21 — Observer: Real-Time Order Status Notifications**
> Ready to implement automatic notifications for order status changes? Let's build a system where interested parties get instant updates without constantly checking!

Chapter 21

Observer — Real-Time Order Status Notifications

Setting The Stage

Your order status changes happen silently. Customers, kitchen staff, and managers have no way to know when orders progress through different stages.

> In this chapter, you'll:
> 1. **Identify Pitfalls:** Identify the silent status change problem in your order processing
> 2. **Learn the Pattern:** Learn the Observer pattern to create publish-subscribe notification system
> 3. **Build Real-time Notifications:** Build automatic real-time notifications for order status changes
> 4. **Create a Flexible System:** Create a flexible system where new subscribers can join without modifying core logic

21.1 Hook: What's the Pain?

"Right now, when an order moves from 'Received' to 'Baking' to 'Delivered', nobody knows unless they constantly check. Customers wonder where their pizza is, kitchen staff don't know when new orders arrive, and managers can't track progress. We need automatic notifications that ping everyone who cares about order status changes!"

21.2 The Problem in Our Pizza App

Silent order status changes (Oops Moment #13)

```
// ❌ OLD: Status changes happen silently
order.Status = "Baking"; // No one knows!
order.Status = "Ready";  // Still no notifications!
order.Status = "Delivered"; // Customer left wondering...

// Manual notifications are scattered and easy to forget
_emailNotifier.Send(...);
_smsNotifier.Send(...);
// What about kitchen display? Manager dashboard? Mobile app?
```

Why This Hurts:

- **Poor Customer Experience:** No updates on order progress
- **Inefficient Operations:** Staff must constantly check order status
- **Missed Notifications:** Easy to forget to notify someone
- **Tight Coupling:** Order class knows about specific notifiers
- **Hard to Extend:** Adding new notification channels requires code changes

OBSERVER

21.3 The Formal Pattern: Observer

Pattern Definition

> "**Observer** is a behavioral pattern that lets you define a subscription mechanism to notify multiple objects about any events that happen to the object they're observing."

In Simpler Terms: The Observer pattern is like setting up a "status update newsletter" for your orders. Any component (email, SMS, kitchen screen) can subscribe to order status changes, and they'll automatically get notified whenever something important happens, without the order needing to know who's listening.

21.4 Understanding the Pattern

The Real-World Analogy: Restaurant Order Board

Imagine a busy pizza restaurant:

- **Without Observer:** Waiters constantly check with chefs, chefs shout across the kitchen, delivery drivers peek into the oven
- **With Observer:** There's a central order board. When a pizza goes in the oven, the board updates. Waiters, chefs, and drivers just watch the board - they automatically know the status without asking

21.5 How the Observer Pattern Solves It

Instead of this manual approach:

```
// ❌ Manual, scattered notifications
order.Status = "Delivered";
_emailNotifier.Send("Order delivered");
_smsNotifier.Send("Pizza arrived!");
_kitchenDisplay.Update(order);
// Forgot to update manager dashboard!
```

We'll create this automatic system:

```
// ✅ Automatic, centralized notifications
order.Status = "Delivered"; // That's it!
// All subscribers automatically notified:
// - Email service
// - SMS service
// - Kitchen display
// - Manager dashboard
// - Mobile app
// - Analytics service
```

21.6 The Implementation Blueprint: Observer Steps

Think of implementing the Observer pattern like setting up a radio station. The order is the broadcaster, and various services are the listeners tuned to your frequency.

1. **Define the Subject Interface:**
   - ***What to do:*** Create *IOrderSubject* with methods for attaching, detaching, and notifying observers
   - ***Why we do it:*** This defines the contract for any observable order
   - ***In simple terms:*** "I'm creating the radio station equipment that can accept listeners and broadcast messages"
2. **Define the Observer Interface:**
   - ***What to do:*** Create *IOrderObserver* with an update method
   - ***Why we do it:*** This defines what it means to be a listener for order updates
   - ***In simple terms:*** "I'm defining what a radio must have to receive our broadcasts (a tuner)"
3. **Make Order Observable:**
   - ***What to do:*** Enhance your *Order* class to implement *IOrderSubject*
   - ***Why we do it:*** This turns orders into broadcasters that can notify subscribers
   - ***In simple terms:*** "I'm upgrading our orders to become radio stations"
4. **Create Concrete Observers:**
   - ***What to do:*** Build observer classes for each notification type
   - ***Why we do it:*** These are the actual listeners that react to order updates
   - ***In simple terms:*** "I'm building different types of radios (email radio, SMS radio, display radio)"
5. **Set Up Subscriptions:**
   - ***What to do:*** Attach observers to orders at the right time
   - ***Why we do it:*** This connects listeners to broadcasters
   - ***In simple terms:*** "I'm tuning all the radios to our order broadcast frequency"
6. **Trigger Notifications:**
   - ***What to do:*** Automatically notify observers when order status changes
   - ***Why we do it:*** This makes the system reactive instead of proactive
   - ***In simple terms:*** "I'm making sure the radio station broadcasts every time something important happens"

21.7 Implementing the Observer Pattern

Step 1: Define Observer Interfaces

IOrderObserver.cs

```
public interface IOrderObserver
{
  void Update(Order order, string
statusChange);
}
```

IOrderSubject.cs

```
public interface IOrderSubject
{
  void Attach(IOrderObserver observer);
  void Detach(IOrderObserver observer);
  void NotifyObservers(string statusChange);
}
```

OBSERVER

Step 2: Make Order Observable

Order.cs

```
public class Order : IOrderSubject
{
  private readonly List<IOrderObserver> _observers = new List<IOrderObserver>();
  private string _status;

  public string Status
  {
    get => _status;
    set
    {
      if (_status != value)
      {
        string oldStatus = _status;
        _status = value;
        NotifyObservers($"Status changed from {oldStatus} to {value}");
      }
    }
  }

  // ... existing Order properties ...

  public void Attach(IOrderObserver observer)
  {
    if (!_observers.Contains(observer))
      _observers.Add(observer);
  }

  public void Detach(IOrderObserver observer)
  {
    _observers.Remove(observer);
  }

  public void NotifyObservers(string statusChange)
  {
    foreach (var observer in _observers.ToList()) // ToList for thread safety
    {
      observer.Update(this, statusChange);
    }
  }
}
```

Step 3: Create Concrete Observers

EmailOrderObserver.cs

```
public class EmailOrderObserver : IOrderObserver
{
  private readonly EmailNotification _emailNotifier;

  public EmailOrderObserver(EmailNotification emailNotifier)
  {
    _emailNotifier = emailNotifier;
  }

  public void Update(Order order, string statusChange)
  {
    if (statusChange.Contains("Delivered"))
    {
      _emailNotifier.Send($"Order #{order.OrderId} delivered successfully!");
    }
    else if (statusChange.Contains("Failed"))
    {
      _emailNotifier.Send($"Order #{order.OrderId} failed: {statusChange}");
    }
  }
}
```

SMSOrderObserver.cs

```
public class SMSOrderObserver : IOrderObserver
{
  private readonly SmsNotification _smsNotifier;

  public SMSOrderObserver(SmsNotification smsNotifier)
  {
    _smsNotifier = smsNotifier;
  }

  public void Update(Order order, string statusChange)
  {
    if (statusChange.Contains("Baking") || statusChange.Contains("Delivered"))
    {
      _smsNotifier.Send($"Order update: {statusChange}");
    }
  }
}
```

KitchenDisplayObserver.cs

```
public class KitchenDisplayObserver : IOrderObserver
{
  public void Update(Order order, string statusChange)
  {
    Console.WriteLine($"[KITCHEN DISPLAY] Order #{order.OrderId}: {statusChange}");
  }
}
```

Step 4: Update OrderProcessor to Use Observers

OrderProcessor.cs

```
public class OrderProcessor : IOrderProcessorFacade
{
  private readonly IOrderHandler _validationChain;
  private readonly IKitchenMediator _mediator;
  private readonly List<IOrderObserver> _globalObservers;

  public OrderProcessor(IOrderHandler validationChain, IKitchenMediator mediator)
  {
    _validationChain = validationChain;
    _mediator = mediator;
    _globalObservers = new List<IOrderObserver>();
  }

  public void AddGlobalObserver(IOrderObserver observer)
  {
    _globalObservers.Add(observer);
  }

  public async Task<bool> PlaceOrder(Order order)
  {
    Console.WriteLine($"[OrderProcessor] Processing order #{order.OrderId}...");

    // Attach global observers to this order
    foreach (var observer in _globalObservers)
    {
      order.Attach(observer);
    }

    if (!_validationChain.Handle(order))
      return false;

    return await _mediator.ProcessOrder(order);
  }
}
```

Step 5: Update Program.cs Setup

Program.cs

```
// In Program.Main():
// Create observers
var emailObserver = new EmailOrderObserver(emailNotifier);
var smsObserver = new SMSOrderObserver(smsNotifier);
var kitchenObserver = new KitchenDisplayObserver();

// Create order processor
var orderProcessor = new OrderProcessor(validationChain, mediator);

// Register global observers
orderProcessor.AddGlobalObserver(emailObserver);
orderProcessor.AddGlobalObserver(smsObserver);
orderProcessor.AddGlobalObserver(kitchenObserver);

// Process order - observers will be notified automatically!
bool success = await orderProcessor.PlaceOrder(order);
```

Key Test Points for Observer Pattern Validation

1. Observer Registration and Notification Test

- **Objective:** Verify observers can register and receive status change notifications.
- **Test Action:** Create order, attach observer, change status, verify notification received.
- **Expected Result:** Observer should receive update with correct order and status change information.

2. Multiple Observers Coordination Test

- **Objective:** Ensure multiple observers receive notifications simultaneously.
- **Test Action:** Attach multiple observers to same order, change status, verify all notified.
- **Expected Result:** All attached observers should receive the same notification.

3. Observer Detachment Test

- **Objective:** Verify detached observers stop receiving notifications.
- **Test Action:** Attach observer, change status, detach observer, change status again.
- **Expected Result:** Observer should only receive notifications while attached.

4. Same Status Change Suppression Test

- **Objective:** Verify no notifications sent for identical status changes.
- **Test Action:** Set same status multiple times consecutively.
- **Expected Result:** Observer should only receive notification for actual changes.

5. Global Observer Registration Test

- **Objective:** Verify OrderProcessor automatically attaches global observers to new orders.

- **Test Action:** Register global observers, process new order, verify attachment.
- **Expected Result:** Global observers should be automatically attached to all new orders.

6. **Observer Message Content Validation Test**
   - **Objective:** Verify notification messages contain correct order details and status changes.
   - **Test Action:** Change order status with specific details, verify message content.
   - **Expected Result:** Messages should include order ID, old status, new status.
7. **Concurrent Modification Safety Test**
   - **Objective:** Verify observer list modifications during notification don't cause errors.
   - **Test Action:** Have observer detach itself during notification process.
   - **Expected Result:** System should handle concurrent modifications gracefully.
8. **Observer Priority and Order Test**
   - **Objective:** Verify observers are notified in consistent order.
   - **Test Action:** Attach multiple observers, track notification sequence.
   - **Expected Result:** Observers should be notified in attachment order or defined priority.
9. **Error Handling in Observers Test**
   - **Objective:** Verify one observer's failure doesn't break notification to others.
   - **Test Action:** Create failing observer among working ones, trigger notification.
   - **Expected Result:** Working observers should still receive notifications despite one failing.
10. **Memory Management and Cleanup Test**
    - **Objective:** Verify observers don't cause memory leaks when orders are completed.
    - **Test Action:** Process multiple orders, check observer references are properly released.
    - **Expected Result:** Completed orders should not retain observer references.

These 10 tests comprehensively validate your Observer pattern implementation while ensuring system reliability and performance.

21.8 Why the Observer Pattern Matters

- **Real-Time Updates:** Automatic notifications without manual checks
- **Loose Coupling:** Subjects and observers don't depend on each other
- **Extensibility:** Easy to add new notification channels without changing core logic
- **Event-Driven Architecture:** Reactive system that responds to state changes
- **Centralized Coordination:** Single source of truth for status changes

21.9 Mini-Exercise: Enhanced Observer Features

Task: Add a "Priority Notification" system where urgent orders (large groups, VIP customers) trigger immediate manager alerts.

Bonus: Implement a "Selective Subscription" feature where customers can choose which notifications they want (SMS only, email only, or both).

21.10 When to Use the Observer Pattern

"Use the Observer pattern when:

- You need to maintain consistency between related objects without making them tightly coupled.
- A change to one object requires changing others, and you don't know how many objects need to be changed
- An object should be able to notify other objects without making assumptions about who those objects are.
- You want to create a one-to-many dependency between objects so that when one object changes state, all its dependents are notified automatically."

21.11 Transition to Chapter 22

"Now that we have real-time automatic notifications working seamlessly with our Observer pattern implementation, let's tackle the chaotic order status management. Next, we'll explore the **State** pattern to bring structure and rules to our order status transitions."

> **Next Up: Chapter 22 — State: Structured Order Status Management**
> Ready to bring order to order status chaos? Let's build a state machine that ensures valid status transitions and encapsulates behavior for each state!

Get Full Code Here

Chapter 22

State — Structured Order Status Management

Setting The Stage

Your order status is managed with raw strings scattered throughout the code. Status transitions happen arbitrarily without validation, and each status has different behaviors but no clear structure.

> In this chapter, you'll:
> 1. **Identify Pitfalls:** Identify the chaos of string-based status management
> 2. **Learn the Pattern:** Learn the State pattern to encapsulate status-specific behavior
> 3. **Build A State Machine:** Build a proper state machine for order lifecycle
> 4. **Ensure Valid State Transitions:** Ensure valid status transitions and centralized behavior

22.1 Hook: What's the Pain?

"Right now, order status is just a string that can be set to anything from anywhere. We've seen 'Deliverd' typos, orders jumping from 'Received' to 'Delivered' without baking, and scattered logic checking if (status == "Baking") everywhere. We need a system that knows the rules of order progression and encapsulates what each status means!"

22.2 The Problem in Our Pizza App

Raw string status with scattered transitions (Oops Moment #11), (Oops Moment #15) , (Oops Moment #23), (Oops Moment #32)

```
// ❌ OLD: String-based status with no validation
order.Status = "Baking"; // Can set anything, anywhere
order.Status = "Delivered"; // Can skip steps!
order.Status = "Deliverd"; // Typos break the system!

// Logic scattered everywhere:
if (order.Status == "Baking") { /* kitchen logic */ }
else if (order.Status == "Packed") { /* packing logic */ }
else if (order.Status == "Delivered") { /* delivery logic */ }
// Adding new status? Change every if/else!
```

Why This Hurts:

- **No Validation:** Invalid status transitions are possible
- **Scattered Logic:** Status behavior spread across multiple classes
- **Brittle Code:** Typos and magic strings break the system
- **No Encapsulation:** Each status doesn't own its behavior
- **Hard to Extend:** Adding new status requires modifying many files

22.3 The Formal Pattern: State

Pattern Definition

> ***"State** is a behavioral pattern that lets an object alter its behavior when its internal state changes. It appears as if the object changed its class."*

In Simpler Terms: The State pattern is like having specialized managers for each phase of your order. When an order is "Received", the *ReceivedManager* handles it. When it moves to "Baking", the *BakingManager* takes over. Each manager knows exactly what should happen in their phase and who should handle it next.

22.4 Understanding the Pattern

The Real-World Analogy: Order Progress in Restaurant

Imagine tracking a pizza order in a real restaurant:

- **Without State:** One person trying to remember all rules: "If it's received, do this. If it's baking, do that. If it's packed, do something else..."
- **With State:** Different specialists: Receiving clerk → Baking chef → Packing staff → Delivery driver. Each specialist knows their job and who to hand off to next.

22.5 How the State Pattern Solves It

Instead of this scattered approach:

```
// ❌ String checks everywhere
if (order.Status == "Received") { /* validation logic */ }
if (order.Status == "Baking") { /* kitchen logic */ }
if (order.Status == "Delivered") { /* notification logic */ }
```

We'll create this encapsulated approach:

```
// ✅ Each state knows its behavior
order.CurrentState.Validate(); // State-specific validation
order.CurrentState.Process();  // State-specific processing
order.CurrentState.Next();     // State knows valid next steps

// States handle their own transitions:
_receivedState.TransitionToBaking();
_bakingState.TransitionToPacked();
_packedState.TransitionToDelivered();
```

22.6 The Implementation Blueprint: State Steps

Think of implementing the State pattern like hiring specialized department managers for your pizza restaurant. Each manager knows everything about their department and the proper handoff procedures.

1. Define the State Interface:

- ***What to do:*** Create *IOrderState* with methods for state behavior and transitions
- ***Why we do it:*** This defines what every state must be able to do
- ***In simple terms:*** "I'm creating a job description that every department manager must follow"

STATE

2. **Implement Concrete States:**
    - ***What to do:*** Create classes for each order state (*ReceivedState*, *BakingState*, *PackedState*, etc.)
    - ***Why we do it:*** Each state encapsulates its specific behavior and valid transitions.
    - ***In simple terms:*** "I'm hiring and training specialized managers for receiving, baking, packing, and delivery".
3. **Refactor Order Class:**
    - ***What to do:*** Replace string Status with State object and delegate behavior.
    - ***Why we do it:*** The order delegates work to its current state instead of checking strings.
    - ***In simple terms:*** "I'm giving each order a current manager who handles all decisions".
4. **Implement State Transitions:**
    - ***What to do:*** Each state knows what states it can transition to and how.
    - ***Why we do it:*** This ensures only valid state progressions can occur.
    - ***In simple terms:*** "I'm teaching each manager who they can hand off to and the proper handoff procedure".
5. **Integrate with Existing System:**
    - ***What to do:*** Update order processing to use state pattern instead of string checks.
    - ***Why we do it:*** This brings the benefits of state pattern to your existing workflow.
    - ***In simple terms:*** "I'm updating our restaurant procedures to use the new department managers".

22.7 Implementing the State Pattern

Step 1: Define State Interfaces

IOrderState.cs

```
public interface IOrderState
{
    string StatusName { get; }
    bool CanTransitionTo(IOrderState nextState);
    void ProcessOrder(Order order);
    void CancelOrder(Order order);
    void UpdateStatus(Order order, IOrderState newState);
    string[] GetPossibleNextStates();
}
```

Step 2: Implement Concrete States

OrderStates.cs

```
public abstract class BaseOrderState : IOrderState
{
   public abstract string StatusName { get; }

   public virtual bool CanTransitionTo(IOrderState nextState)
   {
      return GetPossibleNextStates().Contains(nextState.StatusName);
   }

   public abstract void ProcessOrder(Order order);
   public abstract void CancelOrder(Order order);

   public virtual void UpdateStatus(Order order, IOrderState newState)
   {
      if (CanTransitionTo(newState))
      {
         order.ChangeState(newState);
         Console.WriteLine($"[State] Order #{order.OrderId} transitioned from {this.StatusName} to
{newState.StatusName}");
      }
      else
      {
         throw new InvalidOperationException($"Cannot transition from {StatusName} to
{newState.StatusName}");
      }
   }

   public abstract string[] GetPossibleNextStates();
}

// Concrete State: Received
public class ReceivedState : BaseOrderState
{
   public override string StatusName => "Received";

   public override void ProcessOrder(Order order)
   {
      Console.WriteLine($"[ReceivedState] Starting processing for order #{order.OrderId}");
      // Validation, inventory check, payment processing
      if (order.OrderItem != null)
      {
         this.UpdateStatus(order, OrderStateFactory.BakingState);
      }
   }
```

```
    public override void CancelOrder(Order order)
    {
        Console.WriteLine($"[ReceivedState] Cancelling order #{order.OrderId}");
        this.UpdateStatus(order, OrderStateFactory.CancelledState);
    }

    public override string[] GetPossibleNextStates()
    {
        return new[] { "Baking", "Cancelled" };
    }
}

// Concrete State: Baking
public class BakingState : BaseOrderState
{
    public override string StatusName => "Baking";

    public override void ProcessOrder(Order order)
    {
        Console.WriteLine($"[BakingState] Baking order #{order.OrderId}");

        // Simulate baking process
        Console.WriteLine("🍕 Pizza is in the oven...");
        Thread.Sleep(1000);

        this.UpdateStatus(order, OrderStateFactory.PackedState);
    }

    public override void CancelOrder(Order order)
    {
        Console.WriteLine($"[BakingState] Cannot cancel order #{order.OrderId} - already baking!");
        // Could implement partial refund logic here
    }

    public override string[] GetPossibleNextStates()
    {
        return new[] { "Packed" }; // Can only go to Packed
    }
}

// Concrete State: Packed
public class PackedState : BaseOrderState
{
    public override string StatusName => "Packed";

    public override void ProcessOrder(Order order)
    {
        Console.WriteLine($"[PackedState] Order #{order.OrderId} is packed and ready for delivery");
        this.UpdateStatus(order, OrderStateFactory.OutForDeliveryState);
    }
```

```
    public override void CancelOrder(Order order)
    {
        Console.WriteLine($"[PackedState] Cannot cancel order #{order.OrderId} - already packed and
ready!");
    }

    public override string[] GetPossibleNextStates()
    {
        return new[] { "OutForDelivery" };
    }
}
// Concrete State: OutForDelivery
public class OutForDeliveryState : BaseOrderState
{
    public override string StatusName => "OutForDelivery";

    public override void ProcessOrder(Order order)
    {
        Console.WriteLine($"[OutForDeliveryState] Delivering order #{order.OrderId}");

        // Simulate delivery
        Console.WriteLine("🚚 Order is out for delivery...");
        Thread.Sleep(1500);

        this.UpdateStatus(order, OrderStateFactory.DeliveredState);
    }

    public override void CancelOrder(Order order)
    {
        Console.WriteLine($"[OutForDeliveryState] Cannot cancel order #{order.OrderId} - already out
for delivery!");
    }

    public override string[] GetPossibleNextStates()
    {
        return new[] { "Delivered" };
    }
}

// Concrete State: Delivered
public class DeliveredState : BaseOrderState
{
    public override string StatusName => "Delivered";

    public override void ProcessOrder(Order order)
    {
        Console.WriteLine($"[DeliveredState] Order #{order.OrderId} already delivered - no further
processing");
        order.TimeDelivered = DateTime.Now;
    }
```

```
    public override void CancelOrder(Order order)
    {
        Console.WriteLine($"[DeliveredState] Cannot cancel order #{order.OrderId} - already delivered!");
    }

    public override string[] GetPossibleNextStates()
    {
        return new string[0]; // Final state - no transitions
    }
}

// Concrete State: Cancelled
public class CancelledState : BaseOrderState
{
    public override string StatusName => "Cancelled";

    public override void ProcessOrder(Order order)
    {
        Console.WriteLine($"[CancelledState] Cannot process cancelled order #{order.OrderId}");
    }

    public override void CancelOrder(Order order)
    {
        Console.WriteLine($"[CancelledState] Order #{order.OrderId} already cancelled");
    }

    public override string[] GetPossibleNextStates()
    {
        return new string[0]; // Final state - no transitions
    }
}
```

Step 3: State Factory for Singleton States

OrderStateFactory.cs

```
public static class OrderStateFactory
{
    private static readonly Dictionary<string, IOrderState> _states = new Dictionary<string,
IOrderState>();
    static OrderStateFactory()
    {
        // Create singleton instances of each state
        _states["Received"] = new ReceivedState();
        _states["Baking"] = new BakingState();
        _states["Packed"] = new PackedState();
        _states["OutForDelivery"] = new OutForDeliveryState();
        _states["Delivered"] = new DeliveredState();
        _states["Cancelled"] = new CancelledState();
    }
```

```
        public static IOrderState ReceivedState => _states["Received"];
        public static IOrderState BakingState => _states["Baking"];
        public static IOrderState PackedState => _states["Packed"];
        public static IOrderState OutForDeliveryState => _states["OutForDelivery"];
        public static IOrderState DeliveredState => _states["Delivered"];
        public static IOrderState CancelledState => _states["Cancelled"];

        public static IOrderState GetState(string stateName)
        {
            if (_states.ContainsKey(stateName))
                return _states[stateName];
            throw new ArgumentException($"Unknown state: {stateName}");
        }
    }
}
```

Step 4: Refactor Order Class to Use State Pattern

Order.cs

```
public class Order : IOrderSubject
{
    private IOrderState _currentState;
    private readonly List<IOrderObserver> _observers = new List<IOrderObserver>();

    public int OrderId { get; set; }
    public string CustomerName { get; set; }
    public string Address { get; set; }
    public IOrderItem OrderItem { get; set; }
    public List<IOrderItem> Items { get; set; }
    public List<OrderModifier> Modifiers { get; set; }
    public int Quantity { get; set; }
    public DateTime TimeOrdered { get; set; }
    public DateTime TimeDelivered { get; set; }

    // State-based status (replaces string Status)
    public string Status => _currentState.StatusName;

    public Order()
    {
        // Start in Received state
        _currentState = OrderStateFactory.ReceivedState;
        TimeOrdered = DateTime.Now;
    }
```

STATE

```
    public void ChangeState(IOrderState newState)
    {
        var oldState = _currentState;
        _currentState = newState;

        // Notify observers of state change
        NotifyObservers($"State changed from {oldState.StatusName} to {newState.StatusName}");
    }

    // Delegate state behavior to current state
    public void Process()
    {
        Console.WriteLine($"[Order] Processing order #{OrderId} in {Status} state");
        _currentState.ProcessOrder(this);
    }

    public void Cancel()
    {
        Console.WriteLine($"[Order] Attempting to cancel order #{OrderId}");
        _currentState.CancelOrder(this);
    }

    public bool CanTransitionTo(string stateName)
    {
        var targetState = OrderStateFactory.GetState(stateName);
        return _currentState.CanTransitionTo(targetState);
    }

    public string[] GetPossibleNextStates()
    {
        return _currentState.GetPossibleNextStates();
    }

    // Observer pattern methods (from previous chapter)
}
```

Step 4: Update Commands to use State Pattern

Replace hard-coded status like below:

```
//_order.Status = "Delivered";
//_order.Status = "Packed";
//_order.Status = "Baked";
```

to State Pattern order Process method as below:

```
_order.Process();
```

Step 5: Update OrderProcessor to Use State Pattern

OrderProcessor.cs

```
public class OrderProcessor : IOrderProcessorFacade
{
    private readonly IOrderHandler _validationChain;
    private readonly IKitchenMediator _mediator;
    private readonly List<IOrderObserver> _globalObservers;

    public OrderProcessor(IOrderHandler validationChain, IKitchenMediator mediator){
        _validationChain = validationChain;
        _mediator = mediator;
        _globalObservers = new List<IOrderObserver>();
    }

    public async Task<bool> PlaceOrder(Order order)
    {
        Console.WriteLine($"[OrderProcessor] Placing order #{order.OrderId}");

        // Attach global observers
        foreach (var observer in _globalObservers)
        {
            order.Attach(observer);
        }

        // Validate order using chain of responsibility
        if (!_validationChain.Handle(order))
        {
            Console.WriteLine("❌ Order validation failed");
            return false;
        }

    // 3. Use Mediator for service coordination (inventory, payment, etc.)
    bool mediatorSuccess = await _mediator.ProcessOrder(order);
    if (!mediatorSuccess)
    {
        Console.WriteLine("❌ Mediator coordination failed");
        return false;
    }

    // 4. Use State Pattern for order lifecycle management
    Console.WriteLine("🔄 Processing order through state machine...");
    order.Process(); // This triggers the state machine

    return mediatorSuccess;
    }
  //other methods
}
```


STATE

Step 6: Client Usage Demonstration

Program.cs

```
// In your Program.cs - demonstrate state pattern
private static void DemonstrateStatePattern()
{
    Console.WriteLine("=== State Pattern Demonstration ===");

    var order = new Order
    {
        OrderId = 1001,
        CustomerName = "State Pattern Test",
        Address = "123 Pattern St",
        OrderItem = new SimpleMenuItem("Test Pizza", 15.99m)
    };

    // Show initial state
    Console.WriteLine($"Initial State: {order.Status}");
    Console.WriteLine($"Possible next states: {string.Join(", ", order.GetPossibleNextStates())}");

    // Process through states
    order.Process(); // Received → Baking
    Console.WriteLine($"State after first process: {order.Status}");

    order.Process(); // Baking → Packed
    Console.WriteLine($"State after second process: {order.Status}");

    order.Process(); // Packed → OutForDelivery
    Console.WriteLine($"State after third process: {order.Status}");

    order.Process(); // OutForDelivery → Delivered
    Console.WriteLine($"Final State: {order.Status}");

    // Try to process delivered order
    order.Process(); // Should do nothing

    // Try invalid transition
    try
    {
        Console.WriteLine($"Can transition to Baking from Delivered:
{order.CanTransitionTo("Baking")}");
    }
    catch (Exception ex)
    {
        Console.WriteLine($"Expected error: {ex.Message}");
    }

    Console.WriteLine("=== State Demo Complete ===\n");
}
```

Key Test Points for State Pattern Validation

1. Initial State Test
- **Objective:** Verify order starts in correct initial state.
- **Test Action:** Create new order and check initial state.
- **Expected Result:** Order should start in "Received" state.

2. Valid State Transition Test
- **Objective:** Verify valid state transitions work correctly.
- **Test Action:** Process order through valid state sequence.
- **Expected Result:** States should transition in correct order without errors.

3. Invalid Transition Prevention Test
- **Objective:** Verify system prevents invalid state transitions.
- **Test Action:** Attempt illegal transitions and verify they're blocked.
- **Expected Result:** Invalid transitions should throw exceptions or return false.

4. State-Specific Behavior Test
- **Objective:** Verify each state implements correct behavior.
- **Test Action:** Test *ProcessOrder* and *CancelOrder* in different states.
- **Expected Result:** Each state should exhibit correct behavior.

5. Terminal State Test
- **Objective:** Verify terminal states don't allow further transitions.
- **Test Action:** Reach terminal states and attempt further processing.
- **Expected Result:** Terminal states should have no possible next states.

6. State Factory Test
- **Objective:** Verify state factory provides correct state instances.
- **Test Action:** Request states from factory and verify types.
- **Expected Result:** Factory should return correct state instances.

7. Observer Integration Test
- **Objective:** Verify state changes trigger observer notifications.
- **Test Action:** Attach observer and track state change notifications.
- **Expected Result:** Observers should receive notifications for each state change

8. Command Integration Test
- **Objective:** Verify commands properly use state transitions.
- **Test Action:** Execute kitchen commands and verify state progression.
- **Expected Result:** Commands should advance order through correct states.

9. State Data Consistency Test
- **Objective:** Verify order data remains consistent during state transitions.
- **Test Action:** Transition states and verify order properties are maintained.
- **Expected Result:** Order data should persist correctly through state changes.

10. Error Recovery Test
- **Objective:** Verify system handles errors during state transitions gracefully.
- **Test Action:** Simulate errors during state processing.
- **Expected Result:** System should maintain consistent state and handle errors.

These 10 tests validate that your State Pattern implementation correctly manages order lifecycle with proper transitions, behavior encapsulation, and system integration.

22.8 Why the State Pattern Matters

- **Validated Transitions:** No more invalid status jumps
- **Encapsulated Behavior:** Each state owns its logic
- **Clean Code:** No more string checks scattered everywhere
- **Easy Extensibility:** Add new states without breaking existing code
- **Maintainable:** State logic is organized and centralized
- **Type Safety:** Compile-time checking instead of runtime string errors

22.9 Mini-Exercise: Enhanced State Features

Task: Add a "Paused" state that can occur during baking (oven maintenance) and implement proper resume functionality.
Bonus: Create a "FailedDelivery" state that can retry delivery up to 3 times before going to "Cancelled".

22.10 When to Use the State Pattern

"Use the State pattern when:

- You have an object that behaves differently depending on its current state.
- You have multiple states and complex state transitions.
- You find yourself using multiple conditionals that check the same state property.
- You want to make state transitions explicit and maintainable.
- You need to add new states without changing existing state logic".

22.11 Transition to Chapter 23

"Now that we have a robust state machine managing our order lifecycle with proper validation and encapsulated behavior, let's tackle our pricing strategy. Next, we'll explore the **Strategy** pattern to make our discount and delivery pricing flexible and maintainable."

> **Next Up: Chapter 23 — Strategy: Flexible Pricing and Delivery**
> Ready to make your pricing system as flexible as your pizza toppings? Let's build a strategy-based pricing engine that can handle any discount, promotion, or delivery fee calculation!

Get Full Code Here

Strategy — Flexible Pricing and Delivery

Setting The Stage

Your pricing system is rigid with hardcoded discount rules and fixed delivery calculations. Adding new pricing strategies requires modifying core logic, and delivery costs are calculated the same way for all scenarios.

> In this chapter, you'll:
> 1. **Identify Pitfalls:** Identify the inflexibility in your current pricing system
> 2. **Learn the Pattern:** Learn the Strategy pattern to make pricing algorithms interchangeable
> 3. **Build A Flexible Pricing Engine:** Build a flexible pricing engine that can handle any discount or delivery scenario
> 4. **Create a Well Defined System:** Create a system where new pricing strategies can be added without changing existing code

23.1 Hook: What's the Pain?

"Every time marketing wants to run a new promotion - 'Tuesday Discount', 'Student Discount', 'Family Deal' - we have to dig into the *PricingService* and add more if/else statements. Our delivery pricing is equally rigid - flat rate regardless of distance or urgency. We need a system where we can plug in new pricing strategies like swapping out pizza toppings!"

23.2 The Problem in Our Pizza App

Hardcoded pricing rules that are difficult to extend (Oops Moment #19), (Oops Moment #34)

Why This Hurts:

- **Rigid Logic:** Hard to add new pricing strategies
- **Violates Open/Closed:** Must modify existing code to extend functionality
- **Tight Coupling:** Pricing logic tied to specific day/student checks
- **No Reusability:** Can't easily reuse pricing strategies elsewhere
- **Testing Difficulty:** Hard to test individual pricing rules in isolation

```
// ✗ OLD: Rigid pricing with hardcoded rules
public static decimal CalculateTotal(Order order)
{
    decimal total = order.Pizza.Price;

    // Hardcoded discount rules
    if (DateTime.Now.DayOfWeek == DayOfWeek.Tuesday)
        total *= 0.9m; // 10% off on Tuesday

    if (order.Customer.IsStudent)
        total *= 0.85m; // 15% student discount

    // Hardcoded delivery calculation
    total += 2.99m; // Flat delivery fee

    // Adding new rule? Add another if statement!
    return total;
}
```

23.3 The Formal Pattern: Strategy

Pattern Definition

> *"**Strategy** is a behavioral pattern that lets you define a family of algorithms, put each of them into a separate class, and make their objects interchangeable."*

In Simpler Terms: The Strategy pattern is like having a toolbox of different pricing calculators. Need to calculate a Tuesday discount? Grab the *TuesdayDiscount* calculator. Need rush delivery pricing? Grab the *RushDelivery* calculator. You can swap them in and out without changing your main order processing system.

23.4 Understanding the Pattern

The Real-World Analogy: Restaurant Pricing Menu

Imagine a restaurant with different pricing approaches:

- **Without Strategy:** One fixed menu with prices that never change
- **With Strategy:** Different price sheets - Happy Hour menu, Weekend Brunch menu, Catering menu, Takeout menu. Each has its own pricing rules, and you can switch between them based on the situation.

23.5 How the Strategy Pattern Solves It

Instead of this monolithic approach:

```
// ❌ One big method with all rules
decimal total = CalculateTotal(order);
// Adding new rule? Modify this method!
```

We'll create this flexible approach:

```
// ✅ Composable pricing strategies
var pricingContext = new PricingContext();
pricingContext.AddStrategy(new TuesdayDiscountStrategy());
pricingContext.AddStrategy(new StudentDiscountStrategy());
pricingContext.AddStrategy(new DistanceBasedDeliveryStrategy());

decimal total = pricingContext.CalculateTotal(order);
// New strategy? Just create new class and add it!
```

23.6 The Implementation Blueprint: Strategy Steps

Think of implementing the Strategy pattern like building a modular pizza pricing system. Each pricing rule is a separate ingredient that can be added or removed without affecting the others.

1. Define the Strategy Interface:

- ***What to do:*** Create *IPricingStrategy* with a method to calculate price
- ***Why we do it:*** This defines the contract for all pricing algorithms
- ***In simple terms:*** "I'm creating a standard recipe card that every pricing calculator must follow"

2. **Implement Concrete Strategies:**
   - ***What to do:*** Create classes for each pricing rule (*TuesdayDiscountStrategy*, *StudentDiscountStrategy*, *DeliveryPricingStrategy*, etc.)
   - ***Why we do it:*** Each strategy encapsulates one specific pricing rule.
   - ***In simple terms:*** "I'm writing specific recipes for Tuesday discount, student discount, delivery pricing, etc."
3. **Create the Pricing Context:**
   - ***What to do:*** Build *PricingContext* that composes multiple strategies.
   - ***Why we do it:*** This orchestrates the application of multiple pricing strategies.
   - ***In simple terms:*** "I'm creating a master chef who can combine multiple recipes to create the final price".
4. **Refactor Existing Pricing:**
   - ***What to do:*** Replace hardcoded pricing logic with strategy pattern.
   - ***Why we do it:*** This makes the pricing system flexible and extensible.
   - ***In simple terms:*** "I'm replacing the fixed menu with our new modular pricing system".
5. **Integrate with Order Processing:**
   - ***What to do:*** Update order processing to use the new pricing context.
   - ***Why we do it:*** This brings strategy pattern benefits to your existing workflow.
   - ***In simple terms:*** "I'm training our staff to use the new pricing system".

23.7 Implementing the Strategy Pattern

Step 1: Define Strategy Interface

IPricingStrategy.cs

```
public interface IPricingStrategy
{
   string StrategyName { get; }
   decimal CalculatePrice(Order order, decimal currentTotal);
   bool IsApplicable(Order order);
}
```

STRATEGY

Step 2: Implement Concrete Pricing Strategies

PricingStrategies.cs

```
// Base strategy with common functionality
public abstract class BasePricingStrategy : IPricingStrategy
{
   public abstract string StrategyName { get; }
   public abstract decimal CalculatePrice(Order order, decimal currentTotal);
   public abstract bool IsApplicable(Order order);

   protected void LogApplication(decimal oldPrice, decimal newPrice)
   {
      Console.WriteLine($"[Pricing] Applied {StrategyName}: ${oldPrice} → ${newPrice}");
   }
}

// Discount Strategies
// 1. Day-Based Discount (Runtime: Based on current day)
public class TuesdayDiscountStrategy : BasePricingStrategy
{
   public override string StrategyName => "Tuesday 10% Off";

   public override bool IsApplicable(Order order)
   {
      return DateTime.Now.DayOfWeek == DayOfWeek.Tuesday;
   }

   public override decimal CalculatePrice(Order order, decimal currentTotal)
   {
      return currentTotal * 0.9m; // 10% discount
   }
}

// 2. Customer-Type Discount (Runtime: Based on customer input)
public class StudentDiscountStrategy : BasePricingStrategy
{
   public override string StrategyName => "Student 15% Off";

   public override bool IsApplicable(Order order)
   {
      // This would be set based on user input in Program.cs
      return order.CustomerType == "Student";
   }

   public override decimal CalculatePrice(Order order, decimal currentTotal)
   {
      return currentTotal * 0.85m; // 15% discount
   }
}
```

```
// 3. Payment Method Discount (Runtime: Based on payment choice)
public class CreditCardDiscountStrategy : BasePricingStrategy{
  public override string StrategyName => "Credit Card 5% Off";

  public override bool IsApplicable(Order order){
    return order.PaymentMethod == "CreditCard";
  }

  public override decimal CalculatePrice(Order order, decimal currentTotal){
    return currentTotal * 0.95m; // 5% discount
  }
}

// 4. Order Value Discount (Runtime: Based on cart total)
public class BulkDiscountStrategy : BasePricingStrategy{
  private readonly decimal _threshold;

  public BulkDiscountStrategy(decimal threshold = 50.00m){
    _threshold = threshold;
  }

  public override string StrategyName => $"Bulk Order (Over ${_threshold}) 10% Off";

  public override bool IsApplicable(Order order){
    decimal baseTotal = CalculateBasePrice(order);
    return baseTotal >= _threshold;
  }

  public override decimal CalculatePrice(Order order, decimal currentTotal){
    return currentTotal * 0.9m; // 10% discount
  }

  private decimal CalculateBasePrice(Order order){
    return order.OrderItem?.Price * order.Quantity ?? 0m;
  }
}

// 5. Basic Delivery Fee (Always applicable for delivery)
public class DeliveryFeeStrategy : BasePricingStrategy{
  public override string StrategyName => "Delivery Fee";

  public override bool IsApplicable(Order order) {
    return order.DeliveryType == "Delivery"; // Not pickup
  }

  public override decimal CalculatePrice(Order order, decimal currentTotal){
    return currentTotal + 2.99m; // Flat delivery fee
  }
}
```

Step 3: Create Pricing Context

PricingContext.cs

```
public class PricingContext
{
    private readonly List<IPricingStrategy> _strategies = new List<IPricingStrategy>();

    public void AddStrategy(IPricingStrategy strategy)
    {
        _strategies.Add(strategy);
        Console.WriteLine($"[Pricing] Added strategy: {strategy.StrategyName}");
    }

    public void RemoveStrategy(IPricingStrategy strategy)
    {
        _strategies.Remove(strategy);
        Console.WriteLine($"[Pricing] Removed strategy: {strategy.StrategyName}");
    }

    public void ClearStrategies()
    {
        _strategies.Clear();
        Console.WriteLine("[Pricing] Cleared all strategies");
    }

    public decimal CalculateTotal(Order order)
    {
        // Start with base price from order items
        decimal total = CalculateBasePrice(order);
        Console.WriteLine($"[Pricing] Base price: ${total}");

        // Apply each strategy in sequence
        foreach (var strategy in _strategies)
        {
            if (strategy.IsApplicable(order))
            {
                total = strategy.CalculatePrice(order, total);
            }
        }
        // ✅ CRITICAL: Update the order object with the calculated total
        order.CalculatedTotal = total;
        order.AppliedPricingStrategies = GetAppliedStrategies(order);
        Console.WriteLine($"[Pricing] Final total: ${total:0.00}");
        return total;
    }
```

```
  private decimal CalculateBasePrice(Order order)
  {
    if (order.OrderItem != null)
    {
      return order.OrderItem.Price * order.Quantity;
    }

    // Fallback: sum all items
    return order.Items?.Sum(item => item.Price) * order.Quantity ?? 0m;
  }

  public List<string> GetAppliedStrategies(Order order)
  {
    return _strategies
      .Where(s => s.IsApplicable(order))
      .Select(s => s.StrategyName)
      .ToList();
  }
}
```

Step 4: Create Strategy Factory

PricingStrategyFactory.cs

```
public static class PricingStrategyFactory
{
  public static List<IPricingStrategy> CreateAllApplicableStrategies()
  {
    return new List<IPricingStrategy>
  {
    new TuesdayDiscountStrategy(),      // Applies only on Tuesdays
    new StudentDiscountStrategy(),      // Applies if CustomerType = "Student"
    new CreditCardDiscountStrategy(),   // Applies if PaymentMethod = "CreditCard"
    new BulkDiscountStrategy(40.00m),   // Applies if base price >= $40
    new DeliveryFeeStrategy()           // Applies if DeliveryType = "Delivery"
  };
  }

}
```

STRATEGY

Step 5: Update Order Class

Order.cs

```
public class Order : IOrderSubject
{
    // ... existing properties ...

    // NEW: Properties for runtime strategy decisions
    public string CustomerType { get; set; } = "Regular"; // Student, Senior, Regular
    public string PaymentMethod { get; set; } = "Cash";  // CreditCard, Cash, Digital
    public string DeliveryType { get; set; } = "Pickup"; // Delivery, Pickup

    public decimal CalculatedTotal { get; set; }
    public List<string> AppliedPricingStrategies { get; set; } = new List<string>();

    // Method to calculate price using strategy pattern
    public void CalculatePrice(PricingContext pricingContext)
    {
        this.CalculatedTotal = pricingContext.CalculateTotal(this);
        this.AppliedPricingStrategies = pricingContext.GetAppliedStrategies(this);
    }
}
```

Step 6: Update OrderProcessor

OrderProcessor.cs

```
public class OrderProcessor : IOrderProcessorFacade
{
    //Other Properties
    private readonly PricingContext _pricingContext;
    public OrderProcessor(
        IInventoryService inventory,
        PaymentGatewayAdapter paymentAdapter,
        IKitchenMediator mediator
        )
    {
        _inventory = inventory;
        _paymentAdapter = paymentAdapter;
        _validationChain = BuildValidationChain();
        _mediator = mediator;
        _globalObservers = new List<IOrderObserver>();
        _pricingContext = new PricingContext();

        // Add ALL strategies - they'll auto-apply based on order properties
        var strategies = PricingStrategyFactory.CreateAllApplicableStrategies();
        foreach (var strategy in strategies){
            _pricingContext.AddStrategy(strategy);
        }
    }
```

```
    public async Task<bool> PlaceOrder(Order order)
    {
        Console.WriteLine($"[OrderProcessor] Processing order #{order.OrderId}...");
        _orders.Add(order);

        // Attach global observers to this order
        foreach (var observer in _globalObservers){
            order.Attach(observer);
        }

        // Calculate price using strategy pattern
        Console.WriteLine("[Strategy] Calculating price with strategies...");
        order.CalculatePrice(_pricingContext);

        // Validate Order

        // Use Mediator for service coordination

        // Process through state machine
        Console.WriteLine("[State] Processing order through state machine...");
        order.Process(); // This triggers the state machine

        return mediatorSuccess;
    }

    // ... existing methods ...

    // Method to customize pricing strategies
    public void SetPricingStrategies(List<IPricingStrategy> strategies){
        _pricingContext.ClearStrategies();
        foreach (var strategy in strategies)
        {
            _pricingContext.AddStrategy(strategy);
        }
    }
}
```

Step 7: Update the *PaymentValidationHandler*

Now we need to use the Order's *CalculatedTotal* instead of Old *PricingService*.

PaymentValidationHandler.cs

```
public override bool Handle(Order order){
 // ✅ Use the order's CalculatedTotal that includes strategy discounts
 var total = order.CalculatedTotal;
 var result = _paymentAdapter.ProcessPayment(total, Config.Instance.CurrencySymbol, "card-
token-123");
    //...existing code
}
```

STRATEGY

Step 8: Client Usage in Program.cs

Program.cs

```
// In your Main method, after order is created:

var order = new Order
{
   OrderId = id,
   CustomerName = "Walk-in", // simplified
   Address = "Counter",
   OrderItem = orderItem,
   Items = interpretedOrder?.Items ?? new List<IOrderItem> { orderItem }, // Safe fallback
   Modifiers = interpretedOrder?.Modifiers ?? new List<Modifier> { }, // Safe fallback
   Quantity = interpretedOrder?.Quantity ?? 1, // Safe fallback
   //Status = "Received",
   TimeOrdered = DateTime.Now
};

Console.WriteLine("\n[Pricing Strategy] Please provide some details for best pricing:");

// 1. Customer Type
Console.Write("Are you a student? (yes/no): ");
if (Console.ReadLine().ToLower() == "yes")
{
   order.CustomerType = "Student";
}

// 2. Delivery Type
Console.Write("Delivery or Pickup? (delivery/pickup): ");
order.DeliveryType = Console.ReadLine().ToLower() == "delivery" ? "Delivery" : "Pickup";

// 3. Payment Method
Console.Write("Payment method? (credit/cash): ");
order.PaymentMethod = Console.ReadLine().ToLower() == "credit" ? "CreditCard" : "Cash";

Console.WriteLine("[Strategy] Pricing preferences saved!");

// Price is automatically calculated during order processing
bool orderSuccess = await orderProcessor.PlaceOrder(order);
```

Key Runtime Strategy Applications:

- Tuesday Discount: Auto-applies based on system date.
- Student Discount: Based on user input ("Are you a student?")
- Credit Card Discount: Based on payment method choice.
- Bulk Discount: Auto-applies when order value threshold met.
- Delivery Fee: Based on delivery/pickup choice.

Key Test Points for Strategy Pattern Validation

1. **Strategy Application Test**
    - **Objective:** Verify each strategy applies only when conditions are met.
    - **Test Action:** Create orders with different properties and verify correct strategies apply.
    - **Expected Result:** Strategies should only activate when their applicability conditions are met.
2. **Strategy Calculation Accuracy Test**
    - **Objective:** Verify each strategy calculates prices correctly.
    - **Test Action:** Apply strategies to known amounts and verify calculations.
    - **Expected Result:** Strategies should produce mathematically correct results.
3. **Multiple Strategy Combination Test**
    - **Objective:** Verify multiple strategies can be combined correctly.
    - **Test Action:** Apply multiple applicable strategies in sequence.
    - **Expected Result:** Strategies should compose correctly without interfering.
4. **Strategy Order Independence Test**
    - **Objective:** Verify strategy application order doesn't affect final result.
    - **Test Action:** Apply same strategies in different orders.
    - **Expected Result:** Final price should be the same regardless of application order.
5. **Runtime Strategy Modification Test**
    - **Objective:** Verify strategies can be added/removed at runtime.
    - **Test Action:** Modify strategy list and verify pricing changes.
    - **Expected Result:** Pricing should update immediately when strategies change.
6. **Strategy Isolation Test**
    - **Objective:** Verify each strategy works independently.
    - **Test Action:** Test each strategy in isolation with controlled inputs.
    - **Expected Result:** Strategies should not depend on other strategies or global state.
7. **Edge Cases and Boundaries Test**
    - **Objective:** Verify strategies handle edge cases correctly.
    - **Test Action:** Test with zero values, maximum values, and boundary conditions.
    - **Expected Result:** Strategies should handle edge cases gracefully.
8. **Integration with Order Processing Test**
    - **Objective:** Verify strategy pattern integrates with existing order flow.
    - **Test Action:** Process complete order with strategy-based pricing.
    - **Expected Result:** Pricing should work seamlessly with order validation and processing.
9. **Strategy Factory Test**
    - **Objective:** Verify strategy factory creates correct strategy combinations.
    - **Test Action:** Use factory methods and verify returned strategies.
    - **Expected Result:** Factory should provide appropriate strategy collections.

10. Performance Under Load Test

- **Objective:** Verify pricing calculation performs well with multiple strategies.
- **Test Action:** Calculate prices for many orders with multiple strategies.
- **Expected Result:** Pricing should complete quickly even with complex strategy sets.

23.8 Why the Strategy Pattern Matters

- **Flexible Pricing:** Easy to add, remove, or modify pricing rules
- **Clean Separation:** Each pricing rule is isolated and testable
- **Runtime Configuration:** Can change pricing strategies without recompiling
- **Composable:** Multiple strategies can be combined
- **Maintainable:** New team members can understand pricing rules quickly

23.9 Mini-Exercise: Enhanced Strategy Features

Task: Create a "*LoyaltyPointsStrategy*" that gives 5% discount to customers with over 100 loyalty points.
Bonus: Implement a "*SeasonalPromotionStrategy*" that applies special discounts during holidays.

23.10 When to Use the Strategy Pattern

"Use the Strategy pattern when:

- You have multiple variations of an algorithm and want to switch between them at runtime.
- You need to isolate the implementation details of an algorithm from the code that uses it.
- You have many related classes that differ only in their behavior.
- Your class has multiple conditional statements for selecting different behaviors".

23.11 Transition to Chapter 24

"Now that we have a flexible, strategy-based pricing system that can handle any discount or delivery scenario, let's tackle our kitchen workflow. Next, we'll explore the **Template** Method pattern to create a reusable pizza preparation framework."

> **Next Up: Chapter 24 — Template Method: Standardized Pizza Preparation**
> Ready to create a foolproof pizza preparation process? Let's build a template-based kitchen workflow that ensures every pizza is made perfectly every time!

Get Full Code Here

Template Method — Standardized Pizza Preparation

Setting The Stage

Your pizza preparation steps are hardcoded and scattered across different services. Adding new pizza types or changing preparation sequences requires modifying multiple classes.

In this chapter, you'll:

1. **Identify Pitfalls:** Identify the rigid pizza preparation workflow.
2. **Learn the Pattern:** Learn the Template Method pattern to create reusable preparation templates
3. **Build A Flexible Pricing Engine:** Build a standardized pizza-making process that ensures consistency
4. **Create a flexible system:** Create a flexible system where pizza types can customize specific steps

24.1 Hook: What's the Pain?

"Every time we process a different type of order, we have to remember all the validation, payment, preparation, and delivery steps - and make sure we don't forget anything. Our standard orders, express orders, and pickup orders all follow similar workflows but with crucial differences in sequencing and business rules. The code duplication is massive, and it's too easy to accidentally skip a critical step. We need a standardized 'order processing checklist' that guarantees every order type follows the correct sequence while allowing flexibility for special cases!"

24.2 The Problem in Our Pizza App

Right now, our order processing logic is scattered across multiple classes with no standardized workflow. Different parts of the system handle order steps in different sequences, leading to potential inconsistencies and maintenance headaches. (Oops Moment# 38)

```
// ✗ CURRENT: Order processing scattered everywhere
// In OrderProcessor.PlaceOrder():
if (!_validationChain.Handle(order)) return false;  // Validation
order.CalculatePrice(_pricingContext);              // Pricing
bool mediatorSuccess = await _mediator.ProcessOrder(order);  // Kitchen ops
order.Process();  // State transitions

// In KitchenMediator.ProcessOrder():
var commandProcessor = new KitchenCommandProcessor(maxRetries: 3);
// ... kitchen commands added manually
return await commandProcessor.ProcessQueueAsync();

// In individual commands (BakePizzaCommand, PackPizzaCommand, DeliverPizzaCommand):
// Each handles state transitions differently
_order.Process(); // Sometimes called
// _order.ChangeState() // Sometimes called directly
```

Why This Hurts:

- **Inconsistent Sequencing:** No guarantee that orders always follow the same validation → pricing → preparation → delivery sequence
- **Scattered Logic:** Order workflow steps are spread across *OrderProcessor*, *KitchenMediator*, and individual commands
- **Duplicated Code:** Same pre-processing and post-processing logic repeated
- **Hard to Extend:** Adding new order types (express, catering, pickup) requires modifying multiple classes
- **No Standard Hooks:** No clean way to add cross-cutting concerns like logging, timing, or retry policies across all order types

24.3 The Formal Pattern: Template

Pattern Definition

> *"**Template** Method is a behavioral pattern that defines the skeleton of an algorithm in the base class but lets subclasses override specific steps without changing the algorithm's structure."*

In Simpler Terms: The Template Method pattern is like having a standard pizza recipe card with some blank spaces. Every pizza follows the same basic steps (knead dough, add sauce, bake), but you can fill in the blanks for specific pizza types (wood oven vs regular oven, specific cheese types).

24.4 Understanding the Pattern

The Real-World Analogy: Restaurant Pricing Menu

Imagine a pizza restaurant:

- **Without Template Method:** Each chef has their own way of making pizzas - some forget steps, some do them in different orders
- **With Template Method:** There's a standard recipe card for all pizzas with specific steps. Chefs follow the card but can customize certain steps for different pizza types

24.5 How the Template Pattern Solves It

Instead of this scattered approach:

```
// ❌ Order processing logic duplicated and inconsistent
await PlaceStandardOrder(order);
await PlaceExpressOrder(order);
await PlaceCateringOrder(order);
// Each method has similar but slightly different steps
```

We'll create a standardized template-based approach:

```
// ✅ Single template with consistent workflow
public abstract class OrderProcessingTemplate
{
    // Template method - defines the order processing skeleton
    public async Task<bool> ProcessOrderAsync(Order order)
    {
        if (!await ValidateOrderAsync(order)) return false;
        await CalculatePriceAsync(order);
        if (!await ProcessPaymentAsync(order)) return false;
        if (!await PrepareOrderAsync(order)) return false;
        if (!await DeliverOrderAsync(order)) return false;
        await CompleteOrderAsync(order);
        return true;
    }
```

```
// Steps that can be customized by order type
    protected abstract Task<bool> ValidateOrderAsync(Order order);
    protected abstract Task<bool> ProcessPaymentAsync(Order order);
    protected abstract Task<bool> PrepareOrderAsync(Order order);
    protected abstract Task<bool> DeliverOrderAsync(Order order);
```

```
// Specific order types implement the template
await new StandardOrderProcessing().ProcessOrderAsync(order);
await new ExpressOrderProcessing().ProcessOrderAsync(order);
await new PickupOrderProcessing().ProcessOrderAsync(order);
```

24.6 Implementation Blueprint: Template Method Steps

Think of implementing the Template Method pattern like creating a master pizza recipe that all chefs must follow, but with customizable ingredients for different pizza styles.

1. Create the Abstract Template Class:
- ***What to do:*** Build *PizzaPreparationTemplate* with the preparation algorithm skeleton.
- ***Why we do it:*** This defines the standard pizza-making process.
- ***In simple terms:*** "I'm creating the master pizza recipe card that every chef must use".

2. Define Template Method:
- ***What to do:*** Create the *Prepare()* method that calls the step methods in order.
- ***Why we do it:*** This ensures consistent execution order across all pizza types.
- ***In simple terms:*** "I'm numbering the steps on the recipe card so they're always done in right order".

3. Declare Abstract Steps:
- ***What to do:*** Make key preparation steps abstract for subclasses to implement.
- ***Why we do it:*** This forces specific pizza types to define their unique requirements.
- ***In simple terms:*** "I'm leaving blank lines on the recipe card for chefs to fill in specific ingredients".

4. Provide Hook Methods:
- ***What to do:*** Create optional methods subclasses can override for customization.
- ***Why we do it*:** This allows flexibility without breaking the template structure.
- ***In simple terms:*** "I'm adding optional steps that chefs can include if needed".

5. Implement Concrete Templates:
- ***What to do:*** Create subclasses for each pizza type that implement the specific steps.
- ***Why we do it:*** This provides the actual implementation for different pizza styles.
- ***In simple terms:*** "I'm creating specific recipe cards for Margherita, Pepperoni, etc. using our master template".

24.7 Implementing the Template Pattern

Step 1: Create the Order Processing Template Class

OrderProcessingTemplate.cs

```
public abstract class OrderProcessingTemplate
{
  // Template Method - defines the order processing algorithm skeleton
  public async Task<bool> ProcessOrderAsync(Order order){
    Console.WriteLine($"[Template] Starting order #{order.OrderId} processing...");
    // Standardized order processing sequence
    if (!await PreProcessOrderAsync(order))
      return false;
```

TEMPLATE

```
    if (!await ValidateOrderAsync(order))
        return false;

    await CalculatePriceAsync(order);

    if (!await ProcessPaymentAsync(order))
        return false;

    if (!await PrepareOrderAsync(order))
        return false;

    if (!await DeliverOrderAsync(order))
        return false;

    await CompleteOrderAsync(order);

    Console.WriteLine($"[Template] Order #{order.OrderId} processing completed successfully");
    return true;
}

// Abstract methods - must be implemented by specific order types
protected abstract Task<bool> ValidateOrderAsync(Order order);
protected abstract Task<bool> ProcessPaymentAsync(Order order);
protected abstract Task<bool> PrepareOrderAsync(Order order);
protected abstract Task<bool> DeliverOrderAsync(Order order);

// Concrete methods - common to all order types
protected virtual async Task<bool> PreProcessOrderAsync(Order order)
{
    Console.WriteLine($"[Template] Pre-processing order #{order.OrderId}");
    order.TimeOrdered = DateTime.Now;
    await AttachObserversAsync(order);
    return true;
}

protected virtual async Task CalculatePriceAsync(Order order)
{
    Console.WriteLine($"[Template] Calculating price for order #{order.OrderId}");
    // Use existing pricing context
    var pricingContext = new PricingContext();
    var strategies = PricingStrategyFactory.CreateAllApplicableStrategies();
    foreach (var strategy in strategies)
    {
        pricingContext.AddStrategy(strategy);
    }
    order.CalculatePrice(pricingContext);
    await Task.CompletedTask;
}
```

```
    protected virtual async Task CompleteOrderAsync(Order order)
    {
        Console.WriteLine($"[Template] Completing order #{order.OrderId}");
        order.NotifyObservers("Order completed successfully");
        await Task.CompletedTask;
    }

    // Helper method
    private async Task AttachObserversAsync(Order order)
    {
        // Attach standard observers
        var emailNotifier = new EmailNotification(new SmtpEmailSender());
        var smsNotifier = new SmsNotification(new TwilioSmsSender());

        order.Attach(new EmailOrderObserver(emailNotifier));
        order.Attach(new SMSOrderObserver(smsNotifier));
        order.Attach(new KitchenDisplayObserver());

        await Task.CompletedTask;
    }
}
```

Step 2: Implement Concrete Order Processors

StandardOrderProcessing.cs

```
public class StandardOrderProcessing : OrderProcessingTemplate
{
    private readonly IOrderHandler _validationChain;
    private readonly IKitchenMediator _mediator;
    private readonly PaymentGatewayAdapter _paymentAdapter;

    public StandardOrderProcessing(
        IOrderHandler validationChain = null,
        IKitchenMediator mediator = null,
        PaymentGatewayAdapter paymentAdapter = null)
    {
        _validationChain = validationChain ?? BuildDefaultValidationChain();
        _mediator = mediator ?? CreateDefaultMediator();
        _paymentAdapter = paymentAdapter ?? new PaymentGatewayAdapter();
    }

    protected override async Task<bool> ValidateOrderAsync(Order order)
    {
        Console.WriteLine("[StandardOrder] Validating order structure and inventory...");
        return _validationChain.Handle(order);
    }
```

TEMPLATE

```
    protected override async Task<bool> ProcessPaymentAsync(Order order)
    {
        Console.WriteLine("[StandardOrder] Processing payment...");
        var result = _paymentAdapter.ProcessPayment(
            order.CalculatedTotal,
            Config.Instance.CurrencySymbol,
            "card-token-123");

        return result.IsSuccess;
    }

    protected override async Task<bool> PrepareOrderAsync(Order order)
    {
        Console.WriteLine("[StandardOrder] Preparing order in kitchen...");
        return await _mediator.ProcessOrder(order);
    }

    protected override async Task<bool> DeliverOrderAsync(Order order)
    {
        Console.WriteLine("[StandardOrder] Delivering order to customer...");
        // Standard delivery logic
        var deliveryService = new DeliveryService();
        await deliveryService.DeliverAsync(order);
        order.Process(); // Transition to delivered state
        return true;
    }

    private static IOrderHandler BuildDefaultValidationChain()
    {
        var inventory = new InventoryApiProxy(new InventoryApi());
        var payment = new PaymentGatewayAdapter();

        var orderValidation = new OrderValidationHandler();
        var inventoryValidation = new InventoryValidationHandler(inventory);
        var paymentValidation = new PaymentValidationHandler(payment);

        orderValidation.SetNext(inventoryValidation).SetNext(paymentValidation);
        return orderValidation;
    }

    private static IKitchenMediator CreateDefaultMediator()
    {
        var emailNotifier = new EmailNotification(new SmtpEmailSender());
        var smsNotifier = new SmsNotification(new TwilioSmsSender());
        var pushNotifier = new PushNotification(new FirebasePushSender());

        return new KitchenMediator(emailNotifier, smsNotifier, pushNotifier);
    }
}
```

PickupOrderProcessing.cs

```
public class PickupOrderProcessing : OrderProcessingTemplate
{
  protected override async Task<bool> DeliverOrderAsync(Order order)
  {
    Console.WriteLine("[PickupOrder] Order ready for customer pickup...");
    // No delivery - customer picks up
    order.Process(); // Mark as ready for pickup
    order.NotifyObservers("Order ready for pickup");
    return true;
  }

  protected override async Task CalculatePriceAsync(Order order)
  {
    Console.WriteLine("[PickupOrder] Applying pickup discount...");
    await base.CalculatePriceAsync(order);

    // Apply 10% discount for pickup orders
    order.CalculatedTotal *= 0.9m;
    order.AppliedPricingStrategies.Add("Pickup Discount 10%");
  }

  // Skip payment processing for pickup (pay in store)
  protected override async Task<bool> ProcessPaymentAsync(Order order)
  {
    Console.WriteLine("[PickupOrder] Payment deferred to store pickup");
    return true;
  }

  // Other methods use base implementation
  protected override async Task<bool> ValidateOrderAsync(Order order) => await
base.PreProcessOrderAsync(order);
  protected override async Task<bool> PrepareOrderAsync(Order order)
  {
    var mediator = CreateDefaultMediator();
    return await mediator.ProcessOrder(order);
  }

  private static IKitchenMediator CreateDefaultMediator()
  {
    var emailNotifier = new EmailNotification(new SmtpEmailSender());
    var smsNotifier = new SmsNotification(new TwilioSmsSender());
    var pushNotifier = new PushNotification(new FirebasePushSender());

    return new KitchenMediator(emailNotifier, smsNotifier, pushNotifier);
  }
}
```

ExpressOrderProcessing.cs

```
public class ExpressOrderProcessing : OrderProcessingTemplate
{
    private readonly IKitchenMediator _mediator;
    private readonly PaymentGatewayAdapter _paymentAdapter;

    public ExpressOrderProcessing(
        IKitchenMediator mediator = null,
        PaymentGatewayAdapter paymentAdapter = null)
    {
        _mediator = mediator ?? CreateExpressMediator();
        _paymentAdapter = paymentAdapter ?? new PaymentGatewayAdapter();
    }

    protected override async Task<bool> ValidateOrderAsync(Order order)
    {
        Console.WriteLine("[ExpressOrder] Fast-tracking validation...");
        // Simplified validation for express orders
        return order != null && order.OrderItem != null;
    }

    protected override async Task<bool> ProcessPaymentAsync(Order order)
    {
        Console.WriteLine("[ExpressOrder] Processing express payment...");
        var result = _paymentAdapter.ProcessPayment(
            order.CalculatedTotal,
            Config.Instance.CurrencySymbol,
            "express-card-token");

        return result.IsSuccess;
    }

    protected override async Task<bool> PrepareOrderAsync(Order order)
    {
        Console.WriteLine("[ExpressOrder] Expedited kitchen preparation...");

        // ✅ CORRECT: Use the mediator for consistency
        // The mediator should be configured for express processing internally
        return await _mediator.ProcessOrder(order);
    }

    protected override async Task<bool> DeliverOrderAsync(Order order)
    {
        Console.WriteLine("[ExpressOrder] Priority delivery...");
        var deliveryService = new DeliveryService();
        await deliveryService.DeliverAsync(order);
        order.Process();
        return true;
    }
```

```
    protected override async Task CompleteOrderAsync(Order order)
    {
        Console.WriteLine("[ExpressOrder] Express order complete - sending priority notification");
        order.NotifyObservers("Express order delivered!");
        await base.CompleteOrderAsync(order);
    }

    private static IKitchenMediator CreateExpressMediator()
    {
        var emailNotifier = new EmailNotification(new SmtpEmailSender());
        var smsNotifier = new SmsNotification(new TwilioSmsSender());
        var pushNotifier = new PushNotification(new FirebasePushSender());

        // Create a mediator configured for express processing
        return new ExpressKitchenMediator(emailNotifier, smsNotifier, pushNotifier);
    }
}
```

Step 3: Create an Express Kitchen Mediator

The *ExpressKitchenMediator* acts as our 'priority kitchen coordinator' - it's specifically configured to handle express orders by reducing retries and streamlining operations, ensuring fast-track preparation without compromising our established kitchen workflow patterns.

ExpressKitchenMediator .cs

```
public class ExpressKitchenMediator : KitchenMediator
{
    public ExpressKitchenMediator(
        EmailNotification emailNotifier,
        SmsNotification smsNotifier,
        PushNotification pushNotifier)
        : base(emailNotifier, smsNotifier, pushNotifier)
    {
    }

    protected override async Task<bool> ExecuteKitchenOperations(Order order, List<IPizza> pizzas)
{
        // Express version: faster processing with fewer retries
        var commandProcessor = new KitchenCommandProcessor(maxRetries: 1);

        foreach (var pizza in pizzas) {
            commandProcessor.AddCommand(new BakePizzaCommand(pizza, order));
            commandProcessor.AddCommand(new PackPizzaCommand(pizza, order));
        }
        // Note: No delivery command - that's handled in DeliverOrderAsync

        return await commandProcessor.ProcessQueueAsync();
    }
}
```

Step 4: Update OrderProcessor to Use Template Method

OrderProcessor.cs

```
// In OrderProcessor.cs - update PlaceOrder method
public async Task<bool> PlaceOrder(Order order)
{
  Console.WriteLine($"[OrderProcessor] Processing order #{order.OrderId}...");
  _orders.Add(order);

  // Choose the appropriate processing template based on order properties
  var orderProcessor = CreateOrderProcessor(order);

  // Use template method for consistent order processing
  bool success = await orderProcessor.ProcessOrderAsync(order);

  if (success)
  {
    Console.WriteLine($"[OrderProcessor] Order #{order.OrderId} completed successfully");
  }
  else
  {
    Console.WriteLine($"[OrderProcessor] Order #{order.OrderId} failed");
  }

  return success;
}

private OrderProcessingTemplate CreateOrderProcessor(Order order)
{
  return order.DeliveryType switch
{
   "Pickup" => new PickupOrderProcessing(),
   "Express" => new ExpressOrderProcessing(),
   _ => new StandardOrderProcessing(_validationChain, _mediator, _paymentAdapter)
};
}
```

Step 5: Usage in Program.cs

Program.cs

```
// In your Main method - no changes needed!
// The template method pattern works transparently based on Delivery Type user selected
bool orderSuccess = await orderProcessor.PlaceOrder(order);
```

Key Test Points for Template Pattern Validation

1. **Template Method Sequence Test**
   - **Objective:** Verify the template method executes all steps in correct order.
   - **Test Action:** Create test orders and verify step execution sequence.
   - **Expected Result:** All processing steps execute in predefined order (PreProcess → Validate → CalculatePrice → ProcessPayment → Prepare → Deliver → Complete).
2. **Step Customization Test**
   - **Objective:** Verify concrete classes properly customize template steps.
   - **Test Action:** Test different order types with specialized step implementations.
   - **Expected Result:** Each order type customizes specific steps while maintaining base sequence.
3. **Hook Method Test**
   - **Objective:** Verify optional hook methods work correctly.
   - **Test Action:** Test orders that trigger additional steps via hook methods.
   - **Expected Result:** Hook methods execute when overridden, skip when using default implementation.
4. **Error Handling in Template Flow Test**
   - **Objective:** Verify template method handles step failures gracefully.
   - **Test Action:** Force failures at different steps and verify flow interruption.
   - **Expected Result:** Template method stops processing when any step fails and returns appropriate result.
5. **Template Extension Test**
   - **Objective:** Verify new order types extend template without breaking existing flow.
   - **Test Action:** Create new order processor by extending base template.
   - **Expected Result:** New order type integrates seamlessly while maintaining core sequence.
6. **Cross-Cutting Concerns Test**
   - **Objective:** Verify common functionality in base template works across all order types.
   - **Test Action:** Test pricing calculation and observer attachment across different processors.
   - **Expected Result:** Base template functionality applies consistently to all order types.

24.8 Why the Template Pattern Matters

- **Consistent Order Quality:** Every order type follows the same high-level workflow, ensuring no critical steps are missed
- **Eliminates Duplication:** Common order processing steps (pricing, observer attachment, completion) defined once in base template
- **Flexible Customization:** Specific order types (express, pickup) can override only the steps that differ while inheriting common logic

- **Easy Maintenance:** Changes to base order processing (adding logging, timing) affect all order types automatically
- **Clear Business Rules:** Order workflows are explicit and well-documented through the template structure
- **Scalable Architecture:** New order types can be added by simply extending the base template without modifying existing processors

24.9 Mini-Exercise: Enhanced Template Features

Task: Add a "*CateringOrderProcessing*" template that follows the same pattern but includes additional steps for large order handling and special delivery scheduling.
Bonus: Create a "*PreValidation*" hook method that allows orders to perform custom checks before the main validation step.

24.10 When to Use the Template Pattern

"Use the Template Method pattern when:

- You want to let clients extend only particular steps of an algorithm, but not the whole algorithm or its structure
- You have several classes that contain almost identical algorithms with some minor differences
- You need to control the exact order of algorithm steps to ensure consistency
- You want to avoid code duplication by pulling the skeletal algorithm into a base class".

24.11 Transition to Chapter 25

"Now that we have a standardized, template-based pizza preparation system that ensures every pizza is made perfectly, let's tackle our final challenge: applying complex operations across our object structure. Next, we'll explore the **Visitor** pattern to handle operations like discounts, analytics, and reports without modifying the objects themselves."

> **Next Up: Chapter 25 — Visitor: Universal Operations Across Objects**
> Ready to add new operations to your object structure without changing the classes? Let's build a visitor system that can apply discounts, generate reports, and more across all your pizza objects!

Scan to see Template Pattern in Action

Visitor — Universal Operations Across Objects

Setting The Stage

Your pizza ordering system has a complex object structure with different types (pizzas, drinks, desserts, combos) that need various operations applied to them (discounts, nutritional calculations, inventory checks, etc.). Adding new operations requires modifying every class.

> In this chapter, you'll:
> 1. **Identify Pitfalls:** Identify the challenge of adding operations to existing object structures.
> 2. **Learn the Pattern:** Learn the Visitor pattern to separate operations from object structure
> 3. **Build A Visitor System:** Build a visitor system that can apply operations across your entire menu
> 4. **Create a flexible system:** Create a flexible system where new operations can be added without modifying existing classes

25.1 Hook: What's the Pain?

"Every time we need to add a new operation like 'calculate calories', 'apply loyalty points', or 'generate nutritional report', we have to go and modify every single class in our object hierarchy! Our Pizza, Drink, Dessert, and Combo classes are becoming bloated with unrelated methods. We need a way to add new operations without touching the existing classes!"

25.2 The Problem in Our Pizza App

Adding new operations requires modifying every class (Oops Moment #16)

```
// ✗ OLD: Operations scattered across classes
public class Pizza : IOrderItem
{
    public decimal CalculateCalories() { /* pizza-specific logic */ }
    public void ApplyLoyaltyPoints() { /* pizza-specific logic */ }
    public string GenerateNutritionalReport() { /* pizza-specific logic */ }
    // Adding new operation? Modify this class!
}

public class Drink : IOrderItem
{
    public decimal CalculateCalories() { /* drink-specific logic */ }
    public void ApplyLoyaltyPoints() { /* drink-specific logic */ }
    public string GenerateNutritionalReport() { /* drink-specific logic */ }
    // Also modify this class!
}
// And modify Dessert, Combo, etc. for every new operation!
```

Why This Hurts:

- **Violates Open/Closed:** Must modify existing classes to add new operations
- **Class Bloat:** Classes become large with unrelated methods
- **Tight Coupling:** Operations are tied to specific class implementations
- **Hard to Maintain:** Changing an operation requires modifying multiple classes
- **Poor Separation:** Classes know about operations they shouldn't care about

25.3 The Formal Pattern: Visitor

Pattern Definition

> *"**Visitor** is a behavioral pattern that lets you separate algorithms from the objects on which they operate."*

In Simpler Terms: The Visitor pattern is like having specialized inspectors who can visit different departments in your restaurant. The pizza station doesn't know how to calculate nutritional information, but the nutrition inspector knows how to examine pizzas, drinks, and desserts to calculate their nutritional values.

25.4 Understanding the Pattern

The Real-World Analogy: Restaurant Quality Inspector

Imagine a restaurant with different food stations:

- **Without Visitor:** Each station (pizza, drinks, desserts) must know how to perform quality checks, calorie counting, and health inspections
- **With Visitor:** Specialized inspectors visit each station - a nutritionist checks calories, a quality manager checks preparation standards, a health inspector checks safety. Stations just need to allow access; they don't need to know the inspection details.

25.5 How the Visitor Pattern Solves It

Instead of this scattered approach:

```
// ❌ Operations are methods on the objects
pizza.CalculateCalories();
drink.CalculateCalories();
dessert.CalculateCalories();
// Adding new operation? Add method to every class!
```

We'll create this visitor-based approach:

```
// ✅ Operations are separate visitors
IVisitor calorieVisitor = new CalorieCalculatorVisitor();
pizza.Accept(calorieVisitor);
drink.Accept(calorieVisitor);
dessert.Accept(calorieVisitor);
// New operation? Create new visitor, no class changes!
```

25.6 Implementation Blueprint: Visitor Method Steps

Think of implementing the Visitor pattern like hiring specialized consultants who can work with every department in your restaurant without the departments needing to know the consultant's expertise.

1. Define the Visitor Interface:

- ***What to do:*** Create *IOrderItemVisitor* with *Visit* methods for each element type.
- ***Why we do it:*** This defines what operations can be performed on our object structure.
- ***In simple terms:*** "I'm creating a job description that every specialist must follow".

2. Update Element Interface:

- ***What to do:*** Add *Accept(IVisitor visitor)* method to *IOrderItem*
- ***Why we do it:*** This allows elements to accept visitors and be operated on.
- ***In simple terms:*** "I'm teaching every department how to welcome specialists".

3. Implement Concrete Visitors:

- ***What to do:*** Create visitor classes for each operation (DiscountVisitor, CalorieVisitor, LoyaltyVisitor)
- ***Why we do it:*** Each visitor encapsulates one complete operation across all elements
- ***In simple terms:*** "I'm hiring a discount specialist, a nutrition specialist, and a loyalty specialist"

4. Update Element Classes:

- ***What to do:*** Implement *Accept* method in each element class to call the appropriate visitor method.
- ***Why we do it:*** This connects elements with visitors when they accept them.
- ***In simple terms:*** "I'm training each department to direct specialists to the right area".

5. Use Visitors in Client Code:

- ***What to do:*** Create visitors and make elements accept them.
- ***Why we do it:*** This applies operations to elements without the elements knowing the operation details.
- ***In simple terms:*** "I'm sending specialists to departments to get their work done".

25.7 Implementing the Visitor Pattern

Step 1: Define Visitor Interfaces

IOrderItemVisitor.cs

```
public interface IOrderItemVisitor{
   void VisitPizza(IPizza pizza);
   void VisitDrink(Drink drink);
   void VisitDessert(Dessert dessert);
   void VisitComposite(OrderComposite composite);
}
```

IOrderItem.cs

```
public interface IOrderItem
{
   string Name { get; }
   decimal Price { get; }
   void Accept(IOrderItemVisitor visitor);
}
```

Step 2: Implement Concrete Visitors

OrderItemVisitors.cs

Scan to see Visitor Pattern in Action

```
//1. Loyalty Points Calculator (Business Value)
public class LoyaltyPointsVisitor : IOrderItemVisitor
{
   private int _totalPoints = 0;

   public void VisitPizza(IPizza pizza)
   {
      // Pizzas earn more points (2 per dollar)
      int points = (int)(pizza.Price * 2);
      _totalPoints += points;
      Console.WriteLine($"[Visitor] {pizza.Name}: {points} loyalty points");
   }

   public void VisitDrink(IDrink drink)
   {
      int points = (int)drink.Price;
      _totalPoints += points;
      Console.WriteLine($"[Visitor] {drink.Name}: {points} loyalty points");
   }

   public void VisitDessert(IDessert dessert)
   {
      int points = (int)(dessert.Price * 1.5m);
      _totalPoints += points;
      Console.WriteLine($"[Visitor] {dessert.Name}: {points} loyalty points");
   }

   public void VisitComposite(OrderComposite composite)
   {
      // Composites don't earn points directly
      Console.WriteLine($"[Visitor] Processing composite: {composite.Name}");
   }


   public int TotalPoints => _totalPoints;
}

// 2. Order Summary Visitor (Customer Experience)
public class OrderSummaryVisitor : IOrderItemVisitor
{
   private readonly Order _order;
   private readonly StringBuilder _summary = new StringBuilder();
   private decimal _totalPrice = 0;
```

```
    public OrderSummaryVisitor(Order order)
    {
        _order = order;
    }
    public void VisitPizza(IPizza pizza)
    {
        _summary.AppendLine($"[Visitor] {pizza.Name} - ${pizza.Price:0.00}");
        if (pizza is CustomPizza customPizza){
            var toppings = string.Join(", ", customPizza.GetToppingNames());
            if (!string.IsNullOrEmpty(toppings))
                _summary.AppendLine($"   Toppings: {toppings}");
        }
        _totalPrice += pizza.Price;
    }

    public void VisitDrink(IDrink drink)
    {
        _summary.AppendLine($"[Visitor] {drink.Name} - ${drink.Price:0.00}");
        _totalPrice += drink.Price;
    }

    public void VisitDessert(IDessert dessert)
    {
        _summary.AppendLine($"[Visitor] {dessert.Name} - ${dessert.Price:0.00}");
        _totalPrice += dessert.Price;
    }

    public void VisitComposite(OrderComposite composite)
    {
        _summary.AppendLine($"\n[Visitor] COMBO: {composite.Name}");
        _summary.AppendLine($"   Includes {composite.Count} items");
    }

    public void PrintSummary()
    {
        Console.WriteLine("\n[Visitor] ORDER SUMMARY");
        Console.WriteLine("================");
        Console.WriteLine(_summary.ToString());

        // Show BOTH base total and discounted total
        Console.WriteLine($"==> SUBTOTAL: ${_totalPrice:0.00}");
        Console.WriteLine($"==> DISCOUNTS APPLIED: ${(_totalPrice - _order.CalculatedTotal):0.00}");
        Console.WriteLine($"==> FINAL TOTAL: ${_order.CalculatedTotal:0.00}");

        if (_order.AppliedPricingStrategies.Any())
        {
            Console.WriteLine($"** Applied: {string.Join(", ", _order.AppliedPricingStrategies)}");
        }
    }
}
```

Step 3: Update Element Classes to Accept Visitors

```
// Add this Method in all Pizza Classes
  public void Accept(IOrderItemVisitor visitor)
  {
    visitor.VisitPizza(this);
  }

// Add this Method in all Dessert Classes
public void Accept(IOrderItemVisitor visitor)
{
  visitor.VisitDessert(this);
}

// Add this Method in all Drink Classes
public void Accept(IOrderItemVisitor visitor)
{
  visitor.VisitDrink(this);
}

//Add this method in OrderComposite
public void Accept(IOrderItemVisitor visitor)
{
  visitor.VisitComposite(this);

  //✅ CRITICAL: Also accept the visitor for all children
  foreach (var item in _items)
  {
    item.Accept(visitor);
  }
}
```

Step 4: Create Visitor Manager

VisitorManager.cs

```
public class VisitorManager
{
  private readonly List<IOrderItemVisitor> _visitors = new List<IOrderItemVisitor>();

  public void AddVisitor(IOrderItemVisitor visitor){
    _visitors.Add(visitor);
    Console.WriteLine($"[VisitorManager] Added visitor: {visitor.GetType().Name}");
  }

  public void ApplyTo(IOrderItem item)
  {
    if (_visitors.Count == 0){
      Console.WriteLine("[VisitorManager] No visitors to apply");
      return;
    }
```

```
    Console.WriteLine($"[VisitorManager] Applying {_visitors.Count} visitors to {item.Name}");

    foreach (var visitor in _visitors){item.Accept(visitor);}
  }

  public T GetVisitor<T>() where T : IOrderItemVisitor
  {
    return _visitors.OfType<T>().FirstOrDefault();
  }

  public int VisitorCount => _visitors.Count;
}
```

Step 5: Client Usage in Program.cs

Program.cs

```
private static void ApplyVisitorOperations(Order order)
{
  Console.WriteLine("\n=== Order Confirmation Details ===");

  // Create visitors
  var loyaltyVisitor = new LoyaltyPointsVisitor();
  var summaryVisitor = new OrderSummaryVisitor(order);

  // Create manager and add visitors
  var visitorManager = new VisitorManager();
  visitorManager.AddVisitor(loyaltyVisitor);
  visitorManager.AddVisitor(summaryVisitor);

  // Apply to order
  visitorManager.ApplyTo(order.OrderItem);

  // Display results
  summaryVisitor.PrintSummary(); // This shows the itemized breakdown
  Console.WriteLine($"\n[Visitor] You earned {loyaltyVisitor.TotalPoints} loyalty points!");
}

//In Main Program after order Success Print the reports
bool orderSuccess = await orderProcessor.PlaceOrder(order);

if (orderSuccess)
{
  Console.WriteLine("\nThank you for your order!");
  ApplyVisitorOperations(order);
}
else
{
  Console.WriteLine("\nThere was a problem with your order.");
}
```

Key Test Points for Visitor Pattern Validation

1. Visitor Application Test

- **Objective:** Verify each visitor correctly processes different element types.
- **Test Action:** Create different order items and apply visitors to verify proper handling.
- **Expected Result:** Each visitor should process the correct element type with appropriate calculations.

2. Composite Structure Traversal Test

- **Objective:** Verify visitors correctly traverse and process composite order structures.
- **Test Action:** Create composite orders with multiple items and verify all items are processed.
- **Expected Result:** Visitors should process both the composite and all its child elements.

3. Visitor State Accumulation Test

- **Objective:** Verify visitors maintain and accumulate state correctly across multiple elements.
- **Test Action:** Apply visitors to multiple elements and verify accumulated results.
- **Expected Result:** Visitors should correctly accumulate totals across all processed elements.

4. Visitor Independence Test

- **Objective:** Verify multiple visitors can operate independently on the same elements.
- **Test Action:** Apply different visitors to the same elements and verify they don't interfere.
- **Expected Result:** Each visitor should produce correct results independently.

5. Visitor Manager Integration Test

- **Objective:** Verify Visitor Manager correctly coordinates multiple visitors.
- **Test Action:** Use Visitor Manager to apply multiple visitors and verify coordinated execution.
- **Expected Result:** Manager should apply all visitors and provide access to their results.

6. Error Handling Test

- **Objective:** Verify visitors handle edge cases and invalid elements gracefully.
- **Test Action:** Test visitors with null elements, empty composites, and boundary conditions.
- **Expected Result:** Visitors should handle edge cases without crashing and provide sensible defaults.

These test points ensure the Visitor Pattern works correctly, integrates well with your existing architecture, and provides the expected business value without introducing new issues.

25.8 Why the Visitor Pattern Matters

- **Separation of Concerns:** Operations are separated from object structure.
- **Extensibility:** New operations can be added without changing existing classes.
- **Centralized Logic:** Related operations are grouped in one visitor class.
- **Type Safety:** Visitor methods are type-specific and compile-time checked.
- **Maintainable:** Changes to an operation affect only one visitor class.

25.9 Mini-Exercise: Enhanced Visitor Features

Task: Create a "*InventoryCheckVisitor*" that verifies ingredient availability for each menu item and calculates total preparation time.
Bonus: Implement a "*SeasonalVisitor*" that applies special seasonal modifications (holiday toppings, summer/winter menu adjustments).

25.10 When to Use the Visitor Pattern

"Use the Visitor pattern when:

- You need to perform operations on objects of different types in a complex object structure.
- You want to avoid polluting classes with operations that are not their primary responsibility.
- The object structure is stable, but you want to frequently add new operations.
- You want to keep related operations together in one class.
- You need to perform several unrelated operations on objects without modifying them".

25.11 Transition to Chapter 25

Congratulations! You've successfully implemented a comprehensive set of design patterns that have transformed your pizza ordering system from a messy codebase into a clean, maintainable, and extensible architecture. Each pattern solved specific pain points and together they create a robust system ready for future growth.

Final System Architecture

Your pizza ordering system now exemplifies enterprise-level software design with:

- Clean separation of concerns
- Flexible and extensible architecture
- Maintainable and testable code
- Professional development practices

You're now equipped to tackle complex software design challenges using these proven patterns! 🎉

> This completes our design patterns journey! You've transformed the Delizioso Pizzeria codebase into a masterpiece of software architecture. Well done! 🍕🚀

🏁 PART 5: WRAP-UP

Where It All Comes Together! 🎊
The grand finale! This is where we step back and admire the masterpiece we've built together. From chaotic code to elegant architecture - let's celebrate your transformation into a pattern master!

What We're Celebrating:

- Chapter 26: See the complete pattern symphony in action
- Chapter 27: Test your skills with interview-ready challenges

You'll Master:

- Connecting all 23 patterns into one beautiful system
- Recognizing patterns in real-world problems
- Acing pattern-related interview questions
- Your new superpower: thinking in patterns!

Perfect for cementing your knowledge and:

- Preparing for technical interviews
- Reviewing the complete pattern journey
- Building confidence in your design decisions

Congratulations, Pattern Master! 🎓 Your coding toolkit will never be the same!

Chapter 26

Putting It All Together

26.1 The Journey: From Chaos to Masterpiece

We've traveled an incredible journey together - from a tangled mess of code to an elegant, professional pizza ordering system. Let's step back and admire the architectural masterpiece we've built.

The Transformation Story

Remember our starting point in Chapter 2? A single Program.cs file with over 1000 lines, 37 "Oops Moments," and code that was:

- **Hard to change** - Every modification risked breaking multiple features
- **Hard to understand** - New developers would need weeks to grasp the system
- **Hard to extend** - Adding new features meant rewriting existing code

Now, we have a system that's:

- **Modular** - Each component has a single responsibility
- **Extensible** - New features integrate seamlessly
- **Maintainable** - Changes are localized and predictable
- **Testable** - Each component can be verified independently

26.2 The Final Architecture: A Pattern Symphony

Our system now works like a well-conducted orchestra, with each pattern playing its part in harmony:

High-Level Architecture Overview

```
CUSTOMER INTERFACE LAYER
├── Program.cs (User Interaction)
├── PizzaOrderParser (Interpreter Pattern)
└── MenuBuilder (Composite Pattern)

BUSINESS LOGIC LAYER
├── OrderProcessor (Facade Pattern)
│   ├── Validation Chain (Chain of Responsibility)
│   ├── Pricing Engine (Strategy Pattern)
│   ├── Order Processing (Template Method)
│   └── Analysis Engine (Visitor Pattern)
│
├── Kitchen Management
│   ├── KitchenMediator (Mediator Pattern)
│   ├── Command Processor (Command Pattern)
│   └── State Management (State Pattern)
│
└── Notification System
    ├── Notification Bridge (Bridge Pattern)
    └── Order Observers (Observer Pattern)
```

```
DATA & INFRASTRUCTURE LAYER
├── Object Creation
│   ├── Factories (Factory Method, Abstract Factory)
│   ├── Pizza Builder (Builder Pattern)
│   └── Cloning (Prototype Pattern)
│
├── Structural Patterns
│   ├── Menu Composition (Composite Pattern)
│   ├── Topping Management (Decorator Pattern)
│   ├── Ingredient Optimization (Flyweight Pattern)
│   └── Service Protection (Proxy Pattern)
│
└── Global Services
    ├── Configuration (Singleton Pattern)
    └── ID Generation (Singleton Pattern)
```

Pattern Interaction Flow

```
Customer Order Flow:
1. "2x margherita + coke with extra cheese" → Interpreter Pattern
2. Create Order Items → Factory Method + Builder + Prototype
3. Apply Toppings → Decorator Pattern
4. Process Order → Facade Pattern
   ├── 4.1 Validate → Chain of Responsibility
   ├── 4.2 Price → Strategy Pattern + Visitor Pattern
   ├── 4.3 Coordinate → Mediator Pattern
   │   ├── Bake → Command Pattern
   │   ├── Pack → Command Pattern
   │   └── Deliver → Command Pattern
   ├── 4.4 Track Status → State Pattern
   └── 4.5 Notify → Observer Pattern
5. Generate Summary → Visitor Pattern
```

26.3 Complete Pattern Reference: Every Problem Solved

Here's how we systematically eliminated all 37 "Oops Moments":

Creational Patterns: Building Better Objects

PATTERN	CHAPTER	PROBLEMS SOLVED	KEY BENEFIT
Factory Method	3	#28 (Long if/else creation)	Centralized object creation
Abstract Factory	4	#29 (Manual combo creation)	Family-based object creation
Builder	5	#1, #2 (Complex constructors)	Step-by-step object construction
Prototype	6	#4, #31 (No cloning, instance reuse)	Efficient object copying
Singleton	7	#5, #6, #7, #30 (Config chaos)	Single instance management

Structural Patterns: Organizing Relationships

PATTERN	CHAPTER	PROBLEMS SOLVED	KEY BENEFIT
Adapter	8	#18, #24 (Payment API mismatch)	Interface compatibility
Bridge	9	#20, #25 (Notification coupling)	Implementation separation
Composite	10	#8 (Flat menu structure)	Uniform tree structures
Decorator	11	#2, #17 (Boolean add-ons)	Dynamic feature addition
Facade	12	#33 (God class complexity)	Simplified subsystem access
Flyweight	13	#3 (Duplicate toppings)	Memory optimization
Proxy	14	#9, #26 (Raw API calls)	Access control & caching

Behavioral Patterns: Managing Algorithms & Communication

PATTERN	CHAPTER	PROBLEMS SOLVED	KEY BENEFIT
Chain of Responsibility	15	#10 (Monolithic validation)	Sequential request processing
Command	16	#21, #36 (Direct method calls)	Action encapsulation & queuing
Interpreter	17	#27 (Ad-hoc input parsing)	Language grammar processing

PATTERN	CHAPTER	PROBLEMS SOLVED	KEY BENEFIT
Iterator	18	#14, #15 (Raw list iteration)	Uniform collection traversal
Mediator	19	#37 (Service spaghetti)	Centralized communication
Memento	20	#12 (No undo/redo)	State preservation
Observer	21	#13 (Silent status changes)	Event notification system
State	22	#11, #23, #32 (String statuses)	Behavior by state
Strategy	23	#19, #34 (Hardcoded pricing)	Algorithm interchangeability
Template Method	24	#22, #35, #38 (Inconsistent workflows)	Algorithm skeleton definition
Visitor	25	#16 (Brittle type checks)	Operation-object separation

26.4 The Architecture in Action: A Complete Order Journey

Let's trace a complete order through our pattern-based system:

Scenario: "Student orders 2x Pepperoni Pizza with extra cheese for pickup"

Step 1: Input Interpretation

```
// Interpreter Pattern parses natural language
Input: "2x pepperoni pizza with extra cheese + pickup"
→ ItemExpression("pepperoni pizza", quantity: 2)
→ ModifierExpression("extra cheese", isAddition: true)
→ DeliveryType: "Pickup"
→ CustomerType: "Student"
```

Step 2: Object Creation

```
// Factory Method creates the pizza
var pizza = PizzaFactory.CreatePizza("pepperoni")

// Builder customizes it
pizza = new ExtraCheeseDecorator(pizza);

// Prototype clones for quantity
var secondPizza = pizza.Clone();

// Composite groups the order
var orderComposite = new OrderComposite("Your Order");
orderComposite.AddItem(pizza);
orderComposite.AddItem(secondPizza);
```

Step 3: Order Processing

```
// Facade provides simple interface
var success = await orderProcessor.PlaceOrder(order);

// Inside OrderProcessor (Template Method):
// 1. Chain of Responsibility validates
// 2. Strategy Pattern calculates price with student discount
// 3. PickupOrderProcessing template handles pickup workflow
// 4. Visitor Pattern calculates loyalty points
```

Step 4: Kitchen Operations

```
// Mediator coordinates kitchen
// Command Pattern queues operations
// State Pattern tracks order progress
// Observer Pattern sends notifications
```

26.5 Key Architectural Insights

Insight 1: Patterns Solve Real Problems

Each pattern wasn't applied theoretically - it solved specific, painful "Oops Moments" in our code.

Insight 2: Patterns Work Together

The real power emerged when patterns collaborated:

- **Factory + Builder + Prototype** = Flexible object creation
- **Strategy + Visitor** = Comprehensive pricing and analysis
- **Command + State + Observer** = Robust workflow management

THE JOURNEY

Insight 3: The Architecture Scales

Our system can now easily handle:

- New pizza types (just implement *IPizza*)
- New pricing strategies (implement *IPricingStrategy*)
- New order types (extend *OrderProcessingTemplate*)
- New notification channels (implement *IMessageSender*)

Insight 4: Maintenance Becomes Predictable

- **Bugs are localized** - Issues in pricing won't affect kitchen operations
- **Changes are safe** - Modifying notification logic won't break order processing
- **Testing is thorough** - Each pattern has clear test points

26.6 The Big Picture: Beyond Pizza

While we built a pizza ordering system, the patterns we mastered apply to virtually any software domain:

- **E-commerce:** Same patterns for shopping carts, payments, inventory
- **Banking:** Similar needs for transaction processing, validation, reporting
- **Healthcare**: Patient records, appointment scheduling, billing systems
- **IoT**: Device management, data processing, notification systems

26.7 Your Design Pattern Toolkit

You now have a comprehensive toolkit for tackling software design challenges:

When You Need To:

- **Create objects flexibly** → Creational Patterns
- **Organize object relationships** → Structural Patterns
- **Manage behavior and algorithms** → Behavioral Patterns

Your Decision Framework:

1. **Identify the pain point** (look for "Oops Moments")
2. **Match pattern to problem** (use our reference table)
3. **Implement incrementally** (refactor one concern at a time)
4. **Verify with tests** (use our key test points)

26.8 Final Reflection

Look how far we've come! From a single, overwhelmed *Program.cs* to a sophisticated, enterprise-ready architecture. You've not just learned design patterns - you've experienced their transformative power in a real, working system.

The patterns are now part of your thinking toolkit. When you see complex constructors, you'll think "Builder." When you see hardcoded algorithms, you'll think "Strategy." When you see tangled object communication, you'll think "Mediator."

Remember: Design patterns aren't about making code more complex - they're about making complex requirements manageable. They're the difference between code that works today but breaks tomorrow, and architecture that grows with your business needs.

You're now equipped to build software that's not just functional, but truly professional - software that your teammates will love to work with and your users will love to use.

Congratulations on mastering design patterns through building something real! 🎉

> In our final chapter, we'll reinforce your learning with interview questions and practical exercises to ensure these patterns become second nature in your development career.

Chapter 27

Interview Questions & Exercises

27.1 Deep Dive: Pattern Implementation Questions

Exercise 1: Singleton Pattern Internals

Question: In our Singleton implementation, we used:

```
private static readonly Lazy<Config> _lazyInstance = new Lazy<Config>(() => new Config());
private Config() { }
```

a) Why is the constructor private?
b) Why use Lazy<T> instead of direct instantiation?
c) What would happen if we made the constructor public?

Exercise 2: Factory Method vs. Abstract Factory

Question: Compare these two implementations and explain when you'd use each:

Option A (Factory Method):

```
public abstract class PizzaFactory {
    protected abstract IPizza CreatePizza(string type);
    public IPizza OrderPizza(string type) {
        IPizza pizza = CreatePizza(type);
        pizza.Prepare();
        pizza.Bake();
        return pizza;
    }
}
```

Option B (Abstract Factory):

```
public interface IPizzaFactory {
    IPizza CreatePizza();
    IDrink CreateDrink();
    IDessert CreateDessert();
}
```

When would you choose Factory Method over Abstract Factory?

Exercise 3: Strategy Pattern Application

Question: Given this pricing code, refactor it to use Strategy Pattern:

```
// BEFORE: Hardcoded pricing logic
public decimal CalculateTotal(Order order) {
    decimal total = order.BasePrice;

    if (order.CustomerType == "Student") {
        total *= 0.85m; // 15% discount
    }

    if (DateTime.Now.DayOfWeek == DayOfWeek.Tuesday) {
        total *= 0.90m; // 10% discount
    }

    if (order.PaymentMethod == "CreditCard") {
        total *= 0.95m; // 5% discount
    }

    return total;
}
```

27.2 Pattern Recognition Challenges

Exercise 4: Identify the Pattern

Question: For each code snippet, identify which design pattern is being used. Explain why:

Snippet A:

```
public class PizzaPattern : IPizza {
    protected IPizza _pizza;
    public PizzaPattern(IPizza pizza) { _pizza = pizza; }
    public virtual decimal Price => _pizza.Price + 1.50m;
    public virtual string Name => _pizza.Name + " + Extra Cheese";
}
```

Snippet B:

```
public class KitchenPattern : IKitchenPattern {
    public async Task<bool> ProcessOrder(Order order) {
        // Coordinate between BakeService, PackService, DeliveryService
        await _bakeService.BakeAsync(order);
        await _packService.PackAsync(order);
        await _deliveryService.DeliverAsync(order);
        return true;
    }
}
```

Snippet C:

```
public abstract class OrderProcessingPattern {
    public async Task<bool> ProcessOrderAsync(Order order) {
        await ValidateOrderAsync(order);
        await ProcessPaymentAsync(order);
        await PrepareOrderAsync(order);
        return await DeliverOrderAsync(order);
    }
    protected abstract Task<bool> ValidateOrderAsync(Order order);
    protected abstract Task<bool> ProcessPaymentAsync(Order order);
    // ... other abstract methods
}
```

27.3 Architecture Design Questions

Exercise 5: System Extension Design

Question: How would you extend our pizza system to support:

1. Real-time order tracking for customers.
2. Multiple restaurant locations with different menus.
3. Dynamic pricing based on demand.

Which patterns would you use for each requirement and why?

Exercise 3: Strategy Pattern Application

Question: Given this pricing code, refactor it to use Strategy Pattern:

```
// BEFORE: Hardcoded pricing logic
public decimal CalculateTotal(Order order) {
    decimal total = order.BasePrice;

    if (order.CustomerType == "Student") {
        total *= 0.85m; // 15% discount
    }

    if (DateTime.Now.DayOfWeek == DayOfWeek.Tuesday) {
        total *= 0.90m; // 10% discount
    }

    if (order.PaymentMethod == "CreditCard") {
        total *= 0.95m; // 5% discount
    }

    return total;
}
```

EXERCISES

27.4 Multiple Choice Questions

Exercise 6: Select the Best Answer

1. Which pattern is most appropriate when you need to add new operations to object structures without modifying the classes?

a. Strategy Pattern
b. Visitor Pattern
c. Decorator Pattern
d. Adapter Pattern

2. You have a complex object that requires step-by-step initialization. Which pattern you use?

a. Factory Method
b. Singleton
c. Builder Pattern
d. Prototype

3. Which pattern ensures a class has only one instance and provides global access to it?

a. Factory Method
b. Builder
c. Singleton Pattern
d. Prototype

4. You need to decouple an abstraction from its implementation so both can vary independently. Which pattern helps?

a. Adapter Pattern
b. Bridge Pattern
c. Decorator Pattern
d. Facade Pattern

5. Which pattern is best for handling state-dependent behavior of an object?

a. Strategy Pattern
b. State Pattern
c. Template Method Pattern
d. Command Pattern

6. You notice your code has many if/else statements for creating different pizza types. Which pattern would help eliminate this?

a. Singleton Pattern
b. Factory Method Pattern
c. Observer Pattern
d. Decorator Pattern

7. Your payment gateway has a different interface than what your system expects. Which pattern solves this?

a. Adapter Pattern b. Bridge Pattern c. Proxy Pattern d. Facade Pattern

8. You want to add extra cheese or stuffed crust to pizzas without modifying the pizza class. Which pattern is ideal?

   a. Composite Pattern
   b. Strategy Pattern
   c. Decorator Pattern
   d. Template Method Pattern

9. You need to ensure only one configuration instance exists in your entire application. Which pattern guarantees this?

   a. Factory Method
   b. Builder Pattern
   c. Singleton Pattern
   d. Prototype Pattern

10. Your order validation has multiple steps (customer info, inventory, payment). Which pattern organizes these sequential checks?

   a. Chain of Responsibility Pattern
   b. Command Pattern
   c. Strategy Pattern
   d. State Pattern

11. You want to treat individual pizzas and pizza combos the same way in your menu system. Which pattern enables this?

   a. Adapter Pattern
   b. Composite Pattern
   c. Bridge Pattern
   d. Flyweight Pattern

12. You need to save and restore pizza customization states for undo/redo functionality. Which pattern handles this?

   a. Memento Pattern
   b. Command Pattern
   c. Observer Pattern
   d. State Pattern

13. Different customers (students, seniors, regular) get different discount calculations. Which pattern manages these varying algorithms?

   a. Template Method Pattern
   b. Strategy Pattern
   c. Factory Method Pattern
   d. Visitor Pattern

14. Which pattern is primarily used to reduce memory usage by sharing common data?

   a. Singleton Pattern
   b. Flyweight Pattern
   c. Prototype Pattern
   d. Composite Pattern

15. Your kitchen operations (bake, pack, deliver) need to be queued, retried, and potentially undone. Which pattern encapsulates these operations?

  a. State Pattern
  b. Command Pattern
  c. Strategy Pattern
  d. Template Method Pattern

16. You need to share common topping data across multiple pizzas to save memory. Which pattern optimizes this?

  a. Flyweight Pattern
  b. Proxy Pattern
  c. Decorator Pattern
  d. Composite Pattern

17. Your order processing follows the same steps but with variations for different order types (standard, express, pickup). Which pattern defines this skeleton?

  a. Template Method Pattern
  b. Strategy Pattern
  c. Factory Method Pattern
  d. Builder Pattern

18. You want to add loyalty points calculation and nutritional reporting without modifying your existing menu classes. Which pattern enables this?

  a. Visitor Pattern
  b. Decorator Pattern
  c. Adapter Pattern
  d. Bridge Pattern

19. Your inventory API calls need caching, retry logic, and rate limiting without changing the original API. Which pattern wraps this functionality?

  a. Proxy Pattern
  b. Adapter Pattern
  c. Facade Pattern
  d. Decorator Pattern

20. You need to coordinate communication between kitchen, delivery, and notification services without them directly referencing each other. Which pattern manages this?

  a. Mediator Pattern
  b. Observer Pattern
  c. Chain of Responsibility Pattern
  d. Command Pattern

21. You want to notify customers via email, SMS, and push notifications when their order status changes. Which pattern coordinates this?
   a. Mediator Pattern
   b. Observer Pattern
   c. Command Pattern
   d. Chain of Responsibility Pattern
22. Which pattern allows you to add new operations to existing classes without modifying them?
   a. Decorator Pattern
   b. Visitor Pattern
   c. Adapter Pattern
   d. Bridge Pattern
23. Which pattern helps when you need to provide a simple interface to complex subsystem?
   a. Facade Pattern
   b. Adapter Pattern
   c. Proxy Pattern
   d. Bridge Pattern
24. Which pattern is best for implementing undo/redo functionality?
   a. Command Pattern
   b. Memento Pattern
   c. State Pattern
   d. Observer Pattern
25. Which pattern ensures an object's behavior changes when its internal state changes?
   a. Strategy Pattern
   b. State Pattern
   c. Template Method Pattern
   d. Command Pattern
26. Your e-commerce system needs to calculate shipping costs differently for standard, express, and international orders. Which pattern is most suitable?
   a. Factory Method Pattern
   b. Strategy Pattern
   c. Template Method Pattern
   d. Observer Pattern
27. You're building a document editor that needs to treat individual characters and character groups uniformly. Which pattern helps?
   a. Composite Pattern
   b. Decorator Pattern
   c. Flyweight Pattern
   d. Bridge Pattern

28. Your weather app needs to update multiple display components (temperature, humidity, forecast) when new data arrives. Which pattern coordinates this?

a. Mediator Pattern
b. Observer Pattern
c. Command Pattern
d. Chain of Responsibility Pattern

29. You're creating a game where character abilities change based on power-up states (normal, super, invincible). Which pattern manages these state-dependent behaviors?

a. Strategy Pattern
b. State Pattern
c. Template Method Pattern
d. Command Pattern

30. Your application needs to parse and execute user-created scripts or formulas. Which pattern interprets these custom languages?

a. Interpreter Pattern
b. Command Pattern
c. Visitor Pattern
d. Template Method Pattern

27.5 Code Review & Refactoring Exercises

Exercise 7: Refactor to Patterns

Question: Review this code and identify which pattern(s) could improve it:

```
public class NotificationService {
    public void SendNotification(string type, string message) {
        if (type == "Email") {
            var email = new EmailService();
            if (Config.UseSmtp) {
                email.SendViaSmtp(message);
            } else {
                email.SendViaSendGrid(message);
            }
        }
        else if (type == "SMS") {
            var sms = new SmsService();
            if (Config.UseTwilio) {
                sms.SendViaTwilio(message);
            } else {
                sms.SendViaNexmo(message);
            }
        }
        else if (type == "Push") {
            var push = new PushService();
            push.SendViaFirebase(message);
        }
    }
}
```

27.6 Advanced Pattern Questions

Exercise 8: Pattern Combinations

Question: Describe a scenario where you would combine three patterns and explain how they work together.
Example Scenario: "A configurable order processing pipeline with validation, transformation, and notification"

27.7 Performance & Memory Questions

Exercise 9: Pattern Trade-offs

Question: What are the performance implications of these patterns and when might you avoid them?
a) Singleton Pattern
b) Flyweight Pattern
c) Visitor Pattern
d) Decorator Pattern

27.8 Real-World Problem Solving

Exercise 10: Design a New Feature

Question: Design a "Meal Subscription" feature where customers can:

- Choose weekly meal plans
- Customize dietary preferences
- Skip weeks when needed
- Get automatic deliveries

Which patterns would you use and how?

EXERCISES

Design Patterns Cheat Sheet

Quick Problem-Solution Guide

● Object Creation Problems

Problem	Pattern	Quick Fix
Complex object creation	**Builder**	Step-by-step construction
Multiple related objects	**Abstract Factory**	Create product families
Object variations	**Factory Method**	Let subclasses decide
Expensive object creation	**Prototype**	Clone existing objects
Single instance needed	**Singleton**	One instance globally

🏗 Structure Problems

Problem	Pattern	Quick Fix
Incompatible interfaces	**Adapter**	Convert interface
Too many class combinations	**Bridge**	Separate abstraction or implementation
Tree-like structures	**Composite**	Treat parts & wholes alike
Adding features dynamically	**Decorator**	Wrap with new functionality
Complex subsystem	**Facade**	Simple interface
Too many similar objects	**Flyweight**	Share common data
Controlled access	**Proxy**	Add protection layer

Behavior Problems

Problem	Pattern	Quick Fix
Multiple validation steps	**Chain of Responsibility**	Pass through chain
Action queuing/undo	**Command**	Encapsulate requests
Custom language parsing	**Interpreter**	Define grammar
Collection traversal	**Iterator**	Access elements uniformly
Complex communication	**Mediator**	Centralize communication
Undo/redo functionality	**Memento**	Save/restore state
Event notifications	**Observer**	Subscribe/notify
State-dependent behavior	**State**	Behavior changes with state
Switchable algorithms	**Strategy**	Interchangeable algorithms
Algorithm skeleton	**Template Method**	Define steps, vary details
Add operations to classes	**Visitor**	External operations

Pattern Selection Flowchart

1. Creation Questions:

- "How do I create it?" → **Creational Patterns**
- Complex construction? → **Builder**
- Related objects? → **Abstract Factory**
- Single instance? → **Singleton**
- Copy existing? → **Prototype**

2. Structure Questions:

- "How do I organize it?" → **Structural Patterns**
- Interface mismatch? → **Adapter**
- Add features dynamically? → **Decorator**
- Tree structure? → **Composite**
- Too many objects? → **Flyweight**

3. Behavior Questions:

- "How does it behave?" → **Behavioral Patterns**
- Multiple handlers? → **Chain of Responsibility**
- State changes behavior? → **State**
- Need notifications? → **Observer**
- Different algorithms? → **Strategy**

Quick Decision Matrix

If you need to...	Use this pattern
Create objects flexibly	**Factory Method**
Build complex objects	**Builder**
Ensure single instance	**Singleton**
Make interfaces compatible	**Adapter**
Add features dynamically	**Decorator**
Handle state changes	**State**
Notify multiple objects	**Observer**
Choose algorithms	**Strategy**
Save/restore state	**Memento**
Queue operations	**Command**

Pattern Categories at a Glance

Creational - Object Creation

- **Factory Method:** Delegate creation to subclasses
- **Abstract Factory:** Create related object families
- **Builder:** Construct complex objects step-by-step
- **Prototype:** Clone existing objects
- **Singleton:** Single instance access

Structural - Object Composition

- **Adapter:** Bridge incompatible interfaces
- **Bridge:** Separate abstraction from implementation
- **Composite:** Treat individual and groups uniformly
- **Decorator:** Add responsibilities dynamically
- **Facade:** Simplify complex subsystems
- **Flyweight:** Share common state
- **Proxy:** Control object access

Behavioral - Object Interaction

- **Chain of Responsibility:** Pass requests through chain
- **Command:** Encapsulate requests as objects
- **Interpreter:** Define language grammar
- **Iterator:** Access collections uniformly
- **Mediator:** Centralize object communication
- **Memento:** Capture and restore state
- **Observer:** Notify dependents of changes
- **State:** Change behavior with state
- **Strategy:** Define algorithm families
- **Template Method:** Define algorithm skeleton
- **Visitor:** Add operations to objects

Remember: Patterns are tools, not rules. Choose the simplest solution that solves your problem!

Answers

Exercise 1: Singleton Pattern Internals

a) Why is the constructor private?

Think of the constructor as the "birth certificate" for objects. When we make it private, we're saying: "Only this class can create new copies of itself - nobody else is allowed to make babies!"

What happens:

- ❌ **Without private:** Anyone can do new *Config()* and create unlimited copies
- ■ **With private:** Only the class itself can create instances through its static methods

Real-world analogy:

It's like having a special key that only the building manager has. You can't just walk in and make copies of the master key - you have to ask the manager for access.

b) Why use Lazy<T> instead of direct instantiation?

Lazy<T> is like a "promise" - it says "I'll create this when you actually need it, not before."

Three big benefits:

1. **Thread Safety:** If 100 people ask for the instance at the same time, Lazy<T> ensures only one gets created
2. **Performance:** If nobody ever uses the instance, it never gets created
3. **Clean Code:** The code says "create this only when first used" right in the declaration

Without Lazy<T> problems:

- The instance gets created when your app starts, even if you never use it
- Multiple threads might create multiple instances by accident

c) What would happen if we made the constructor public?

Chaos! It would be like telling everyone "feel free to make as many copies as you want" - completely breaking the "single instance" promise.

What would go wrong:

```
// DISASTER SCENARIO:
var config1 = new Config();  // First instance
var config2 = new Config();  // Second instance - OOPS!

config1.CurrencySymbol = "$";
config2.CurrencySymbol = "€";

// Now different parts of your app see different currency symbols!
// Some orders calculate in dollars, others in euros - total confusion!
```

Real-world consequence:

- Different parts of your app would have different configuration values
- Orders might calculate prices differently
- Reports would show inconsistent data
- The entire "single source of truth" concept breaks down

The private constructor + Lazy<T> combo is like having a well-trained security guard who:

- Only lets one person in at a time (thread safety)
- Only opens the door when someone actually needs to come in (lazy loading)
- Never lets anyone make copies of the key (private constructor)

This ensures your configuration stays consistent, safe, and efficient throughout your entire application! 🔒

Exercise 2: Factory Method vs. Abstract Factory

Factory Method: "One Product, Multiple Ways"

<u>When to use:</u> When you have one main product but need different ways to create it.

<u>Simple example:</u> Different pizza styles

- New York Pizza Shop → creates thin crust pizzas
- Chicago Pizza Shop → creates deep dish pizzas
- Each shop makes pizzas differently, but they're all still pizzas

<u>Key idea:</u> Let subclasses decide exactly which type of single product to create.

Abstract Factory: "Complete Packages"

<u>When to use:</u> When you need multiple related products that work together.

<u>Simple example:</u> Meal combos

- Family Combo → large pizza + big soda + cookie platter
- Date Night Combo → medium pizza + wine + chocolate dessert
- Each combo includes coordinated items that belong together

<u>Key idea:</u> Create families of products that are designed to work together.

Quick Comparison:

<u>Factory Method:</u>

- Creates one type of product
- Example: Different pizza styles
- Best for: "I need this thing, but in different variations"

<u>Abstract Factory:</u>

- Creates multiple related products
- Example: Complete meal packages
- Best for: "I need a set of things that work together"

Remember: Factory Method = single product variations | Abstract Factory = product family packages

Exercise 3: Strategy Pattern Application

```
// AFTER: Strategy Pattern implementation
public interface IPricingStrategy {
    string StrategyName { get; }
    decimal CalculatePrice(Order order, decimal currentTotal);
    bool IsApplicable(Order order);
}

public class StudentDiscountStrategy : IPricingStrategy {
    public string StrategyName => "Student 15% Off";
    public bool IsApplicable(Order order) => order.CustomerType == "Student";
    public decimal CalculatePrice(Order order, decimal currentTotal) => currentTotal * 0.85m;
}

public class TuesdayDiscountStrategy : IPricingStrategy {
    public string StrategyName => "Tuesday 10% Off";
    public bool IsApplicable(Order order) => DateTime.Now.DayOfWeek == DayOfWeek.Tuesday;
    public decimal CalculatePrice(Order order, decimal currentTotal) => currentTotal * 0.90m;
}

public class CreditCardDiscountStrategy : IPricingStrategy {
    public string StrategyName => "Credit Card 5% Off";
    public bool IsApplicable(Order order) => order.PaymentMethod == "CreditCard";
    public decimal CalculatePrice(Order order, decimal currentTotal) => currentTotal * 0.95m;
}

// Usage in PricingContext:
public decimal CalculateTotal(Order order) {
    decimal total = order.BasePrice;
    foreach (var strategy in _strategies) {
        if (strategy.IsApplicable(order)) {
            total = strategy.CalculatePrice(order, total);
        }
    }
    return total;
}
```

Exercise 4: Identify the Pattern

Snippet A: Decorator Pattern
Why: Wraps an object to add new functionality dynamically.
Key indicators: Constructor takes same type, delegates to wrapped object.

Snippet B: Mediator Pattern
Why: Centralizes communication between multiple services.
Key indicators: Coordinates between multiple dependencies.

Snippet C: Template Method Pattern
Why: Defines algorithm skeleton with customizable steps.
Key indicators: Abstract methods in fixed sequence within template method.

Exercise 5: System Extension Design

1. **Real-time Order Tracking:**
    - **Pattern:** Observer Pattern + State Pattern
    - **Why:**
        - Observers can push updates to customer dashboards
        - State pattern can expose tracking events (Preparing, OutForDelivery, etc.)
    - **Implementation:**

```
public class OrderTracker : IOrderObserver {
    public void Update(Order order, string statusChange) {
        // Push to customer UI, mobile app, etc.
    }
}
```

2. **Multiple Restaurant Locations:**
    - **Pattern:** Abstract Factory + Strategy Pattern
    - **Why:**
        - Abstract Factory can create location-specific menu families
        - Strategy can handle location-specific pricing rules
    - **Implementation:**

```
public interface ILocationFactory {
    IMenu CreateMenu();
    IPricingStrategy CreatePricingStrategy();
}
```

3. **Dynamic Pricing:**
    - **Pattern:** Strategy Pattern + Observer Pattern
    - **Why:**
        - Strategy can implement different demand-based algorithms
        - Observer can notify when demand changes occur
    - **Implementation:**

```
public class DemandBasedPricingStrategy : IPricingStrategy {
    public decimal CalculatePrice(Order order, decimal currentTotal) {
        var demandMultiplier = GetCurrentDemandLevel();
        return currentTotal * demandMultiplier;
    }
}
```

ANSWERS

Exercise 6: Select the Best Answer

1) b	2) c	3) c	4) b	5) b	6) b	7) a	8) c	9) c	10) a
11) b	12) a	13) b	14) b	15) b	16) a	17) a	18) a	19) a	20) a
21) b	22) b	23) a	24) a	25) b	26) b	27) b	28) b	29) b	30) a

Exercise 7: Refactor to Patterns

```
// Apply Bridge Pattern + Factory Method

// Bridge: Separate abstraction (notification type) from implementation (provider)
public interface IMessageSender {
    void SendMessage(string message);
    string ProviderName { get; }
}

public abstract class Notification {
    protected IMessageSender _messageSender;
    protected Notification(IMessageSender messageSender) {
        _messageSender = messageSender;
    }
    public abstract void Send(string message);
}

// Concrete implementations
public class EmailNotification : Notification {
    public EmailNotification(IMessageSender messageSender) : base(messageSender) { }
    public override void Send(string message) {
        Console.Write("Email: ");
        _messageSender.SendMessage(message);
    }
}

// Factory for creating notifications
public static class NotificationFactory {
    public static Notification CreateEmailNotification() {
        IMessageSender sender = Config.UseSmtp ? new SmtpEmailSender() : new SendGridEmailSender();
        return new EmailNotification(sender);
    }

    public static Notification CreateSmsNotification() {
        IMessageSender sender = Config.UseTwilio ? new TwilioSmsSender() : new NexmoSmsSender();
        return new SmsNotification(sender);
    }
}

// Clean usage:
var emailNotification = NotificationFactory.CreateEmailNotification();
emailNotification.Send("Your order is ready!");
```

Exercise 8: Pattern Combinations

```
// Combined Patterns: Chain of Responsibility + Strategy + Observer

// 1. Chain of Responsibility - Sequential validation steps
public interface IOrderHandler {
    IOrderHandler SetNext(IOrderHandler handler);
    bool Handle(Order order);
}

// 2. Strategy Pattern - Different processing strategies
public interface IOrderProcessingStrategy {
    Task<bool> ProcessAsync(Order order);
}

// 3. Observer Pattern - Status notifications
public interface IOrderObserver {
    void Update(Order order, string status);
}

// Implementation:
public class OrderProcessor {
    private readonly IOrderHandler _validationChain;
    private readonly IOrderProcessingStrategy _processingStrategy;
    private readonly List<IOrderObserver> _observers;

    public async Task<bool> ProcessOrder(Order order) {
        // Chain of Responsibility: Validate
        if (!_validationChain.Handle(order)) return false;

        // Notify observers
        _observers.ForEach(o => o.Update(order, "Validated"));

        // Strategy: Process based on order type
        bool success = await _processingStrategy.ProcessAsync(order);

        // Notify observers of result
        _observers.ForEach(o => o.Update(order, success ? "Completed" : "Failed"));
        return success;
    }
}
```

Exercise 9: Pattern Trade-offs

a) Singleton Pattern

Performance Impact:

- ■ Good: Saves memory (only one instance)
- ■ Good: Fast access (no object creation needed after first use)
- ✕ Bad: Can become a bottleneck if many threads access it simultaneously
- ✕ Bad: Hard to unit test (global state causes issues)

When to Avoid:

- When you need multiple instances (different configurations)
- When writing unit tests (hard to mock)
- When the object holds heavy resources that should be cleaned up

ANSWERS

b) Flyweight Pattern

Performance Impact:

- ✅ Good: Greatly reduces memory usage by sharing data
- ✅ Good: Faster creation (reuses existing objects)
- ❌ Bad: More complex code
- ❌ Bad: Thread-safety concerns with shared data

When to Avoid:

- When objects don't share enough common data
- When memory isn't a concern
- When the code complexity outweighs memory benefits

c) Visitor Pattern

Performance Impact:

- ✅ Good: Easy to add new operations
- ✅ Good: Keeps operations organized in one place
- ❌ Bad: Performance overhead from method calls
- ❌ Bad: Hard to add new element types

When to Avoid:

- When you frequently add new element types
- When performance is critical (too many virtual calls)
- When you have only a few simple operations

d) Decorator Pattern

Performance Impact:

- ✅ Good: Flexible runtime customization
- ✅ Good: Follows open/closed principle
- ❌ Bad: Many small objects can clutter memory
- ❌ Bad: Debugging becomes harder (many wrapper layers)

When to Avoid:

- When you need to know the exact object type
- When performance is critical (too many method delegations)
- When you have only a few simple variations

Bottom Line: Every pattern has trade-offs. Choose based on your specific needs - flexibility vs performance, memory vs complexity.

Exercise 10: Design a New Feature

```
// Pattern Solution:

// 1. Builder Pattern - For constructing complex meal plans
public class MealPlanBuilder {
    private MealPlan _plan = new MealPlan();

    public MealPlanBuilder AddPizza(string type) { /* ... */ return this; }
    public MealPlanBuilder SetDietaryPreference(string preference) { /* ... */ return this; }
    public MealPlanBuilder SkipWeek(DateTime week) { /* ... */ return this; }
    public MealPlan Build() => _plan;
}

// 2. Template Method - For subscription processing workflow
public abstract class SubscriptionProcessor {
    public async Task ProcessSubscription(Subscription sub) {
        await ValidateSubscription(sub);
        await GenerateMealPlan(sub);
        await ScheduleDelivery(sub);
        await ProcessPayment(sub);
    }
    // ... abstract methods for each step
}

// 3. Strategy Pattern - For different subscription types
public interface ISubscriptionStrategy {
    decimal CalculatePrice(MealPlan plan);
    DateTime GetNextDeliveryDate();
}

// 4. Observer Pattern - For subscription events
public class SubscriptionObserver : IObserver<SubscriptionEvent> {
    public void OnNext(SubscriptionEvent value) {
        // Handle subscription changes, skipped weeks, etc.
    }
}

// Usage:
var mealPlan = new MealPlanBuilder()
    .AddPizza("Margherita")
    .SetDietaryPreference("Vegetarian")
    .SkipWeek(DateTime.Now.AddDays(7))
    .Build();

var processor = new WeeklySubscriptionProcessor();
await processor.ProcessSubscription(customerSubscription);
```

ANSWERS

A Small Note from the Author

Thank you for joining me on this delicious journey through the world of design patterns! I hope this book made these often-intimidating concepts feel approachable, practical, and maybe even a little bit fun. 🍕

A quick note about the code: While we've built a complete working pizza app together, you might spot areas where the code could be optimized or implemented differently. That's intentional! Remember, our main goal was to demonstrate design patterns clearly, not to build the most perfect pizza app in the universe. Think of it as a learning playground where we prioritized pattern education over production perfection.

If this book helped you finally "get" design patterns, made you smile with our pizza analogies, or gave you that "aha!" moment you've been searching for — please consider leaving a positive review or rating. Your support helps this book reach more developers and keeps the Logic Ladder series growing strong! Every review truly makes a difference for indie authors like me. 🤍

Stay curious, keep coding, and remember — even the messiest code can become a masterpiece with the right patterns!

See you in the next coding adventure! 🚀

Warm wishes,

Humna Ansari

Author of Design Patterns Served Hot in C#

www.ingramcontent.com/pod-product-compliance
Lightning Source LLC
LaVergne TN
LVHW080029210926
848481LV00011B/3143
9798232322007